Networks Social Studies

United States Modern Times

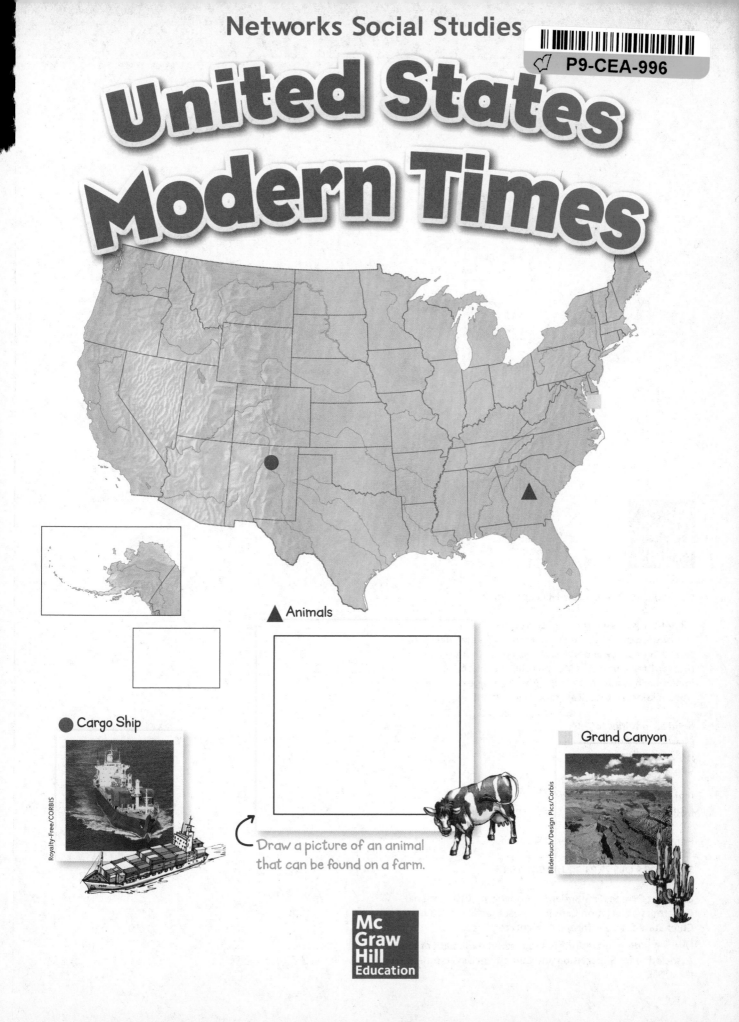

▲ Animals

● Cargo Ship

Draw a picture of an animal that can be found on a farm.

Grand Canyon

Mc Graw Hill Education

Send all inquiries to:
McGraw-Hill Education
8787 Orion Place
Columbus, OH 43240

ISBN: 978-0-02-144857-9
MHID: 0-02-144857-4

Printed in the United States of America.

3 4 5 6 7 8 9 QVS 22 21 20 19 18 17 16 15

My Book

My Cover

Find a geographic feature on your cover. Describe what you found. What fun things might you do there?

_____

_____

_____

_____

Explore! UNIT 2 Reconstruction

BIG IDEA 💡 Conflict causes change.

My Book

Keep going!
Next we'll explore how
The Nation Grows!

My Cover

Find an image from a former Confederate state on your cover.
Tell what it is and in what region you found it.

_____

_____

My Book

My Cover

Find the image of a cowboy on a horse. Why might he have moved west as the nation grew?

_____

_____

_____

_____

BIG IDEA Culture influences the way people live.

My Book

Keep going!
Next we'll explore
World War II.

My Cover

Find the mountains of Alaska, a state added at this time. Contrast Alaska with Hawaii, another new state.

BIG IDEA Conflict causes change.

My Book

My Cover

Find the image of the place where our federal government is. Tell what major acts the President took during this time period.

_____

_____

_____

_____

Explore! UNIT 6 The Modern Era

BIG IDEA Culture influences the way people live.

My Book

My Cover

Find the rocket blasting off. The Space Race started an age of rapid technological change. How does technology affect you?

_____

_____

_____

EXplore! Skills and Maps

Skills

Reading Skills

Primary and Secondary Sources

Chart and Graph Skills

My Cover

Count the number of buildings, ships, people, and animals on your cover. Draw a chart or graph to show this information.

Notes

Notes

Maps

UNIT

1 Introduction

BIG IDEA Relationships affect choices.

The United States has many different cultures. Much of this is due to our immigrant population. In this unit, you will read about our state's economy and government. Businesses and people are attracted to the many opportunities the U.S. offers them. As you read this unit, think about how our people, economy, and government influence the way we live.

The Capitol is where the U.S. Congress meets to make our nation's laws. ▶

networks

connected.mcgraw-hill.com
● Skill Builders
● Vocabulary Flashcards

2

Show As You Go! After you read each lesson in this unit, choose a public issue that is related to the topic of the lesson. Describe the issue below. You will use your notes here to help you complete a project at the end of this unit.

Fold page here

Lesson 1

Lesson 2

Lesson 3

Common Core Standards
RI.3: Explain the relationships or interactions between two or more individuals, events, ideas, or concepts in a historical, scientific, or technical text based on specific information in the text. **RI.5:** Compare and contrast the overall structure (e.g., chronology, comparison, cause/ effect, problem/solution) of events, ideas, concepts, or information in two or more texts.

Fact and Opinion

When people write about events, they often include both facts and opinions. Facts are statements that can be proven true. Opinions state feelings and beliefs. Opinions cannot be proven true or false. Being able to distinguish facts from opinions will help you understand what you read in social studies.

LEARN IT

- Facts can be checked and proven true.
- Opinions are personal views. They cannot be proven true or false.
- Clue words such as *think, felt, believe,* and *it seems* often state opinions.
- Now read the passage below. Look for facts and opinions.

The Underground Railroad

In 1849 Harriet Tubman heard that she and other enslaved workers on her Maryland plantation were to be sold farther south. Tubman believed that life there would be more difficult. She fled from the plantation in the middle of the night. After traveling 90 miles, she reached the free soil of Pennsylvania. She later said, "I felt like I was in heaven."

Fact
After traveling 90 miles, she reached the free soil of Pennsylvania.

Opinion
I felt like I was in heaven.

TRY IT

Copy and complete the chart below. Fill in the chart with two facts and two opinions from the paragraph about the Underground Railroad on page R2.

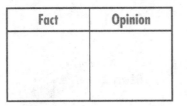

Fact	Opinion

How did you figure out which phrases were facts and which were opinions?

APPLY IT

- Review the steps for understanding fact and opinion from Learn It.
- Read the paragraph below. Then make a chart that lists two facts and opinions from the paragraph.

Ulysses S. Grant was Lincoln's best general, and he seemed fearless. Lincoln decided to put Grant in charge of the entire Union army. He hoped Grant would bring the ugly war to an end.

Grant had two major goals. First, he planned to destroy Lee's army in Virginia. After that, he planned to capture Richmond, the capital of the Confederacy.

For 40 days, from April to June 1864, Grant battled Lee again and again across Virginia. Finally, Grant surrounded Lee in Petersburg, and put the city under siege. In the end, Grant captured Richmond. But he wasted the lives of thousands of Union troops. The Confederacy would have fallen without Grant's attacks.

Words to Know

Common Core Standards
RI.4 Determine the meaning of general academic and domain-specific words and phrases in a text relevant to a grade 5 topic or subject area.

The list below shows some important words you will learn in this unit. Their definitions can be found on the next page, Read the words.

amendment (uh • MEHND • muhnt)

ratify (RAT • a • fi)

federal (fed • ur • uhl)

interest (IN • tur • ist)

productivity (PRO • dak • TI • vah • tee)

scarcity (SKAR • si • tee)

budget (BUJ • it)

dividend (DI • va • dend)

FOLDABLES®

The **Foldable** on the next page will help you learn these important words. Follow the steps below to make your Foldable.

Step 1 Fold along the solid red line.

Step 2 Cut along the dotted lines.

Step 3 Read the words and their definitions.

Step 4 Complete the activities on each tab.

Step 5 Look at the back of your Foldable. Choose ONE of these activities for each word to help you remember its meaning:

- Draw a picture of the word.
- Write a description of the word.
- Write how the word is related to something you know.

An **amendment** is an addition to the U.S. Constitution.	**Give an example of a Constitutional amendment you know. Tell what change it made to our law.** _____ _____
To **ratify** means to officially approve.	**Give an antonym (word that means the opposite) for _ratify_.** _____
Federal is another word for national.	**Write a sentence using the word _federal_.** _____
Interest is money that is paid for the use of borrowed or deposited money.	**Write _interest_ below and circle its prefix.** _____
Productivity is the amount of goods and services that are produced.	**Write the root word of _productivity_.** _____
Scarcity is a shortage of available goods and services.	**Circle the words that belong with scarcity.** Lack rare common Few many poor
A **budget** is a plan for spending and saving money.	**What is one positive aspect of staying on a budget?** _____
A **dividend** is a share of the profit a company makes paid to shareholders.	**Who receives dividends, shareholders or companies?** _____

FOLD

amendment	amendment
ratify	ratify
federal	federal
interest	interest
productivity	productivity
scarcity	scarcity
budget	budget
dividend	dividend

CUT HERE

Primary Sources

Learn about the United States through primary and secondary sources! Primary sources are written or made by someone who witnessed an event. They teach us about people, places, and events.

In contrast, secondary sources are sources that are written or made after an event happens. Secondary sources include encyclopedias, biographies, textbooks, and other books.

Maps

A historical map can be a primary source. A historical map shows what an area looked like at a particular time in the past. Maps can be secondary sources too. For example, maps made today that show what a place looked like long ago are secondary sources. Maps, both primary and secondary ones, help you understand the past.

You can see many different kinds of maps in an atlas. An atlas is a book of maps. You can find an atlas at the back of this book.

DBQ Document-Based Questions

Look at the map. It was made in 1594.
Use it to answer the following questions.

1. Why is trade an industry in the region shown on the map?

_____

_____

2. Is this map a primary source? Why or why not?

_____

_____

networks
connected.mcgraw-hill.com
• Skill Builders
• Resource Library

(t)Fuse/Getty Images, (b)Culture Club/Hulton Archive/Getty Images

The Constitution

How does the Constitution protect the rights of Americans? Tell what you know about the Constitution.

_____

_____

_____

_____

_____

_____

_____

_____

_____

The Constitution guarantees our freedom to speak out about issues.

Words To Know

List the part of speech for each of the following:

____ **amendment**

____ **ratify**

____ **federal**

____ **checks and balances**

____ **Electoral College**

A Living Document

The United States is a nation governed by laws. The highest and most important set of laws in the country is the U.S. Constitution.

Many of the events in U.S. history involve government and the economy. This introduction will help you learn how our government and economy work.

When the leaders of the new nation declared independence from Great Britain in 1776, they wrote a plan of government called the Articles of Confederation. This plan did not work well. In 1787 delegates from 12 states met to write a new plan—the Constitution of the United States.

The writers of the Constitution knew this new plan was not perfect. They also knew the country would change in the years ahead. They designed a way to change the Constitution when necessary. These changes or additions are called **amendments**. The writers made sure that a wide majority of Americans would have to agree on an amendment.

The Amendment Process

An amendment can be made in two different ways. One way is for two-thirds of the Senate and the House of Representatives to vote for it in Congress. The amendment then goes to the states for approval. Three-fourths of the states must **ratify**, or approve, it before it becomes part of the U.S. Constitution.

Another way to add an amendment is for two-thirds of the state legislatures to propose, or ask for it. Congress then organizes a national convention to approve the amendment. This way of amending the Constitution has not yet happened in our country, however.

> **How is the Constitution amended? What do you think of this process?**
>
> _____
>
> _____

Amending the Constitution

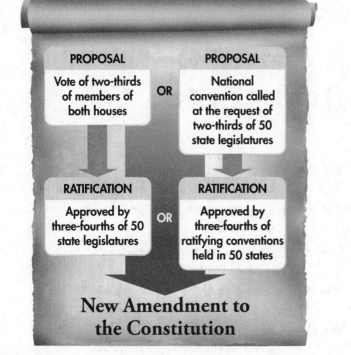

PROPOSAL

Vote of two-thirds of members of both houses

OR

PROPOSAL

National convention called at the request of two-thirds of 50 state legislatures

RATIFICATION

Approved by three-fourths of 50 state legislatures

OR

RATIFICATION

Approved by three-fourths of ratifying conventions held in 50 states

New Amendment to the Constitution

Reading Skill

How can an amendment to the Constitution be proposed?

_____

_____

_____

A Plan For All People

After the Constitution was approved by the delegates of the Constitutional Convention, the states had to vote to approve it. Many of those who had fought for rights during the Revolutionary War were not happy with it. They wanted the Constitution to more clearly protect the rights of citizens. In 1791, the states had approved the first 10 amendments to the Constitution, protecting these rights. Today we know them as the Bill of Rights.

The Bill of Rights

The Bill of Rights begins by protecting basic rights. The First Amendment guarantees five freedoms: freedom of religion, freedom of speech, freedom of the press, freedom of assembly, and freedom to petition, or complain about government policies. Many Americans find this to be the most important amendment.

Just as important as basic freedoms is the right to "due process of the law." Due process of the law means the government must follow rules established by law. Together, the Fourth through Eighth Amendments protect the right to due process. They make sure that people are not arrested unfairly. They also guarantee people fair trials and fair punishment.

Responsibilities

The Bill of Rights does not just talk about rights; it also outlines citizens' responsibilities. For example, the Sixth Amendment guarantees the right to a trial by jury. This means that citizens must be willing to serve as jurors.

Other responsibilities of citizens include voting, paying taxes, following the law and serving in the military.

> (Circle) the two amendments that are the most important. Why?
>
> _____
>
> _____
>
> _____

∞ Bill of Rights ∞

First Ten Amendments

First People have freedom of religion, freedom of speech, freedom of the press; the right to assemble peacefully; the right to complain to the government

Second People have the right to own and use firearms lawfully

Third Prevents the government from forcing people to house soldiers

Fourth People cannot be searched or have property taken without reason

Fifth Protects the rights of people who are accused of crimes

Sixth Guarantees the right to a speedy trial by jury and a lawyer in criminal cases

Seventh Guarantees the right to trial by jury in civil cases

Eighth Prohibits high bail, fines, and cruel or unusual punishment

Ninth The rights of the people are not limited to those listed in the Constitution

Tenth Powers not given to the federal government belong to the states or to the people

Other Limits of Government

The writers of the Constitution did not want the national government to become too powerful. They decided to divide power among the states and the **federal**, or national government.

Some powers only belong to the federal government, such as coining money or regulating foreign trade. The Tenth Amendment of the Bill of Right reserves all other powers for the states, because they affect only the citizens of that state. These powers include establishing schools or creating rules for drivers on roadways.

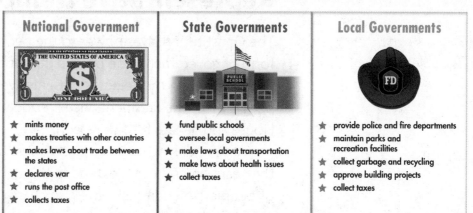

Main Responsibilities Under Federalism

National Government	State Governments	Local Governments
★ mints money ★ makes treaties with other countries ★ makes laws about trade between the states ★ declares war ★ runs the post office ★ collects taxes	★ fund public schools ★ oversee local governments ★ make laws about transportation ★ make laws about health issues ★ collect taxes	★ provide police and fire departments ★ maintain parks and recreation facilities ★ collect garbage and recycling ★ approve building projects ★ collect taxes

Which level of government approves the building of malls?

_____

_____

_____

Separation of Powers

The separation of powers is another way that the United States Constitution prevents the national government from becoming too powerful. The federal government is divided into three branches that have different functions: legislative, executive, and judicial.

The legislative branch consists of members of Congress. They make the laws for our nation. The President heads the executive branch. The executive branch carries out our nation's laws. The judicial branch decides if laws follow the rules stated in the Constitution.

The writers of the Constitution did not want any one branch to become more powerful than the others, so they developed a system of **checks and balances**. Each branch of the federal government can check, or stop, the power of another branch. For example, the President must sign a law before it becomes effective. The President also can veto, or reject, a law. Congress has the power to override, or cancel, a veto with a two-thirds majority. Finally, the Supreme Court can declare a law unconstitutional.

Reading Skill

Fact and Opinion. Name a task of your local government. Do they perform it well? Why or Why not?

_____

_____

_____

Representative Democracy

The Constitution gives power to the people. This is a democratic form of government. The people do not run the government directly, though. Instead, they elect representatives to do this for them. The people elect the President, Vice President, and representatives in the House and Senate for this reason.

At first, only white male landowners had the right to vote. Over the years, amendments extended this right to many more groups of people. Amendments have also changed how some officials are elected, who is allowed to vote, and how elections are run.

Electing Presidents and Senators

The writers of the Constitution did not want the people to vote directly for the President. They were worried that the people could be fooled into voting for an unacceptable candidate too easily. Some suggested that Congress elect the President. Yet, they did not want to give all the power to Congress.

Their solution was the **Electoral College**. In the Electoral College, each state has a certain number of electoral votes based on the number of representatives it has in Congress. The number of representatives is based on a state's population. When people vote for a presidential candidate, they are also voting for a member of the Electoral College, or elector, to vote for their candidate.

Amendments have changed and improved our representative democracy. The Constitution said that the candidate with the most electoral votes would become President, and the candidate with the next-highest number would become Vice President. The Twelfth Amendment, ratified in 1804, changed this. Since then, presidential candidates have chosen their own running mates.

Senators are also elected differently today. Before 1913 the state legislatures selected their state's senators. The Seventeenth Amendment let the people of each state elect senators directly. This is the same way that representatives are chosen.

Extending Voting Rights

Amendments have also extended voting rights. The Fifteenth Amendment helped guarantee African American males the right to vote shortly after the end of the Civil War. You will learn more about the years following the Civil War in Unit 1.

Circle the paragraph that describes the Electoral College.

_____

_____

_____

▼ The original, handwritten Constitution is displayed at the National Archives in Washington, D.C.

National Archives and Records Administration;

14

Women had to wait much longer. It was not until 1920 that the Nineteenth Amendment, giving all women the right to vote, was ratified.

Until the Twenty-sixth Amendment, most states required voters to be at least 21 years old. In the 1960s, many younger Americans fought in a war the United States was waging in Vietnam. Many agreed that if these people were old enough to fight for their country, they should be old enough to vote in their country. In 1971 the voting age was lowered to 18, and millions more Americans voted for the first time.

Securing Voting Rights

Although African Americans were guaranteed the right to vote with the Fifteenth Amendment, some states made it difficult for them to vote. Voters had to pay money, called a poll tax, before they were allowed to vote.

Most African Americans did not have the money to pay this poll tax. Many other people also could not afford this tax. This left many Americans without representation. Finally, in 1964 the Twenty-fourth Amendment ended poll taxes.

Protecting the Right to Vote

Amendment	Year Ratified	What It Did
Fifteenth Amendment	1870	Gave all male citizens the vote regardless of race
Nineteenth Amendment	1920	Gave the vote to women
Twenty-third Amendment	1961	Gave residents of Washington, D.C., the right to vote for President
Twenty-fourth Amendment	1964	Made poll taxes illegal
Twenty-sixth Amendment	1971	Lowered the voting age to 18

Why is it important to have the right to vote?

_____

_____

_____

Which amendment made it illegal to charge people a tax to vote?

Lesson 1

(?) Essential Question How Does the Constitution protect the rights of Americans?

_____

_____

_____

Go back to *Show As You Go!* on pages 2–3.

2 Our Economy

? Essential Question

How does the economy affect people's lives? What do you think?

_____

_____

_____

_____

_____

_____

_____

_____

_____

Words To Know

(Circle) each word with a prefix or suffix.

voluntary exchange

_____

price incentives

_____

specialization

_____

interest

_____

productivity

_____

This couple is shopping for something they want but don't need.

Businesses and Consumers

People make economic choices every day. Economics is the study of how we make decisions in a world where resources are limited. Knowing how the economy works will help you make wise decisions.

The economic system in the United States is called capitalism. In this system, individuals make decisions about what to make, how much to produce, and what price to charge.

Entrepreneurs are people who risk their money to start a new business. They may make or sell goods, such as bicycles or books. Others offer services, such as cutting hair or mowing lawns. When they succeed, entrepreneurs can make a lot of money. However, if they fail, they may lose all the money they invested.

Many people work and in return receive an income. With this income, consumers can purchase the goods and services they need and want.

Purestock/SuperStock

Competition, Markets, and Prices

In capitalism consumers decide for themselves what they want to buy and at what prices. This is called demand. Businesses, in turn, decide what goods or services they want to sell and at what prices. This is called supply.

At markets you will find people who freely buy and sell goods and services. This is called **voluntary exchange**.

Businesses compete with each other when they sell the same product. This leads to **price incentives**. Price incentives happen when a price encourages people to buy or sell a good or service. When supply is high and demand is low, prices decrease. When demand is high and supply is low, prices increase. Some people see high prices as an incentive to start a business and make money.

Why is competition good for consumers?

_____

_____

_____

_____

Write About It!

Tell about a time when you or your family wanted something that was in limited supply.

_____

_____

_____

_____

_____

_____

Sectors of the Economy

Businesses form just one of the four major sectors, or parts, of the United States economy. Households, banks, and the government are the other major sectors. Sectors have important functions, or roles, in the economy.

Households

Households include all the people in the United States. Single people, couples, and families all form households. The people in each household do all major things together. They live in one place and combine their money to buy groceries and pay utilities.

The people in households work to earn a living so that they can pay their bills. Their labor is an important resource in our economy. The people in households act as consumers when they spend their money. They consume goods, such as groceries and clothes. They also consume services by going to the doctor or getting their cars washed. Even you are a consumer! You consume a service by learning from your teacher at school.

Businesses

Businesses form the part of the United States economy where most goods are made and services are provided. They can come in all sizes. Some businesses consist of only a few people, while others may employ thousands.

Businesses often make or sell only one or a few goods or services. They learn to make these products very well. This is called **specialization**. Specialization keeps people from wasting time or resources by making or doing things they are not good at. Businesses can also make these products more cheaply because they put all their resources together.

> **How do banks interact with households?**
>
> _____
>
> _____
>
> _____
>
> _____

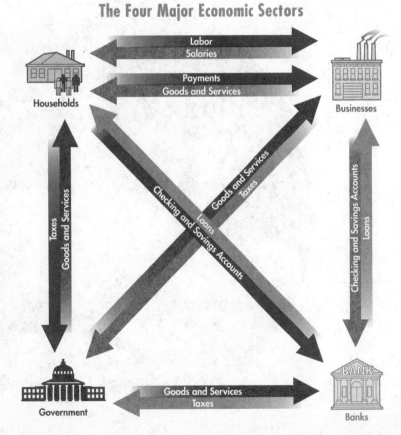

The Four Major Economic Sectors

Households — Labor / Salaries — Businesses
Payments / Goods and Services
Taxes / Goods and Services
Checking and Savings Accounts / Loans
Goods and Services / Taxes
Checking and Savings Accounts / Loans
Government — Goods and Services / Taxes — Banks

Banks

When households and businesses interact, a lot of money changes hands. People receive an income for their work and businesses get paid for their goods and services. Banks are businesses that make money by handling this money.

Banks offer two main kinds of accounts to handle money: checking accounts and savings accounts. With a checking account, you have easy access to all of your money at all times. You can write checks to pay bills and buy products. You can also get cash. Checking accounts help people track and organize their money. They also keep money safe from loss and theft.

To keep money for a longer time, you might put it in a savings account. Banks usually have limits on how often and how much you can take out of that money. In return, you earn **interest**. Interest is money the bank pays you for keeping your money in the account.

Banks use this money to make loans. People borrow money to help them buy expensive items, such as houses. Some borrow money to start a new business, and businesses might use loans to buy new equipment. When they pay back borrowed money, they also have to pay interest. Banks earn money by charging higher interest rates on loans than they pay on savings accounts.

▲ This new bridge is being built with government funds.

> **Why can taxes be considered positive? Why can they be considered negative?**
>
> _____
>
> _____
>
> _____

Government

The government gets its money by collecting taxes. Taxes are money that people and businesses pay for the goods and services they receive from the government. People pay income tax on the money they earn. Businesses also pay taxes on their earnings.

In turn, the government provides goods and services that businesses and people do not usually provide. These include roads and bridges, military and police protection, mail delivery, healthcare, education, and courts.

The government also provides a service by regulating, or setting rules, on how businesses operate. Some regulations protect consumers. Others protect the environment.

The government also works to stabilize, or make steady, the economy. It does this by managing how much money is available in the market. It also sets the interest rate at which banks borrow money from the government.

Trade and Technology

The United States economy has grown greatly since the country started. Some of that growth came when the country grew from 13 states to 50 states. Other things have also helped: trade and technology.

International Trade

During the early years of our country, most communities manufactured or grew almost everything they needed locally. This is no longer true. Many of the foods or clothes we buy today are produced in other parts of the country and even the world.

Americans rely on international trade, or trade between countries, for many goods. The United States imports many raw materials that it does not have from other countries. It also imports products. Importing goods provides a variety of items and encourages competition among businesses, which lowers prices.

The United States also exports both raw materials and many of the products it makes. Exports bring money into the economy, create jobs, and lead to more **productivity**. Productivity is the amount of goods and services that are produced.

Today, the economies of the world are closely interconnected through trade. When one country has an economic problem, it can affect the economies of countries around the world.

U.S. Imports and Exports of Goods — Top 10 Countries

Imports

Rank	Country	Dollars (in billions)	Percentage of Total
1	China	337.8	16.1%
2	Canada	335.6	16.0%
3	Mexico	215.9	10.3%
4	Japan	139.2	6.6%
5	Germany	97.6	4.6%
6	United Kingdom	58.6	2.8%
7	Saudi Arabia	54.8	2.6%
8	Venezuela	51.4	2.4%
9	South Korea	48.1	2.3%
10	France	44.0	2.1%
Total Top 10 Countries		1383.0	65.8%
Total All Countries		2100.4	100.0%

Exports

Rank	Country	Dollars (in billions)	Percentage of Total
1	Canada	261.4	20.1%
2	Mexico	151.5	11.7%
3	China	71.5	5.5%
4	Japan	66.6	5.1%
5	Germany	54.7	4.2%
6	United Kingdom	53.8	4.1%
7	Netherlands	40.2	3.1%
8	South Korea	34.8	2.7%
9	Brazil	32.9	2.5%
10	France	29.2	2.2%
Total Top 10 Countries		796.6	61.2%
Total All Countries		1300.5	100.0%

1. What is the difference in the value of imports and exports with China?

_____

2. Add up the percentage of imports from the top three countries. What does that tell you?

_____

On the other hand, when one country has economic growth, it can help the economies of other countries.

Trade and Specialization

You learned earlier about specialization. Specialization is the main reason why trade occurs. Some countries have resources that other countries do not have. Some are good at producing a particular item better or cheaper. These countries will specialize in those goods or services. They then export them and in turn import those goods or services they do not have or do not make as well or as cheaply.

With specialization, everyone benefits. Countries that specialize in making a product make money selling it. Countries that buy products from countries that specialize in making them benefit because they pay less.

Trade Agreements

Some countries have agreed to make trade easier among them. They have signed formal agreements to easily move goods across borders. This makes the products cheaper and easier to get. All member countries benefit. Businesses gain new customers and consumers can enjoy new, cheaper products.

Technology

New technology also has helped the United States economy grow. Inventions have improved productivity in many ways. Improvements to the plow helped settlers. In 1837 John Deere made a plow that could cut through the roots of prairie grasses. This made farming easier and allowed settlers to farm land that they had not been able to use.

Other technology allows businesses to do things faster and cheaper. For example, machines now do many of the things people once did by hand. Cars and airplanes allow us to get to places quickly. Washers and refrigerators help us with household chores.

Communication also has changed greatly. Many of these changes have come in recent years, with the invention of computers and cell phones. As you read your textbook, you will learn how technology has improved life throughout our country's history.

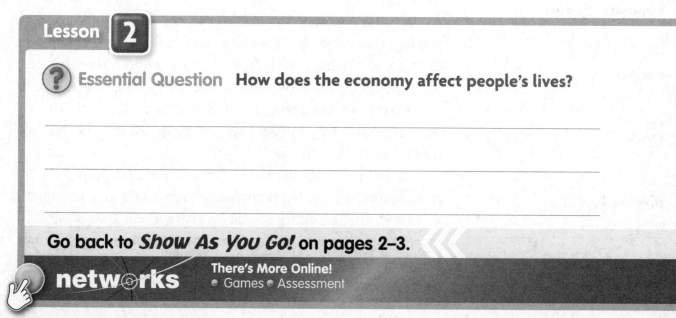

Lesson 2

(?) Essential Question   How does the economy affect people's lives?

_____

_____

_____

Go back to *Show As You Go!* on pages 2–3. «««

netw⊚rks   **There's More Online!**
   ● Games ● Assessment

Personal Finance

Essential Question

How do financial decisions affect how people live? Write two good financial decisions and share them with a partner.

_____

_____

_____

_____

_____

_____

Words To Know

Circle each word with a prefix or suffix.

scarcity

_____

opportunity cost

_____

budget

_____

stock

_____

dividend

_____

bond

_____

Consumers face many choices when buying the things they want and need.

Ed-imaging

Making Choices

We all use money to purchase the goods and services we need and want. Before we decide what to buy, we have to think about how the decision to buy something will affect us now and into the future.

Because we cannot afford to purchase all the things we want and need, we have to make choices. We call things such as food, clothing, and shelter needs. You can't live without them. Once you have met these most basic needs, everything else is a want.

A want, such as a skateboard, is something you can live without. Wants might make your life easier or more fun, but you do not need them to live.

Sometimes you can't have what you want because of **scarcity**. Scarcity happens when there isn't enough of what you want. The reason for scarcity is that we will always want more things than we can produce. There simply are not enough resources to satisfy everybody's wants. Scarcity means that we all have to make choices.

22

People must also decide whether the value they receive is worth the money they spend. For example, a bicycle may cost hundreds of dollars. However, having a bike allows a person to travel faster than walking, saving time. It will also help the person stay healthy. This is a cost-benefit decision. If the benefits are greater than the cost, a consumer may decide to buy the product or service.

When consumers make decisions about what to buy, they also make decisions about what they will not buy. For example, you might want to buy both a pair of jeans and a T-shirt, but you only have enough money for one. The value of the second-best choice—the item you don't buy—is called your **opportunity cost**. If you buy the pair of jeans, the opportunity cost is the value of the T-shirt.

What do consumers consider when spending money? What is important to you?

_____

_____

▼ Scarcity can affect the price of gas.

Image Farm Inc./Alamy Images;

Saving and Budgeting

One way to save money is to put it in a piggy bank. A better way to save is to open a savings account in a bank. Savings accounts help you track how much you are saving. Better yet, you also earn interest! Savings accounts are also safer than a piggy bank. Another way to track your money is with a checking account. After each check is written, your bank records the item and amount in your account.

Making a Budget

When people save money, they are choosing to give up spending that money now in order to be able to buy something in the future. But many people find it difficult to save money. Having a **budget** can help. A budget is a plan for spending and saving money. A budget will make saving money easier.

A budget includes a list of all the expenses and income a person has. Your family's expenses include things like mortgage payments or rent, groceries, car payments, and utilities such as gas and electric. Your personal expenses include the things you buy. You should never spend more than you have. Look at the sample personal budget below.

Income is money you have or plan to have during a certain period of time. Expenses are things you plan to spend your money on during a certain period of time.

THINK · ABOUT · NUMBERS

Suggest two ways for this person to be able to contribute 15 more dollars to her savings.

© Corbis

My Budget		
Category	Planned Expenses	Income
Allowance		+20
Birthday money		+40
Washing cars		+15
To savings	-25	
Gifts	-10	
Books	-5	
Music	-8	
Games	-10	
Snacks	-10	
Other	-7	
Balance		0

Investing

Savings accounts are just one way to save extra money. They help people track their money and keep it in a safe place. If you plan on saving your money for several years, you may want to invest it in stocks. A **stock** is a share of ownership in a company.

If the company does well, the price of the stock increases in value. Then stock can be sold for a profit. Some stocks pay **dividends**, a small share of the profits a company makes, to the stockholders. Buying stock can be risky, however. There is no guarantee that the value of the stock will go up. If it goes down, investors will lose some or even all of the money they have invested.

Bonds are another way of investing. When buyers purchase bonds they loan money in exchange for a fixed amount of money they will get back in the future. Corporations, local governments, state governments, and the federal government sell bonds as a way of raising money to pay for the services they provide. When individuals or communities buy bonds, they are loaning money to the seller. There is less risk in buying bonds than in buying stocks, but the amount of money an investor can make is usually less too.

▲ Wall Street, the Big Apple

What are some advantages to using a savings account to save money?

_____

_____

_____

Lesson **3**

(?) Essential Question **How do financial decisions affect how people live?**

_____

_____

_____

Go back to *Show As You Go!* on pages 2–3. ◀◀◀

networks **There's More Online!**
• Games • Assessment

Beside each number, write the word from the list that matches the description.

specialization	interest	amendment	ratify
federal	scarcity	budget	stock

_____ **1.** A change or addition to the Constitution.

_____ **2.** The national government.

_____ **3.** A shortage of available goods and services.

_____ **4.** To officially approve.

_____ **5.** Money paid when money is kept in a savings account.

_____ **6.** A share of ownership in a company.

_____ **7.** A plan to use money.

_____ **8.** Producing only a few kinds of products.

BIG IDEA

Unit Project

Think about what you have learned about government and economics in this unit. For your unit project, create your own advertisement. You can choose to sell anything you want. Use pages to review what you've learned and apply it to your project. Read the list below to see what should be included in your advertisement.

Your advertisement should...   **Yes it does!**

show what good or service you are selling.

encourage people to buy your product.

explain what currency you will accept for your product.

explain what you want in trade for your product.

use at least two vocabulary terms from this unit.

be colorful and fun!

Think about the Big Idea

BIG IDEA Relationships affect choices.

What have you learned about how government and economics affect choices?

Read the passage before answering Numbers 1 through 6.

The United States government must follow rules established by law. Together, the Fourth through Eighth Amendments protect these rights. They make sure that people are not unfairly arrested. They also guarantee people fair trials and fair punishment. No one—not even the President—is above the law.

1 This passage explains

Ⓐ the limits of the Constitution.

Ⓑ the purpose of the Constitution.

Ⓒ the responsibilities of citizens.

Ⓓ due process of the law.

2 When the price of an item is reduced, more people are likely to buy it. Which term below describes how price encourages people to buy or sell a good or service?

Ⓕ price incentive

Ⓖ voluntary exchange

Ⓗ opportunity cost

Ⓘ specialization

3 When you buy an item, the value of the next best item you did not buy is your

Ⓐ cost benefit decision.

Ⓑ opportunity cost.

Ⓒ price incentive.

Ⓓ voluntary exchange.

4 Many people who had fought for rights during the Revoluntionary War wanted a bill of rights to more clearly protect the rights of citizens. Which of these rights is found in the Bill of Rights?

Ⓕ the right to vote

Ⓖ freedom from slavery

Ⓗ freedom of speech

Ⓘ the right to elect senators

5 Who makes laws?

Ⓐ police officers

Ⓑ teachers

Ⓒ President

Ⓓ lawyers

6 What is an amendment?

Ⓕ a change or addition to the Constitution

Ⓖ to officially approve

Ⓗ a plan to use money

Ⓘ voting rights

UNIT 2 Reconstruction

 Conflict causes change.

In the early 1800s, conflicts brought about many changes. The biggest conflict in American history, the Civil War, changed the way of life of African Americans and many others throughout the South. As you read this unit, think about the changes that happened because of these conflicts. Does war always lead to change?

During Reconstruction African Americans were able to vote and run for office for the first time.

networks
connected.mcgraw-hill.com
● Skill Builders
● Resource Library

U.S. Senator H.R. REVELS, of Mississippi   BENJ. S. TURNE

THE FIRST COLOR

In the

Show As You Go! After you read each lesson, choose an important event from that lesson. Draw a picture to represent the event in the related lesson box. Be sure to include the year and name of the event.

Fold page here.

Lesson 1

Date	Event

Lesson 2

Date	Event

Lesson 3

Date	Event

D SENATOR AN   NTATIVES,

st and 42nd Congress of the United States.

Common Core Standards
RI.5.7: Draw on information from multiple print or digital sources, demonstrating the ability to locate an answer to a question quickly or to solve a problem efficiently.

Draw Conclusions

Reading for understanding is more than noticing the details in a passage. Readers need to think about what the details tell them. Often the details in a passage will help you draw a conclusion. Drawing a conclusion is reaching an opinion based on the details you read.

LEARN IT

- Gather details and other evidence in a reading passage.

- Identify the subject of the passage.

- Look for connections between the pieces of information. Ask yourself what the evidence says about the subject.

- Draw a conclusion based on what you have read.

- Read the passage below and think about what conclusions you can draw from it.

The South's Economy

Text Clue
Confederate money was worthless.

Text Clue
The South no longer had a workforce of enslaved people.

Text Clue
Farmers could not repay debts.

The Confederacy printed its own money. After the war, the money was gone or worthless. Some wealth had been in the form of enslaved workers who were now free. Plantation owners found themselves with no workers and no money to pay hired laborers.

Most farmers in the South owned small farms. Their lands were damaged, and their homes were destroyed. After the war, cotton crops failed several years in a row, leaving farmers with no income to repay their loans.

TRY IT

Complete the graphic organizer below. Fill in lines on the left with the text clues. Fill in the box on the right with a conclusion based on the evidence you gathered.

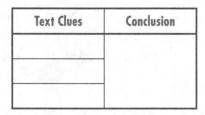

Text Clues	Conclusion

What conclusion did you draw about the Southern economy after the war?

APPLY IT

- Review the steps for drawing conclusions in Learn It.
- Read the paragraphs below. Then use a graphic organizer to draw a conclusion about how African Americans were denied their newly-won rights.

Some white Southerners were determined to not share power with African Americans. They believed in white supremacy, or the idea that white people are superior to other races.

These people began making it harder for African Americans to vote. They created special requirements, such as literacy tests. Literacy is the ability to read and write. In other places, African Americans were required to pay a poll tax. This was a tax people had to pay to before being allowed to vote. Many people were too poor to pay.

Words to Know

Common Core Standards
RI.5.4: Determine the meaning of general academic and
domain-specific words and phrases in a text relevant to a
grade 5 topic or subject area.

The list below shows some important
words you will learn in this unit. Their
definitions can be found on the next page.
Read the words.

impeach (ihm • PEECH)

carpetbagger (kar • pet • bag • uhr)

profit (prof • IT)

tenant (ten • ent)

sharecropping (SHAR • kro • ping)

pardon (par • den)

segregation (seg • reh • GAY • shen)

discrimination (di • skrim • i • NAY • shen)

FOLDABLES®

The **Foldable** on the next page will help you
learn these important words. Follow the steps
below to make your Foldable.

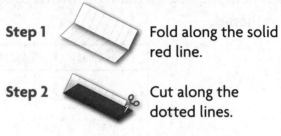

Step 1 Fold along the solid
red line.

Step 2 Cut along the
dotted lines.

Step 3 Read the words and their definitions.

Step 4 Complete the activities
on each tab.

Step 5 Look at the back of your Foldable.
Choose ONE of these activities for
each word to help you remember
its meaning:

- Draw a picture of the word.

- Write a description of the word.

- Write how the word is related to
something you know.

To **impeach** is to charge an official with wrongdoing.	Define *impeach* in your own words.
A **carpetbagger** is the Southern name for Northerners who went south during Reconstruction to help local governments or schools.	If you were a *carpetbagger*, how would you have chosen to help?
Profit is the money made on goods that exceeds the cost of production.	Write a synonym for *profit*. _____
A **tenant** is someone who pays rent.	Circle the part of *tenant* that is a number. Underline the part of *tenant* that is an insect.
Sharecropping is a system in which farmers rented land in exchange for crops.	How many syllables does sharecropping have?
A **pardon** is forgiveness for an offense.	Use the word *pardon* in a sentence.
Segregation is the practice of keeping racial groups separate.	Name some places that have been *segregated*.
Discrimination is an unfair difference in the treatment of people.	List the prefix and suffix contained in *discrimination*.

impeach

impeach

carpetbagger

carpetbagger

profit

profit

tenant

tenant

sharecropping

sharecropping

pardon

pardon

segregation

segregation

discrimination

discrimination

CUT HERE

The Gettysburg Address

"Four **score** and seven years ago our **fathers** brought forth on this continent, a new nation, **conceived** in liberty, and **dedicated** to the **proposition** that all men are created equal.

Now we are engaged in a great civil war, testing whether that nation, or any nation so conceived and so dedicated, can long endure. We are met on a great battlefield of that war. We have come to dedicate a portion of that field, as a final resting place for those who here gave their lives that that nation might live. It is altogether fitting and proper that we should do this.

But, in a larger sense, we cannot dedicate—we can not **consecrate**—we can not **hallow**—this ground. The brave men, living and dead, who struggled here, have consecrated it far above our poor power to add or detract. The world will little note nor long remember what we say here, but can never forget what they did here.

It is for us the living, rather, to be dedicated here to the unfinished work which they who fought here have thus far so nobly advanced. It is rather for us to be here dedicated to the great task remaining before us—that from these honored dead we take increased devotion to that cause for which they gave the last full measure of devotion; that we here highly resolve that these dead shall not have died in vain; that this nation, under God, shall have a new birth of freedom; and that government of the people, by the people, for the people, shall not perish from the earth."

by Abraham Lincoln • Gettysburg, Pennsylvania 1863

score times twenty
fathers forefathers or ancestors
conceived formed
dedicated set apart for a special purpose
proposition intention or plan
consecrate set apart as holy
hallow consider holy

Library of Congress American Memory Collection

netw⊙rks
There's More Online!
⦿ Skill Builders
⦿ Resource Library

Lesson

1 Rebuilding the South

Essential Question

How did political changes affect life after the Civil War? What do you think?

_____

_____

_____

_____

_____

_____

_____

Words To Know

Write a synonym for each of the words below.

Freedmen's Bureau

_____

impeach

_____

scalawag

_____

carpetbagger

_____

The Freedmen's Bureau started schools, such as this one.

A Plan For Reconstruction

After the Civil War, President Lincoln wanted to allow the defeated Confederate states back into the Union. However, they first had to take an oath to support the Constitution and the Union.

Before his death, President Lincoln had been working on a plan for Reconstruction, or rebuilding the South. He felt that reuniting the country was more important than punishing the South for the war. Lincoln asked Americans to

"bind up the nation's wounds, to . . . achieve and cherish a just and lasting peace."

Confederate states had to do two things to reenter the Union. First, 10 percent of each state's voters had to swear loyalty to the Union. Each state could then hold elections and create state governments.

Second, each state also had to ratify, or approve, the Thirteenth Amendment. This amendment abolished slavery in the United States and its territories.

After Lincoln's assassination, President Andrew Johnson moved forward with Lincoln's plan. By December 1865, most Southern states had agreed to the terms. They were once again part of the Union.

Library of Congress Prints and Photographs Division [LC-USZ62-121633]

The Freedmen's Bureau

In March 1865, Lincoln created the **Freedmen's Bureau**. This agency helped newly freed African Americans start new lives. It provided food, clothing, medical care, and legal help to African Americans and whites.

The Bureau started over 4,000 schools for African American adults and children. African Americans also set up colleges and universities in the South. Among these were Fisk University in Tennessee and Spelman College in Georgia.

How were African Americans affected by the Freedmen's Bureau?

_____

_____

_____

_____

_____

Andrew Johnson

Battles On Capitol Hill

When he took office, President Johnson thought the most important task was to restore Southern loyalty to the Union. He preferred to call the process of rebuilding the South "restoration" rather than "Reconstruction."

Some Southern land had been given to freed people. Johnson ordered the land to be restored to its former owners if they swore an oath of loyalty to the Union. He also allowed Southerners to run for political office again.

Johnson's plan upset many Northerners. Many Northerners blamed the South for the war and wanted to punish former Confederate leaders. Others pointed out that people who had led the Confederacy were now leading the new Southern state governments.

President Johnson

Johnson refused to support equal rights for African Americans. In 1866 he vetoed, or rejected, the renewal of the Freedmen's Bureau bill.

In March 1866 Johnson vetoed the Civil Rights Act. He believed it was the job of the states to protect rights.

Johnson believed that Congress was limiting the power of the President. He again vetoed the Freedman's Bureau bill. Johnson also vetoed the Reconstruction Act.

In February 1868, Johnson fired a member of his staff who supported Congress's plan.

Which President thought healing was more important than punishment? _____

Which President vetoed the Freedmen's Bureau bill twice? _____

These Northerners were afraid that under Johnson's plan, little would change for formerly enslaved people. They were right. Almost immediately, the new state governments in the South began to pass new laws called "black codes." These laws were made to limit the rights of African Americans.

In most places, African Americans could not vote, travel freely, or own certain kinds of property. Some codes even forced them to work without pay. Other codes allowed officials to jail unemployed African Americans.

How did black codes limit the rights of formerly enslaved people?

_____

_____

Congress

Congress was angered by Johnson's veto of the Freedmen's Bureau bill and the passage of the black codes in the South. It passed a Civil Rights Act.

Congress overturned the veto of the Civil Rights Act. This is the first time in history a Presidential veto is overturned. In 1867 Congress passed the Reconstruction Act, dividing the South into five districts under Northern military rule. Southern states had to write new constitutions that give all men the right to vote.

Congress wrote and passed the Fourteenth Amendment, which guaranteed all citizens equal protection under the law. Congress also overturned the President's vetoes of the Freedmen's Bureau bill and the Reconstruction Act.

The House voted to **impeach** Johnson. To impeach means to charge an official with wrongdoing. On May 16, 1868, the Senate failed to convict Johnson by one vote.

Congress In Charge

The Reconstruction Act of 1867 divided the South into five military districts. The act said that all males over the age of 21 could vote or hold office, except for those who had served as Confederate officers. The act also required each former Confederate state to write a new constitution and form a new government.

Moving South

The military districts were under the control of martial law. This meant that Union soldiers stayed in cities and towns and made sure the rules were followed. Other Northerners also went to the South. Some went to help the Freedmen's Bureau. Many teachers from the North, such as Charlotte Forten, moved to the South to teach African Americans. Northerners also helped the new state and local governments get started.

Many Northerners moved to the South to start businesses. These people saw a chance to make money, and they did not always do so honestly. Most Southerners resented these Northerners and referred to them as **carpetbaggers**. This name came from the suitcases made of carpeting that many Northerners carried.

Some Southerners cooperated with carpetbaggers and African Americans. Some of these Southerners wanted to gain power or make money. Others simply wanted the South to get back on its feet as soon as possible and thought cooperation was the best way. These people were sometimes called traitors and **scalawags** by other Southerners.

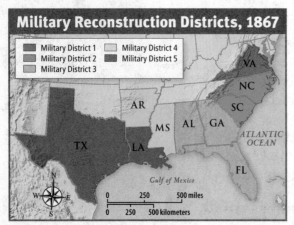

Military Reconstruction Districts, 1867

Military District 1
Military District 2
Military District 3
Military District 4
Military District 5

VA
NC
AR
SC
MS AL GA
TX LA
ATLANTIC OCEAN
FL
Gulf of Mexico

0   250   500 miles
0   250   500 kilometers

Map and Globe Skills

1. How many military districts were there?

_____

2. Which contained the most states?

_____

▲ Blanche K. Bruce (left), Frederick Douglass (center), and Hiram R. Revels (right)

African American Leaders

Northern soldiers in the military districts made sure that African Americans were able to vote. As a result, more than 600 African American leaders were elected to Southern state legislatures. Many more served in local government. In total, 16 African American men served in the United States Congress. Two of them, Hiram R. Revels and Blanche K. Bruce, were elected to the Senate.

Revels was an educator and clergyman. He was born in North Carolina to free parents and attended college in Illinois. During the Civil War, he served as a Union military chaplain for an African American regiment.

After the war, Revels settled in Mississippi and worked to establish schools for African Americans. He was elected to Mississippi's state legislature in 1869. One year later, Revels became the first African American to serve as a U.S. Senator.

Bruce was born into slavery but escaped to Kansas. After the Civil War, he moved to Mississippi and was elected to the Senate in 1875. During his six-year term, Bruce worked for the fair treatment of African Americans and Native Americans. He also opposed U.S. policies that were unfair to Chinese immigrants. Later, he served in other positions in the federal government.

How did the Reconstruction Act affect African Americans?

_____

_____

Constitutional Amendments

During Reconstruction Congress passed three very important amendments to the Constitution. These amendments work together to guarantee equal protection under the law for all citizens.

Making Slavery Illegal

The Thirteenth Amendment was approved in 1865, before the Civil War ended. The Thirteenth Amendment made slavery illegal throughout the United States and its territories. In order for the Southern states to be accepted back into the Union, they had to ratify this amendment.

Granting Equal Protection

Congress soon realized that the Thirteenth Amendment did not do enough to protect the rights of African Americans. In 1868 the passage of the Fourteenth Amendment granted citizenship to everyone born in the United States, except Native Americans.

This amendment also promised that no one, not even the government, had the power to take away a citizen's "life, liberty, or property" without due process of law. This means that the government must follow the rules and rights guaranteed by the Constitution. This amendment also guarantees equal protection under the law to all citizens.

Providing Voting Rights

Finally, in 1869 Congress approved the Fifteenth Amendment. This amendment ensured all citizens the right to vote regardless of "race, color, or previous condition of servitude," or condition of enslavement.

DID YOU KNOW?

As an American citizen, you have the responsibility to protect not only your own rights, but also the rights of others. For example, all citizens of voting age have the responsibility to be informed and to vote. You have the right to let your voice be heard and to ask questions of your government. You also have the responsibility to respect the ideas and opinions of others.

▲ Voters in Delaware, OH

Explain the responsibilities citizens have when voting and what might happen if people were not allowed to vote.

▲ The State Capitol of South Carolina in Columbia, South Carolina today.

The Fifteenth Amendment had a major effect on politics in the United States. For the first time, hundreds of thousands of African Americans were able to vote.

While this amendment protected the voting rights of African American men, Native Americans and women were still excluded. They would not receive the right to vote until much later.

How did these three amendments influence the country's beliefs?

_____

_____

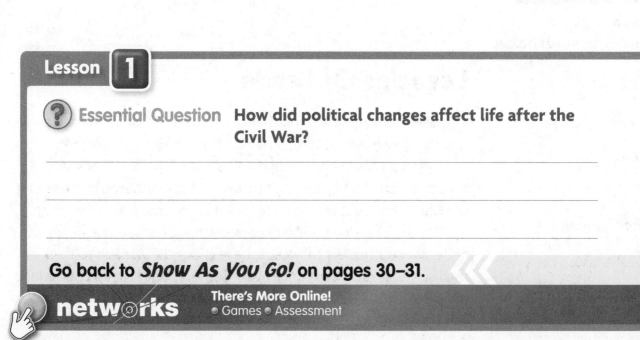

Lesson **1**

(?) Essential Question **How did political changes affect life after the Civil War?**

_____

_____

_____

Go back to _Show As You Go!_ on pages 30–31. ◀◀

netw⊙rks **There's More Online!**
● Games ● Assessment

Life During Reconstruction

? Essential Question

How did life in the South change during Reconstruction? Who thought it was better for them?

_____

_____

_____

_____

_____

_____

_____

Words To Know

Write a synonym for each of the words below.

profit

_____

tenant

_____

sharecropping

_____

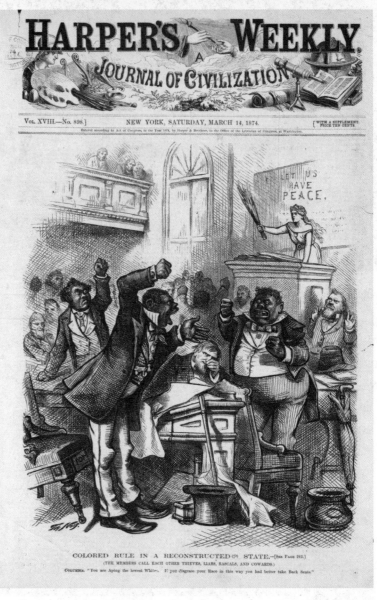

◀ Many newly freed African Americans fought for civil rights.

Legacies Of Leaders

The Civil War and its aftermath made leaders out of many men and women. Three leaders left legacies that will long be remembered.

Although Abraham Lincoln died just days after the Civil War ended, he left a lasting legacy. Above all, Lincoln believed in preserving the Union. He thought it was important to reconcile with the South.

Robert E. Lee led the Confederate Army. After the war, he urged his fellow Southerners to accept the result of the war and to think of themselves as Americans once again. Lee left public life and became the president of Washington College in Lexington, Virginia. The school was later renamed Washington and Lee University in his honor.

A Powerful Voice

Frederick Douglass was an abolitionist leader who had once been enslaved. During the Civil War, he asked President Lincoln to allow African American men to fight for the Union. Once the war ended, Douglass fought for the adoption of the Thirteenth, Fourteenth, and Fifteenth Amendments.

Douglass was a great speaker. Through his many speeches, he sought civil rights for all people. In later years, he worked for women's rights and against the mistreatment of Native Americans and Chinese immigrants. In a speech he gave in 1892, Douglass challenged Americans to

"have loyalty enough, honor enough, [and] patriotism enough to live up to their own Constitution."

▲ Frederick Douglass worked for civil rights during the 1800s.

Why is Frederick Douglass remembered today?

_____

_____

_____

_____

DID YOU KNOW?

Arlington House belonged to General Lee and was taken by Union forces in 1861. Three years later, the property became the site for a national cemetery. More than 300,000 Americans are buried at **Arlington National Cemetery.**

Arlington National Cemetery

The Postwar Economy

Most of the battles of the Civil War had been fought in the South. As a result, many of the South's railroads, buildings, and bridges lay in ruins. The cities of Charleston, South Carolina; Richmond, Virginia; and Atlanta, Georgia, were almost completely destroyed.

Financial Losses

During the secession of the Southern states, the Confederacy had printed its own money, but this money was not recognized by the United States. After the war, the once-wealthy plantation owners of the South were financially ruined. Their money was gone or worthless. Some of their wealth had been in the form of enslaved workers who now were free. Plantation owners found themselves with no workers and no money to pay hired laborers.

Most farmers in the South owned small farms. They had never been wealthy, but they suffered losses as a result of the war as well. Their lands were damaged, and their homes were destroyed. These farmers had to borrow money to rebuild their farms.

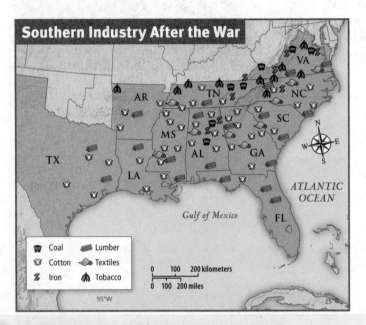

Southern Industry After the War

Coal Lumber
Cotton Textiles
Iron Tobacco

0 100 200 kilometers
0 100 200 miles

95°W

ATLANTIC OCEAN

Gulf of Mexico

Map and Globe Skills

1. What industries were present in Georgia after the Civil War?

_____

_____

Imagine you were a shopkeeper in this city. How would your business have changed?

_____

_____

Many cities in the South were destroyed during the Civil War, such as Richmond, Virginia.

Following the war, the cotton crop failed several years in a row, leaving farmers with no income to repay their loans. Across the South, farmers fell deeper into debt.

Rebuilding

Immediately after the war, the South began to rebuild. Between 1865 and the early 1870s, more than 8,000 miles of railroad track were laid in the South. Funding for this project came mostly from the federal government and Northern investors. Shipping ports, bridges, and communication systems were also built or repaired during this time.

Before the war, there had been few factories in the South. Slowly, with the help of Northern money, the South's textile, tobacco, and steel industries began to grow.

The Economy in the North

Meanwhile, the economy of the North was prospering. Few battles had been fought in the North, so there was little need for rebuilding.

During the war, Northern factories were busy turning out supplies for the Union Army. Factory owners and banks **profited**, or made money, from the war. During Reconstruction these factories were producing more than ever.

More goods to sell meant more profit. This money was reinvested into inventions and the construction of new factories. As more factories were built, there were many opportunities for jobs. This led to an increase in the number of immigrants arriving from Europe. In turn, Northern cities grew quickly.

Postwar Economic Growth

Use the graphs below to answer the questions about postwar economic growth.

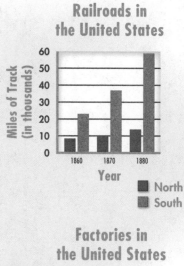

Railroads in the United States

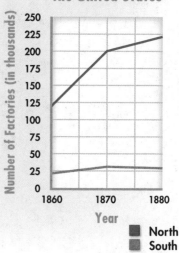

Factories in the United States

1. Which part of the country had both more factories and more miles of railroads?

2. How would having fewer railroads affect the growth of manufacturing?

Life After The War

The end of the Civil War brought other changes. Much of the pre-war economy of the South had depended on enslaved workers.

Sharecropping

Newly freed African Americans had no land, and Southern landowners needed workers. Landowners rented land to African Americans who would live and work on it as **tenant** farmers. A tenant is someone who pays rent.

One form of tenant farming was **sharecropping**. Tenants paid a portion of their crops as rent—sometimes as much as half of the crop. Landowners also loaned money for seeds and tools, which caused more debt.

There were many problems with this system. Sharecroppers often did not have enough crops to sell after they paid their rent and debt. Some borrowed money to survive, which caused more debt. Slavery was over, but many African Americans were poor and had little hope of improving their economic conditions.

▼ House wall of an Alabama sharecropper.

Women and Family

During the war, the wives and daughters of wealthy plantation owners often had to run the plantations by themselves. After the war, many wives were widowed. This caused women to take on new roles and responsibilities.

Many African American women worked as sharecroppers, as servants, or as factory workers. Those with a place to live often took in relatives or orphans, or they joined with other single women to support one another.

How was sharecropping like slavery? How was it different?

_____

_____

_____

_____

_____

_____

Lesson 2

? Essential Question **How did life in the South change during Reconstruction?**

_____

_____

_____

Go back to *Show As You Go!* on pages 30–31.

Reconstruction Ends

National Archives and Records Administration

Essential Question

How did discrimination affect life in the South? What do you think?

_____

_____

_____

_____

_____

_____

Words To Know

Tell a partner what you know about each word.

pardoned

segregation

discrimination

The 15th Amendment to the U.S. Constitution

Political Changes

During Reconstruction, Congress made an effort to build a society that was fair to all. The results did not last.

Most white Southerners accepted the Confederacy's loss and the end of slavery after the war. However, many were not ready to accept the social changes taking place in the South. For some, accepting African Americans as equals meant admitting that slavery was wrong and that the South was unjustified in seceding from the Union.

Many Southerners were unhappy with the new state governments. They also did not like African Americans holding public office. The use of tax money to provide services to and fund programs for African Americans was another issue that many Southerners disliked.

Pardons and Amnesty

While in office, President Johnson **pardoned**, or forgave, the offenses of many high-ranking Confederate leaders. He even pardoned Jefferson Davis, who had been president of the Confederacy. Other Confederate leaders, however, were not pardoned.

Then, in 1872 Congress passed the Amnesty Act. This law pardoned all former Confederate soldiers, except the highest ranking officers, and restored their right to vote. Some former leaders of the Confederacy won elections into Congress and state legislatures. Almost immediately they began trying to remove the rights African Americans had gained.

> **Why was it difficult for white Southerners to accept social changes in the South?**
>
> _____
>
> _____
>
> _____

DID YOU KNOW?

In 1875 Congress passed a **Civil Rights Act**, which guaranteed African Americans full and equal access to public facilities. The law was overturned by the Supreme Court in 1883.

The End Of Reconstruction

Some white Southerners were determined not to share power with African Americans. They believed in white supremacy, or the idea that white people were superior to other races.

These people began making it harder for African Americans to vote by creating special requirements, such as literacy tests. Literacy is the ability to read and write. In other places, African Americans were required to pay a poll tax. This was a tax people had to pay before being allowed to vote. Many people were too poor to pay.

Violence in the South

Some whites used violence and terror to keep African Americans from voting or from otherwise exercising their rights. In 1866 six former Confederate officers formed the Ku Klux Klan. Disguised in white hoods, they terrorized African Americans, driving them from their homes and destroying their property. They also kept African Americans and their white supporters from voting.

When local authorities did nothing to stop the growing violence in the South, Congress passed the Enforcement Acts. These laws banned the use of terror or bribery to keep people from voting. It also gave the federal government the right to punish those who broke these laws.

McGraw-Hill Education

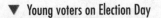

▼ Young voters on Election Day

List three methods people used to prevent others from voting during Reconstruction.

_____

_____

Library of Congress, Prints and Photographs Division [LC-US262-28024]

◄ Ku Klux Klan

The Compromise of 1877

In the presidential election of 1876, Democrat Samuel J. Tilden of New York won the popular vote. The electoral vote, however, was in question in some states, including three in the South. In March of the following year, leaders in Congress worked out a deal that became known as the Compromise of 1877.

According to this deal, the Republican candidate, Rutherford B. Hayes, promised to remove all Union troops from the South if the electoral votes were cast for him. The Democrats from the South, who were white, promised to uphold the rights that African Americans had gained. Congress declared Hayes the winner. President Hayes quickly ordered the removal of federal troops. Reconstruction ended.

Legal Separation in the South

At this time, Southern states began to take control of state governments. They also started a policy called **segregation**. Segregation is the separation of people based on their race. The states created laws called "Jim Crow laws" to make segregation legal in the South. These laws were based on **discrimination**, an unfair difference in the way people are treated.

Under the Jim Crow laws, African Americans had to ride in separate railroad cars, eat at separate restaurants, stay in separate hotels, and use separate drinking fountains and public toilets. Although the Jim Crow laws were aimed mostly at African Americans, they also affected other groups, such as Asian Americans and Native Americans.

Segregation also existed in the North, but it was mostly from custom and was not legally enforced. In many communities, African American and white children went to the same schools and sat in the same classrooms. On the other hand, African Americans in the North were often not accepted in public places.

Why did white Southerners create Jim Crow laws?

_____

_____

_____

_____

_____

_____

_____

55

Life After Reconstruction

Because of Jim Crow laws, most Southern towns had separate schools for white children and African American children. Schools for most white children were in sturdy buildings. These schools had better teachers and received adequate funding. Schools for African Americans were often run down. These schools did not receive much funding and had old, tattered books, if any at all.

Unequal Treatment

In the 1800s, some people in Louisiana tried to change the laws. They asked Homer Plessy to sit in the white section of a railroad car. Homer Plessy had light skin, but by law he was considered African American because one of his great-grandparents was African American. When Plessy was arrested, the case went all the way to the Supreme Court. The case was called *Plessy* v. *Ferguson*.

In 1896 the Supreme Court upheld the Louisiana law. It said "separate" facilities for African Americans and whites were constitutional as long as they were "equal." One justice disagreed with the decision. You can read his words in the Primary Source box. The Court's decision meant that Jim Crow laws would stand. The Supreme Court would not change its decision until 1954.

Although the Fourteenth Amendment had granted equal citizenship, segregation resulted in unequal treatment. African Americans did not enjoy many of the rights guaranteed by the Thirteenth, Fourteenth, and Fifteenth Amendments until the civil rights movement of the 1950s and 1960s.

Library of Congress Prints and Photographs Division [LC-USZ62-61855]

Primary Source

"In view of the Constitution, in the eye of the law, there is in this country no superior, dominant, ruling class of citizens. There is no caste here. Our Constitution is color-blind, and neither knows nor tolerates classes among citizens. In respect of civil rights, all citizens are equal before the law."

—from the dissenting opinion, written by Justice John Marshall Harlan, in the 1896 *Plessy* v. *Ferguson* ruling

Write a sentence explaining Justice Harlan's statement.

_____

_____

A segregated school in South Carolina ▶

New Leaders

Some African Americans were determined to succeed despite the obstacles they faced. Ida B. Wells was a journalist and a teacher from Mississippi. She was part owner of a newspaper called the *Free Speech and Headlight*. Wells used this newspaper to write about the violence and discrimination African Americans faced across the country. She later worked to end segregation in schools.

Booker T. Washington and W.E.B. Du Bois had different opinions about how African Americans should achieve equality.

Booker T. Washington was an African American teacher and author. In 1881 he founded the Tuskegee Institute in Alabama. Students learned bricklaying, carpentry, and teaching. Washington didn't believe that African Americans should fight for equal rights. He thought the best way to achieve equality was to learn a skill and gain economic freedom.

Another African American leader, W.E.B. Du Bois, disagreed with Washington's ideas. Du Bois believed that African Americans deserved equality and should demand it immediately. Like Washington, Du Bois was an educator and author. He also worked as a magazine editor. Du Bois cofounded the National Association for the Advancement of Colored People (NAACP). The purpose of this organization is to seek equality of rights.

Lesson 3

(?) Essential Question How did discrimination affect life in the South?

_____

_____

_____

Go back to *Show As You Go!* on pages 30–31. «««

networks **There's More Online!** • Games • Assessment

Reconstruction

Read the words in the box and the speech bubbles below. Decide which word fits on each blank. Write the word below the speech bubble.

scalawag	impeach	carpetbagger
tenant	sharecropper	pardoned

President Johnson did this to the offenses of many Confederate leaders.

_____

President Johnson was charged with wrongdoing.

_____

A white Southerner who worked with Northerners and African Americans during Reconstruction.

_____

A Northerner who went south during Reconstruction.

_____

Someone who pays rent.

_____

Someone who rents the land to farm and pays with some of the crops.

_____

BIG IDEA

Unit Project

A museum has hired you and a partner to create an exhibit about an event from Reconstruction. Make an exhibit on one of the events you learned about in this unit. Before you begin working, look back at **Show as You Go!** on to review your notes. Read the list below to see what information should be included in your museum exhibit. As you work, check off each item as you include it.

Your museum exhibit should...   **Yes it does!**

include text that describes what happened
during the event and why the event was important.   ☐

include at least one image that supports your text.   ☐

include research from primary sources.   ☐

include research from secondary sources.   ☐

be neat and legible.   ☐

be interesting to look at and appealing to visitors.   ☐

Think about the Big Idea

BIG IDEA Conflict causes change.

What did you learn in this unit that helps you understand the BIG IDEA?

_____

_____

_____

_____

Read the passage "Steam Engines" before answering Numbers 1 through 8.

Steam Engines

by Kim Lee

The history of the invention of the steam engine started a long time ago. A man named Hero of Alexandria, who lived in ancient Egypt, was the first person to experiment with a steam engine. In the early 1700s, Thomas Newcomen made the first useful steam engine in England. In 1765 James Watt made important improvements to the steam engine. By the early 1800s, steam engines were being used in the United States. The first steam engine was used in Florida in 1827.

It might not seem like it now, but the steam engine was a very important invention. For one thing, the steam engine changed transportation. Before the steam engine, people used sailboats, animals, or walked to get from place to place. The steam engine created new, faster modes of transportation for people and goods. For instance, boats powered by steam engines, called steamboats, traveled faster than sailboats could. Steamboats had another advantage over sailboats too. Steamboats didn't have to rely on the wind to move people and goods.

Steam engines also helped the development of another important form of transportation—railroads. Steam engines powered trains as they moved across land. Unlike steamboats, railroads could reach inland places that weren't located along the coasts. Now moving people and goods across land became easier and faster.

1 Which event in the passage happened FIRST?

Ⓐ A steam engine was used in Florida.

Ⓑ Steam powered railroads were built.

Ⓒ James Watt improved the steam engine.

Ⓓ Thomas Newcomen built a steam engine.

2 Read this paragraph from the passage.

> **In 1765 James Watt made important improvements to the steam engine. By the early 1800s, steam engines were being used in the United States. The first steam engine was used in Florida in 1827.**

Which overall text structure did the author use in this paragraph?

Ⓕ chronology

Ⓖ comparison

Ⓗ cause and effect

Ⓘ problem and solution

3 According to the text, why were steamboats better than sailboats?

Ⓐ Steamboats were faster than railroads.

Ⓑ Steamboats traveled faster than sailboats.

Ⓒ Steamboats looked better than sailboats.

Ⓓ Steamboats could reach inland places and sailboats couldn't.

4 Read this sentence from the passage.

The steam engine created new, faster modes of transportation for people and goods.

What does the author mean by the word *modes*?

Ⓕ bridges

Ⓖ kinds

Ⓗ roads

Ⓘ sailboats

5 Which of the following is the best summary for the ENTIRE passage?

Ⓐ Trains changed transportation.

Ⓑ Thomas Newcomen made a very important invention.

Ⓒ The steam engine was an important invention that improved people's lives.

Ⓓ Steamboats and trains are two forms of transportation that people use today.

6 According to the passage, which type of transportation did the steam engine help create?

Ⓕ airplanes

Ⓖ canoes

Ⓗ cars

Ⓘ trains

7 What was the effect of the steam engine on people's lives?

Ⓐ The steam engine made people rich.

Ⓑ The steam engine made transportation faster and easier.

Ⓒ The steam engine used windpower to help people travel.

Ⓓ The steam engine powered household appliances.

8 According to the passage, how are steamboats and trains DIFFERENT?

Ⓕ Steamboats move faster than trains.

Ⓖ Steamboats and trains use steam engines.

Ⓗ Steamboats travel on water and trains travel on land.

Ⓘ Steamboats and trains were invented by different people.

3 The Nation Grows

BIG IDEA Location affects how people live.

Americans began to move westward in the mid-1800s. They wanted more. In this unit, you will read about why people started heading west and what happened to the people along the way. You will also read about the Native Americans that already lived there and what happened when these different cultures met. As you read, think about how location can change a person's life.

networks connected.mcgraw-hill.com
● Skill Builders
● Vocabulary Flashcards

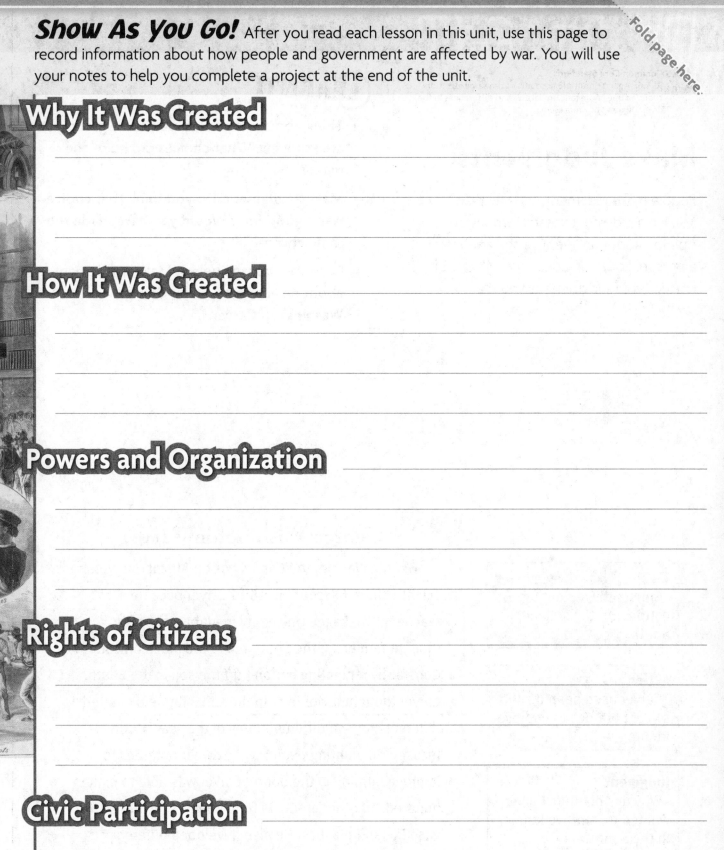

Show As You Go! After you read each lesson in this unit, use this page to record information about how people and government are affected by war. You will use your notes to help you complete a project at the end of the unit.

Fold page here.

Why It Was Created

How It Was Created

Powers and Organization

Rights of Citizens

Civic Participation

Common Core Standards
RI.5.6: Analyze multiple accounts of the same event or topic, noting important similarities and differences in the point of view they represent.

Make Judgments

People make judgments as they read. Making a judgment means forming an opinion about an event or the actions of a person. Look for clues that support or correct your judgment as you read.

LEARN IT

- Think about a historical person or group you are studying. What choices did he or she make?

- Make a judgment. Do you think that choice was a good one? Would you have made the same choice?

- Read the passage below. Make a judgment about an action taken by George Washington Carver.

| **Clue** |
| Constantly replanting cotton hurt the soil in the South. |

| **Action** |
| Carver used peanuts and sweet potatoes to improve farming. |

| **Judgment** |
| Why do you think Carver wanted to improve farming in the South? |

George Washington Carver

George Washington Carver was an African American scientist from Missouri. In 1896 Carver became a teacher at Tuskegee University in Alabama. Carver thought farmers in the South relied too much on cotton. Constantly replanting cotton hurt the soil in the South. Carver thought it would help the soil if farmers planted different crops at different times of the year. Carver focused on planting peanuts and sweet potatoes to improve farming in the South. Carver was able to make hundreds of other products from peanuts, including gasoline and plastics. He also developed different methods for farming to improve the soil and maximize crop growth.

TRY IT

Copy the graphic organizer below. Complete it with actions and judgment about the paragraph on the previous page.

Action	→	Judgement
	→	
	→	
	→	

What judgment would you make about George Washington Carver?

APPLY IT

- **Review the steps for making judgments. Complete a chart for the paragraph below. Make a judgment about Ida Tarbell.**

Action	→	Judgement
	→	
	→	
	→	

Ida Tarbell was a journalist who wrote about dishonest businesses and politicians. In 1903 Tarbell wrote a book about John D. Rockefeller and his Standard Oil Company. She showed how Rockefeller had taken unfair advantage of his competitors. Tarbell accused Rockefeller of forming trusts to get rid of competition. Several chapters from her book were published as articles in a magazine. People across the country read these articles. Not long after Tarbell's articles appeared, Congress broke Standard Oil into several smaller companies.

Words to Know

Common Core Standards
RI.5.4: Determine the meaning of general academic and domain-specific words and phrases in a text relevant to a *grade 5 topic or subject area*.

The list below shows some important words you will learn in this unit. Their definitions can be found on the next page. Read the words.

homesteader (HOHM • sted • uhr)

poverty (PAV • uhr • tee)

cattle drive (KAT • al dryv)

reservation rez • uhr • VAY • shen)

monopoly (MA • nahp • uhl • ee

commute (KA • mute)

slum (slum)

suffrage (SUF • raj)

Foldables®

The Foldable on the next page will help you learn these important words. Follow the steps below to make the Foldable.

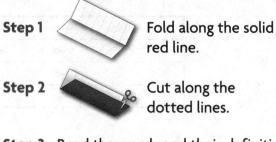

Step 1 Fold along the solid red line.

Step 2 Cut along the dotted lines.

Step 3 Read the words and their definitions.

Step 4 Complete the activities on each tab.

Step 5 Look at the back of your Foldable. Choose ONE of these activities for each word to help you remember its meaning:

- Draw a picture of the word.

- Write a description of the word.

- Write how the word is related to something you know.

	FOLD
A **homesteader** is a person who claimed land on the Great Plains under the Homestead Act of 1862.	Circle a synonym for house contained in *homesteader*.
Poverty is the condition of being poor.	Write an antonym for *poverty*.
A **cattle drive** is the movement of large herds of cattle, by cowboys, from ranches to railroad stations.	Draw a small picture of a *cattle drive*.
A **reservation** is a territory set aside for Native Americans.	Do you know another meaning of the word *reservation* other than the one we gave you? Write it below.
Monopoly means total control of a type of industry by a person or company.	*Mono* means one. Write a definition of *monopoly* using the word one.
To **commute** means to travel back and forth regularly.	What *commute* do you have five days a week?
A **slum** is a rundown neighborhood.	Circle the words that belong with *slum*. disrepair pretty new old fancy broke
Suffrage is the right to vote.	Define *suffrage* in your own words.

homesteader	homesteader
poverty	poverty
cattle drive	cattle drive
reservation	reservation
monopoly	monopoly
commute	commute
slum	slum
suffrage	suffrage

CUT HERE

Primary and Secondary Sources

Artifacts

Objects created by humans long ago are called artifacts. Scientists called archaeologists study artifacts to learn about how people lived in the past. To understand artifacts, you must know the geography of the area where it was found. You then need to study the design of the artifact. Next, think about how someone might have used it in the past.

In this unit, you will learn that as the American West was settled, the Native Americans lost much of their land and were moved to reservations. In that process, artifacts were lost and destroyed.

▲ Anasazi artifacts

DBQ Document-Based Questions

Study the artifacts. Then complete the activities.

1. Choose an artifact and describe how it was most likely used in the past.

   _____

   _____

   _____

▲ Mound Builder artifact

2. Imagine that scientists in the future are studying our culture. Draw an artifact from your life that would give them clues about how you live.

© George H.H. Huey / Alamy

networks
There's More Online!
● Skill Builders
● Resource Library

Settling the West

Essential Question

How did westward expansion change the United States?
What do you think?

_____

_____

_____

_____

_____

Words To Know

Define these terms in your own words.

manifest destiny

_____

transcontinental railroad

_____

homesteader

_____

exoduster

_____

poverty

_____

cattle drive

_____

Cowboys rode well-trained horses and used ropes, called lariats, to herd cattle on long drives.

The Rush to the West

Americans began to move westward in the mid-1800s. The West offered new economic opportunities and new ways of life.

Even before the Civil War, many Americans looked to the West. This area was called the frontier, or unsettled land near the country's boundaries. Some moved west for the opportunity to own land. Others headed west in the hopes of making fortunes.

The Mining Industry

In the mid-1800s, deposits of gold, silver, and copper were discovered in the West. Many of these minerals were important to the rapidly growing industries of the eastern United States.

Many people saw the mineral deposits as a way to make a lot of money. They packed their bags and moved out West to make their fortunes. Towns quickly grew. These "boomtowns," as they were known, were good for the growth of businesses. Stores, hotels, saloons, and restaurants provided goods, services, and jobs to the local community.

When mineral deposits dried up, the economy of these towns failed. Miners moved on in search of new deposits elsewhere. Some boomtowns then became "ghost towns."

Manifest Destiny

In the 1840s, Americans began moving into the upper Midwest and the Great Plains. They believed in **manifest destiny**, the idea that the United States should rule from the Atlantic Ocean to the Pacific Ocean. After Reconstruction, many more people headed west. Some were immigrants from Europe. Others came from the East looking for a new life and the chance to own land.

The last part of the frontier to settle was Oklahoma. After that, in 1890, the government declared the frontier settled and part of the United States.

> Why did some towns quickly grow and fall in the West?
>
> _____
>
> _____

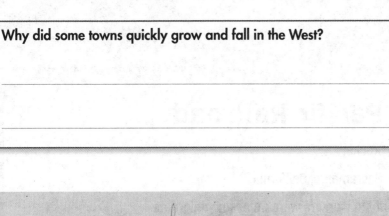

DID YOU KNOW?

At noon on April 22, 1889, the U.S. government opened the Oklahoma Territory for settlement. In a single day, more than 50,000 people raced into the territory to claim land. They found some people already there. The people who had sneaked in before the starting time came to be called "Sooners."

The Transcontinental Railroad

After the 1848 discovery of gold in California, there was greater need for a **transcontinental railroad**, or a railroad that crosses the continent. Congress passed the Pacific Railway Act in 1862 granting two railroad companies land to build the railroad. Congress added amendments that offered money and land for every mile completed.

From the start, building the railroad proved difficult, because many workers were fighting in the Civil War. By 1865, neither company had laid more than 50 miles of track.

Central Pacific Railroad

Led by Charles Crocker

Starting Point Sacramento, California

Labor Nine out of ten workers were Chinese immigrants.

Dangers and Obstacles The Central Pacific made slow progress because workers had to cross the Sierra Nevada. Chinese workers blasted tunnels through the mountains using gunpowder. Thousands died from explosions, freezing temperatures, and avalanches.

Great Achievement On April 28, 1869, Central Pacific workers laid ten miles of track across the desert in 12 hours! This was an all-time record.

The Golden Spike

Finally, after six years, the Union Pacific and the Central Pacific railways met at Promontory Point, Utah. The tracks were joined by a spike made of gold. Five days later, train service began. Ticket prices were $111 for first class, $80 for second class, and $40 for third class.

The trip from New York to San Francisco was still uncomfortable, but now it took one week instead of many months.

Why did the Central Pacific Railroad make slower progress than the Union Pacific?

_____

_____

_____

Union Pacific Railroad

Led by Grenville Dodge

Starting Point Omaha, Nebraska

Labor Many were Irish and German immigrants who were paid low wages but received food and shelter.

Dangers and Obstacles Work was easier on the Union Pacific Railroad because track was built across the Great Plains. The Lakota and Cheyenne often attacked the railroad workers because the tracks were cutting across their traditional hunting grounds. The Union Pacific began to post soldiers along the track as the railroad continued west.

Great Achievement Grenville Dodge had been a general in the Union Army. He organized his work teams like army units. They were able to lay track more quickly than the Central Pacific Railroad.

Architect of the Capitol

Homesteading on the Plains

Imagine you are one of the people in this photo, write a sentence describing your house. Tell what you like and don't like about it.

_____

_____

_____

In 1862 President Lincoln signed the Homestead Act. Under this act, a head of a household who was at least 21 years old could claim 160 acres of land.

The people who claimed land under this act became known as **homesteaders**. Homesteaders agreed to live on the land for at least five years, improve the land, build at least a 12-foot by 14-foot home, grow crops, and pay a small fee.

The Homestead Act made claims to land legal and secure. Settlers were now more willing to move to the West. Eventually, 270 million acres, about 10 percent of the area of the United States, were settled under this act.

Life was hard, yet homesteaders wanted the chance of a better life. There were few trees for lumber and little to no fresh water. In order to access groundwater, wells were dug up to 300 feet deep. In the cold winters, bitter winds made snow drifts high enough to cover houses. Summers were extremely hot and dry, causing prairie fires and droughts.

The settlers called themselves sodbusters because of the tough ground, called sod, which they had to break, or "bust," through to plant crops. Because there were no trees for wood, homesteaders made houses made of sod called soddies. They also used tough prairie grass to strengthen walls and roofs.

▼ Dowse Sod House located in Comstock, Custer County, Nebraska.

This photograph shows Washington Street in Nicodemus, Kansas, a town settled by exodusters.

Succeeding on the Great Plains

Even though people faced many hardships on the plains, some were able to make a profit. Farming the plains became a little easier in the mid-1800s, when Scottish immigrant James Oliver invented the chilled-steel plow. This new plow did not crack or break if it hit a stone in the field.

As farming technology improved, farmers struggled to find a crop able to withstand the dry summer months on the Great Plains. In the 1880s, farmers began planting wheat. Wheat fields were naturally suited to the dry, rocky soil of the plains. By the late 1800s, the United States produced so much wheat that it became the world's leading wheat exporter.

African Americans in the West

The end of Reconstruction also meant the end of federal protection for African Americans in the South. As a result, many felt that the only way to be truly free was to leave the South. Henry Adams, an African American leader from Louisiana, encouraged African Americans to move to Kansas. People who followed his advice called themselves **exodusters**. The root word, exodus, means a journey to freedom.

Thousands of African American families from the South joined what became known as the Kansas Fever Exodus. Most exodusters faced hard times and **poverty**, or lack of money and property, just as they had in the South. Despite these hardships, Kansas's African American population continued to grow.

African Americans also became miners in the West. In California they set up communities to help protect their claims on mineral deposits.

Why would homesteaders be willing to move to the Great Plains?

_____

_____

_____

_____

The Growth of the Cattle Business

The cattle market continued to grow in the United States. Study the two graphs below. One is about Texas cattle, and the other is about all cattle in the United States.

Texas Cattle Drives, 1867–1880

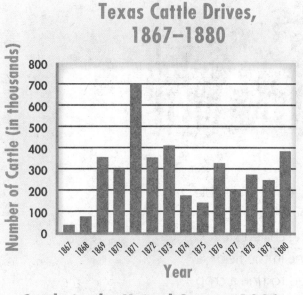

Cattle in the United States, 1880

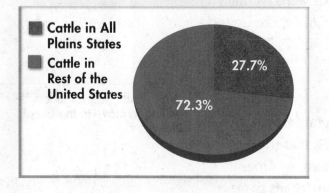

Cattle in All Plains States

Cattle in Rest of the United States

27.7%

72.3%

1. When did cattle drives begin to decline?

2. What do the graphs tell you about the cattle business in the late 1800s?

The Cattle Kingdom

The Spanish who settled Texas and Mexico brought a specific breed of cattle, the longhorn, to the Americas. This tough breed was well suited to the open ranges of the Southwest. The cattle grazed freely, tended by herders on horseback. In Mexico herders were called *vaqueros*, or cowboys.

After the Civil War, the growing demand for beef became an economic opportunity for Texas cattle ranchers. In order to sell their cattle, ranchers needed to move cattle to the rail lines.

Cattle Drives

The long journeys guiding cattle north from Texas were called **cattle drives**. The most-used route, the Chisholm Trail, was hundreds of miles long, and stretched north from Texas, through Oklahoma, and into Kansas. Another route, the Great Western Cattle Trail, was even longer and went further north.

Eight to twelve cowboys usually drove a herd of about 2,500 head of cattle. They kept the herd together, protected it, and kept it moving. Most herds moved about 12 miles a day.

The value of a head of longhorn was about $3 on a ranch but up to $40 at market. As the business thrived, cattle ranching spread throughout the West.

Cowboy Life

Cowboys led rough lives. They spent months on the trail, facing bad weather, risky river crossings, stampedes, occasional attacks from Native Americans, and raids from cattle thieves, called rustlers.

Cowboys needed special skills for their hard lives. They had to be able to rope and control cattle weighing between 1,000 and 1,500 pounds each.

About a third of all cowboys were African American or Mexican. Nat Love, a well-known African American cowboy, said

> "The test of a cow boy's worth is his . . . nerve. He is not supposed to know what fear means, and I assure you there are very few who know the meaning of the word."

The cattle industry affected society after the Civil War. Some African Americans learned to be cowboys from vaqueros. There was a group of famous African American cowboys known as the Black Cowboys of Texas.

The late nineteenth century saw fewer cattle drives. Many farmers refused to let cattle cross their lands. Some states passed laws preventing cattle from crossing state borders. Since railroads had begun to reach into Texas, ranchers soon began shipping their cattle by train directly to meatpacking plants.

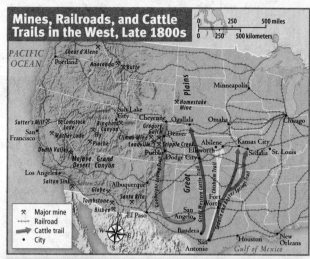

Mines, Railroads, and Cattle Trails in the West, Late 1800s

Map and Globe Skills

Where does the Great Western Cattle Trail end?

_____

Why did the cattle business spread throughout the West?

_____

_____

_____

Lesson 1

? **Essential Question** How did westward expansion change the United States?

_____

_____

_____

Go back to _Show As You Go!_ on pages 62–63.

Conflicts On The Plains

❓ Essential Question

How did growth in the West affect Native American groups? What do you think?

_____

_____

_____

_____

_____

Words To Know

Write a number to show how much you know about the meaning of each word.

1 = I have no idea!

2 = I know a little

3 = I know a lot

_____ **reservation**

_____ **property rights**

General Custer was defeated at the Battle of the Little Bighorn.

Library of Congress Prints and Photographs Division [LC-DIG-pga-04166]

Native American Lands

A brown ocean of buffalo once covered Native American lands. When the settlers and railroads came, the buffalo disappeared. The Native Americans' way of life was threatened.

The Homestead Act, which you have read about, gave settlers on the Great Plains **property rights** to the land. Property rights are the rights to own or use something for sale. Some Native American groups did not believe that land could belong to a person or that it could be sold. These different views of land and property led to major conflicts.

Losing a Way of Life

Native American groups, such as the Lakota and Cheyenne, had been hunting buffalo on the Great Plains for centuries. These large animals were the most important part of Native American life on the Great Plains. They provided food, shelter, tools, and clothing.

Before settlers and railroads arrived, around 50 million buffalo roamed the Great Plains. Over a period of about 40 years, settlers and railroad workers killed most of the huge animals. By 1900, fewer than 1,000 buffalo were left.

In the 1860s, settlers and Native Americans fought over land. The United States government moved Native Americans to **reservations** to make more land available for settlers and railroads. A reservation is land set aside for a Native American group or groups.

Native Americans felt they had to fight for their way of life or it would be lost forever. The clashes between Native Americans and settlers during this period of westward expansion are called the Plains Wars.

Why do you think Native Americans and settlers had different views about owning land?

_____

_____

_____

_____

▲ The buffalo was an important natural resource.

Conflicts Over Land

In 1868 the United States signed a treaty with the Lakota, granting them large areas of land. The grant included the Black Hills area of what is now South Dakota. This area had deep religious meaning to the Lakota. Then, in 1874, gold was discovered in the Black Hills. Immediately, thousands of miners flooded into this sacred part of the Lakota territory. Violence quickly followed.

Little Bighorn

The Lakota chiefs, including Sitting Bull and Crazy Horse, refused to allow miners to dig in the Black Hills. As a result, U.S. soldiers were sent to drive Sitting Bull and the Lakota out of the area and onto reservations.

On June 25, 1876, Colonel George Custer attacked Sitting Bull's camp on the Little Bighorn River. Custer discovered that he was outnumbered, four to one. Hundreds of Lakota warriors counterattacked, killing Custer and all of his troops at the Battle of Little Bighorn. It was the last major Native American victory on the Great Plains.

March of the Nez Perce

Fighting between the U.S. Army and Native Americans soon reached the Northwest region. In 1877 Chief Joseph and the Nez Perce began a 1,200-mile march from eastern Oregon to Canada. They were trying to avoid being forced onto a reservation. Only 40 miles from Canada, the Nez Perce encountered a force of 500 American soldiers. Cold and hungry, the Nez Perce held out for five days. Finally, Chief Joseph surrendered on October 5, 1877.

Wounded Knee

The United States government moved the Sioux to a reservation in North Dakota. At their reservation the Sioux performed a ritual called the Sun Dance. To stop the ritual, officials attempted to arrest their chief, Sitting Bull. In the

▲ Chief Joseph surrendered after many of his people were killed.

Library of Congress Prints & Photographs Division [LC-US262-132047]

Why were the Lakota willing to fight for the Black Hills?

_____

_____

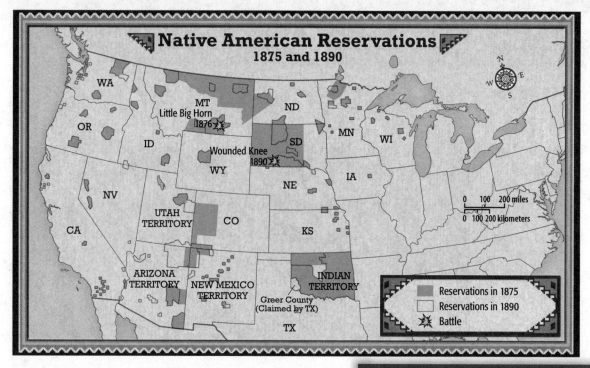

Native American Reservations
1875 and 1890

WA

MT
Little Big Horn
1876

OR

ID

ND

MN

WI

Wounded Knee
1890

SD

WY

NV

IA

NE

UTAH
TERRITORY

CO

KS

CA

ARIZONA
TERRITORY

NEW MEXICO
TERRITORY

Greer County
(Claimed by TX)

INDIAN
TERRITORY

TX

0   100   200 miles
0 100 200 kilometers

Reservations in 1875
Reservations in 1890
Battle

scuffle, Sitting Bull was shot. Many historians believe Sitting Bull was assassinated by the army. Hundreds of Sioux fled fearing for their lives. The army soon arrived to collect the Sioux's weapons. Shots rang out again, killing more than 200 Sioux and 25 soldiers.

Native American Losses

Despite the losses of traditional lands, Native Americans continued to fight for their rights. They continue to honor their history and many have kept their traditions alive. Traditional clothing, dances, and stories preserve the history of the Plains groups.

Map and Globe Skills

In which territories did reservations change the most between 1875 and 1890?

_____

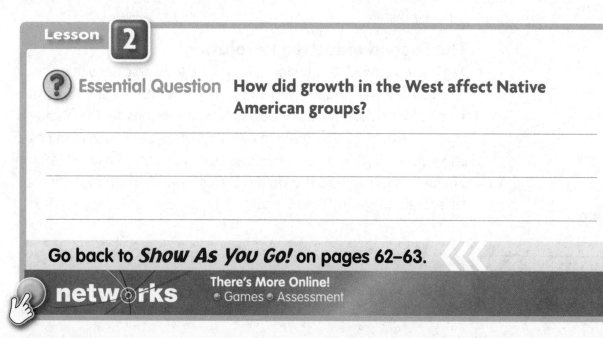

Lesson 2

? Essential Question How did growth in the West affect Native American groups?

_____

_____

_____

Go back to *Show As You Go!* on pages 62–63.

networks
There's More Online!
● Games ● Assessment

3 Big Business

Library of Congress, Prints and Photographs Division (LC-USZC2-3394)

? Essential Question

How did technology affect American life in the late 1800s? What do you think?

_____

_____

_____

_____

_____

_____

_____

▲ The 1893 World's Columbian Exposition in Chicago, Illinois, introduced electricity to millions of people.

Words To Know

Write the plural form of each word on the line.

corporation

_____

monopoly

_____

trust

_____

labor union

_____

Business Takes Over

After Reconstruction ended, big business began to boom. Entrepreneurs took risks investing their money in new businesses, and transformed the United States into an industrial nation.

As the West expanded, the rest of the nation changed too. The United States was becoming a modern nation based on business and industry. Some of these businesses produced large amounts of wealth for their owners.

The Second Industrial Revolution

Beginning in the 1700s, the factories of the Industrial Revolution changed the way people lived and worked. During the late 1870s, a second Industrial Revolution began. New inventions and technology made mass production faster, easier, and less expensive. As businesses and industries grew, so did the cities around them. As a result, millions of immigrants came to the United States to work in cities, such as Pittsburgh, Cleveland, and Chicago.

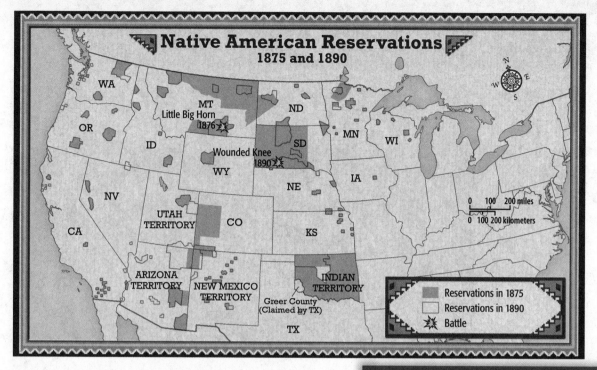

Native American Reservations
1875 and 1890

WA
OR
ID
MT
Little Big Horn
1876
ND
MN
WI
WY
Wounded Knee
1890
SD
NV
UTAH
TERRITORY
CO
NE
IA
CA
ARIZONA
TERRITORY
NEW MEXICO
TERRITORY
KS
Greer County
(Claimed by TX)
INDIAN
TERRITORY
TX

0   100   200 miles
0 100 200 kilometers

Reservations in 1875
Reservations in 1890
Battle

scuffle, Sitting Bull was shot. Many historians believe Sitting Bull was assassinated by the army. Hundreds of Sioux fled fearing for their lives. The army soon arrived to collect the Sioux's weapons. Shots rang out again, killing more than 200 Sioux and 25 soldiers.

Native American Losses

Despite the losses of traditional lands, Native Americans continued to fight for their rights. They continue to honor their history and many have kept their traditions alive. Traditional clothing, dances, and stories preserve the history of the Plains groups.

Map and Globe Skills

In which territories did reservations change the most between 1875 and 1890?

_____

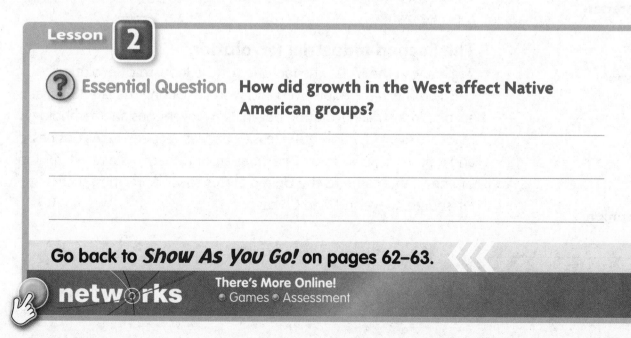

Lesson 2

? **Essential Question** How did growth in the West affect Native American groups?

_____

_____

_____

Go back to *Show As You Go!* on pages 62–63.

networks **There's More Online!**
● Games ● Assessment

Big Business

 Essential Question

How did technology affect American life in the late 1800s? What do you think?

_____

_____

_____

_____

_____

_____

▲ The 1893 World's Columbian Exposition in Chicago, Illinois, introduced electricity to millions of people.

Words To Know

Write the plural form of each word on the line.

corporation

_____

monopoly

_____

trust

_____

labor union

_____

Business Takes Over

After Reconstruction ended, big business began to boom. Entrepreneurs took risks investing their money in new businesses, and transformed the United States into an industrial nation.

As the West expanded, the rest of the nation changed too. The United States was becoming a modern nation based on business and industry. Some of these businesses produced large amounts of wealth for their owners.

The Second Industrial Revolution

Beginning in the 1700s, the factories of the Industrial Revolution changed the way people lived and worked. During the late 1870s, a second Industrial Revolution began. New inventions and technology made mass production faster, easier, and less expensive. As businesses and industries grew, so did the cities around them. As a result, millions of immigrants came to the United States to work in cities, such as Pittsburgh, Cleveland, and Chicago.

The Gilded Age

Americans wanted better lives. Soon, inventions that made life easier, such as electric lights and telephones, came into people's homes. As new technologies made factories more efficient, some business owners made huge profits. In many cases, however, workers were treated poorly and paid very low wages.

New technologies, the growth of cities, and improvements in industry made it seem like America was prospering, or achieving economic success. But there were many problems that were hidden by all of this prosperity, including poverty.

This era of American history is known as the Gilded Age. That name comes from the 1873 book *The Gilded Age: A Tale of Today*, by Mark Twain and Charles Warner. Something that was "gilded" was covered in gold. However, under the gold was cheaper material.

What were the positives and negatives of industrial growth?

_____

_____

_____

_____

_____

Ohio Steel Works and furnaces, 1905 ▼

Library of Congress Prints and Photographs Division [6a15357]

Inventing The Future

As the nation grew, American inventors looked for ways to improve peoples' lives. By the late 1800s, companies began to specialize. They made one product better and cheaper instead of making several different products.

New Forms of Communication

Inventors often built upon the ideas of those who came before them. For example, Samuel Morse discovered how to send messages over just one wire. Along with his partner, Alfred Vail, Morse developed what came to be called Morse Code. In 1866 the code was used to send the first telegraph message to Europe.

Alexander Graham Bell and his assistant, James Watson, invented the telephone in 1876. Bell was able to make a call to Watson in the next room, something that had not been done before. The next year, Bell created the country's first telephone company, the Bell Telephone Company. This would later become the American Telephone and Telegraph Company (AT&T).

However, other inventors also claimed the idea for the telephone. For example, Granville Woods came up with a way to send messages from moving trains that combined features of both the telegraph and the telephone. He called the system "telegraphony."

Thomas Edison

Thomas Edison was known as the "Wizard of Menlo Park." He created hundreds of devices. Among them were the first machine for recording sound and the first moving picture projector. After many attempts, Edison made a useful electric lightbulb. You can read about his reaction to the successful lightbulb in the Primary Source box on this page. He and his assistants developed more than 1,000 inventions. Edison said:

> "Genius is one percent inspiration and ninety-nine percent perspiration."

"We sat and looked, and the lamp continued to burn, and the longer it burned the more fascinated we were. None of us could go to bed, and there was no sleep for any of us for forty hours. . . . I said, 'If it will burn that number of hours now, I know I can make it burn a hundred.'"

—Thomas Edison, 1907

Write a sentence explaining how you would have reacted to seeing an electric lightbulb for the first time.

_____

_____

Edison was also an entrepreneur who brought several of his business interests together to form Edison General Electric. In 1892 Edison General Electric merged with Thomson-Houston Company to form General Electric. General Electric continues to make many of Edison's inventions today.

The Camera for Everyone

As new technologies were enhanced or improved, life became more enjoyable for Americans. In 1884 George Eastman invented roll film for cameras. This made it much easier and quicker to develop film.

In 1888 Eastman created a box that used his roll film. The camera could be sent to the factory for processing. He founded the Eastman Kodak camera company. Twelve years later, he began selling a new camera, the Brownie, for a dollar. Now millions of people could visually capture life.

How did inventions improve life for Americans?

_____

_____

George Washington Carver

George Washington Carver was an African American scientist from Missouri. In 1896 Carver became a teacher at Tuskegee University. Carver thought that constantly replanting cotton hurt the soil in the South. He believed it would help the soil if farmers planted different crops.

Carver focused on the use of peanuts and sweet potatoes to help farmers improve soil. He was able to make hundreds of other products from peanuts, including gasoline and plastics. Carver also developed different methods for farming to maximize crop growth.

North Carolina

KY
VA
Kitty Hawk
TN
Raleigh ★
Charlotte
NC
GA
SC
ATLANTIC OCEAN

The Sky Is the Limit

Brothers Orville and Wilbur Wright were bicycle mechanics from Ohio. Wilbur became interested in aeronautics, or the operation of aircraft. After he identified what was needed to keep an object in the air, he and his brother Orville began testing his ideas using a kite.

Map and Globe Skills

What direction is Kitty Hawk from Raleigh?

_____

Wilbur's ideas worked! After building several prototypes, or models, in 1902 the brothers launched a glider that flew 620 feet. Then they set out to make an engine-powered airplane. A year later, in windy Kitty Hawk, on the outterbanks of North Carolina, Orville piloted the world's first powered flight. The plane traveled 120 feet in just 12 seconds.

Wright brothers and friends in front of a plane.

The Rise Of Corporations

With improved technology, the challenge became getting these improvements to American homes. Some entrepreneurs took risks investing their money and turned small businesses into **corporations**. Corporations are large businesses in which people invest their money and share ownership.

As corporations became successful, they were better able to sell stocks, or shares of ownership. Corporations then could continue the improvement and development of new technologies. Large corporations in the oil, steel, railroad, and banking industries soon dominated American business. Sometimes people who had invested a lot of money controlled a corporation. As businesses grew, so did the power of these corporate heads.

Carnegie Steel Company

One of these people was Andrew Carnegie. As a twelve-year-old, he came to the United States from Scotland in 1848. He worked several jobs, eventually working his way through the ranks of a railroad company. In his early thirties, he left the railroad and bought a steel mill near Pittsburgh, Pennsylvania. Nearby natural resources made Pittsburgh an ideal location for making steel. Steel was used for railroads, buildings, and bridges. Carnegie used a new cheaper method of making steel. His company came to rule the American steel industry.

Rockefeller and Standard Oil

John D. Rockefeller was an equally successful businessman in Cleveland, Ohio. Located on Lake Erie, Cleveland's location was ideal for shipping goods across the Atlantic Ocean. In the 1860s, Rockefeller bought an oil refinery business on the shores of Lake Erie. He and his brother, William, opened a New York office to handle the exporting of the Standard Oil Company's products overseas.

▼ Carnegie steel plant in Homestead, Pennsylvania

Library of Congress LC-D401-10924 LC

Rockefeller then bought other oil companies or forced them out of business. As his wealth grew, he purchased railroads to transport his products. By the early 1880s, Rockefeller controlled the oil business in the United States.

▲ John D. Rockefeller

The Billion Dollar Corporation

Money itself became an industry during the late 1800s. Banks and their investors profited by loaning money. J.P. Morgan, a banker, arranged capital for several railroad corporations. Capital is the money a business needs to run or expand.

Morgan gained increasing control of some of these businesses. As the deals he made grew larger, so did his influence, power, and wealth. Morgan joined with Rockefeller and other investors to combine electric, steel, and manufacturing businesses. The result was the world's first billion- dollar corporation, U.S. Steel.

Monopolies and Trusts

Some people opposed the power of people like Carnegie, Rockefeller, and Morgan. They feared the unfairness that **monopolies** could bring to businesses and the public. A monopoly is a business that completely controls an industry. Most Americans believed that the only way to have fair prices was for businesses to compete. Without competition, a monopoly could set high prices or treat workers poorly.

Many state governments passed laws to try to stop monopolies. For example, many states made it illegal for one company to own stock in another company.

Some businesspeople, such as Rockefeller, tried to find ways around these laws. They set up **trusts**. A trust is a way of merging a number of businesses so that one person, called a trustee, could manage another person's property. Since trustees only managed companies and did not own them, no laws were broken.

Trustees could control a group of companies as if the companies were merged, without actually merging the companies. Trusts prevented competition. Trusts were used to create and protect monopolies. These arrangements were made by Standard Oil trustees to control a group of companies as if they were one large merged company.

When some trusts became too powerful, the government passed the Sherman Antitrust Act of 1890. The act was supposed to eliminate trusts. However, the Supreme Court ruled that the act did not apply to manufacturing. As a result, the act did little to stop trusts.

Draw a box around the first billion dollar corporation.

What risks do monopolies present?

_____

_____

_____

Labor Unions

Library of Congress Prints and Photographs Division [LC-USZ62-96506]

Reading Skill

Why would a worker join a large labor union?

While business owners grew rich, workers struggled. Laborers received low wages and had to work long hours in harsh and often dangerous conditions. One factory in Connecticut had 16,000 accidents in one year. In 1900 an average laborer worked a 60-hour week and earned around $400 a year. Yet, an average family of four needed about $800 a year to survive.

Workers Join Together

At the time, workers had little power. Those who complained could simply be fired. There were other people willing to take their places. Workers realized that they needed to act together to improve their lives. They formed **labor unions**, or groups that represented workers, to gain better working conditions.

One of the first effective unions was the Knights of Labor. It was organized in 1869. The leader of the Knights of Labor was Terrence Powderly. The Knights wanted an 8-hour workday. They also supported equal pay for women. The union organized against companies, particularly railroads. Other unions sprang up as well, but they were often too small to be effective.

American Federation of Labor

In 1886 Samuel Gompers founded the American Federation of Labor (AFL). The AFL represented trade and craft workers across the country, and it pushed for fair pay and better working conditions. The AFL took direct action against employers, using tactics to hurt businesses that refused to respond.

▼ In 1894 the Pullman Strike in Chicago, Illinois, stopped railroad traffic to the West. The strike led to riots, and federal troops were called in.

Strikes and Violence

The main tactic used by unions was to go on **strike**. A strike is when workers refuse to work in order to force an employer to meet their demands. Strikes could shut down businesses and cost their owners millions of dollars. For that reason, many employers used violence against strikers to force them back to work. Unions won small battles but had little power, overall, against large corporations.

Women and Immigrants

Another change in society was the growing presence of women in the workforce. Women worked the same long hours and in many of the same jobs as men but were paid less.

Many labor unions did not allow women to become members. Women took part in organizing their own unions and seeking better conditions. The Collar Laundry Union was organized in 1864. The Cigar Makers' Union and a printers' union admitted women in 1867 and 1869. Augusta Lewis and Susan B. Anthony founded the Working Women's Association. Lewis later became president of the Women's Typographical Union.

Most labor unions did not allow immigrants to join. Some unions were afraid that immigrants would take jobs from other Americans. Many immigrants found jobs working in steel mills and in other industries. Some immigrants worked long hours in sweatshops for little pay. Sweatshops were crowded workshops for making clothing. They had dangerous working conditions.

DID YOU KNOW?
Mary Harris "Mother" Jones was a fierce union organizer. She was involved in many strikes and demonstrations, especially on behalf of coal miners. Once, when asked where she lived, she replied, "Well, wherever there is a fight." In 1903 Jones led a children's march to President Theodore Roosevelt's home in Oyster Bay, New York to support abolishing child labor.

Lesson 3

(?) **Essential Question** How did technology affect American life in the late 1800s?

_____

_____

_____

Go back to *Show As You Go!* on pages 62–63. ◀◀

networks   There's More Online!
● Games ● Assessment

Growing Cities

? Essential Question

How did the growth of cities affect the United States?
What do you think?

_____

_____

_____

_____

_____

Elevated trains in New York City carried people to work. In the late 1800s, cities became the center of American life.

Words To Know

Rank the words (1-3) to show how well you understand them.

commute

_____

slum

_____

tenement

_____

Americans Move to Cities

In 1860 fewer than one in five Americans lived in communities larger than 8,000 people. By 1920, more than half of all Americans lived in major industrial areas.

New cities had growing pains—sewage in the streets, overcrowded buildings, and crime. Cities, however, were the centers of the industrial age. Many people moved to cities in search of work.

The Changing City

Many cities grew up around a single industry. Minneapolis milled flour and Milwaukee brewed beer. New England cities manufactured clothes and shoes. Chicago, St. Louis, and Denver became railroad centers where produce, goods, and people moved in and out in great clouds of locomotive steam.

Fast-growing cities such as Chicago, New York, and St. Louis created markets for American inventions and industry. These cities needed Carnegie's steel for buildings and Edison's lights for streets, homes, and businesses.

New technology brought other changes to daily life in cities. In crowded cities, waste collected fast. City planners tried to solve the problem with indoor plumbing that carried waste and water to underground sewage pipes.

As cities grew, many city officials also had to solve transportation problems. Workers had to **commute**, or travel to their jobs. In the 1890s, Chicago and New York established the first electric streetcar system. Boston moved its transportation underground in 1897 with the first subway system in the United States.

The most impressive change in city life was overhead, not underground. Thanks to inexpensive steel and the invention of a practical elevator, a ten-story building went up in Chicago in 1884. The Home Insurance Building became the nation's first skyscraper.

What was city life like in the late 1800s?

_____

_____

DID YOU KNOW?
In 1871 most of Chicago's residents lived in wooden buildings. On October 8, fire swept through the city. Nearly a third of the city's people were left homeless. At least 250 died. By 1873 the city was entirely rebuilt.

The New Americans

Pretend you are an immigrant. Write a diary entry describing a typical day at Hull House.

Except for Native Americans, the United States is a country of people who can trace their history to immigrants. Most immigrants came here between 1870 and 1924. During those years, more than 25 million immigrants entered the United States. They came on steamships, packed into crowded, bad-smelling quarters. Most came through Ellis Island in New York or Angel Island in San Francisco.

During this time, most immigrants came from Southern and Eastern Europe. Many were Jewish or Catholic. Other immigrants came from China and Japan. Most arrived with little money, in search of a better life.

Hard Life in Cities

The majority of immigrants settled where there were jobs—in the cities of the Northeast. The streets of Boston, New York, Philadelphia, and later Chicago were filled with people speaking foreign languages.

Many new immigrants settled in **slums**—crowded neighborhoods with narrow, dirty streets. They were packed into rundown apartment buildings, called **tenements**. In tenements residents could get only very small amounts of fresh air and sunlight through tiny windows that looked out on the brick walls of neighboring buildings. Whole families often were forced to live in small, single-room apartments.

Despite new sewage systems, waste found its way into city drinking water. Diseases such as cholera and typhus spread quickly. A section of New York was called the "lung block" because so many people had tuberculosis.

Many new immigrants were proud to be in the United States. Yet, American life was harder than they had expected. Most immigrants struggled with the English language or didn't speak it at all. They had trouble communicating with landlords and employers. Many of them struggled to feel like Americans. One immigrant from Bulgaria wrote,

> "In Bulgaria I am not wholly a Bulgarian. In the United States I am not wholly an American."

Settlement Houses

In the late 1880s, Jane Addams, the daughter of a wealthy Illinois state senator, wanted to improve conditions in Chicago's slums. In 1889 Addams rented an old, red-brick house surrounded by tenements. Educated women moved into the building. They helped immigrants find housing. They taught English and job skills to adults. They opened schools for children that featured music and food from many different countries.

▲ Peace Delegates on NOORDAM -- Mrs. P. Lawrence, Jane Addams, Anita Molloy

Settlement houses worked to improve basic living conditions as well as promote education. Addams, along with Ida B. Wells, worked to end segregation in schools. At settlement houses, workers did everything from making sure the city picked up garbage to inviting well-known speakers. The *Chicago Tribune*, a newspaper, described the settlement houses as "A Project to Bring Rich and Poor Together." Hull House became one of the first settlement houses in the United States.

By 1910, more than 400 settlement houses served immigrants in U.S. cities. Jane Addams went on to campaign for child labor laws, better housing, and world peace. In 1931 she was awarded the Nobel Peace Prize.

▲ Families crowded together in tenements. Entire families sometimes lived in a single room.

Why did reformers help immigrants adjust to life in the United States?

_____

_____

(t)Library of Congress, Prints & Photographs Division [LC-DIG-ggbain-18848], (b)Library of Congress, Prints & Photographs Division [LOT 7481, no. 3123]

Limits on Immigration

Americans have long been proud of their hospitality to immigrants. A famous poem carved into the base of the Statue of Liberty in New York City welcomes the world's "poor," its "homeless," and its "huddled masses." Yet, by the early 1900s, many people felt it was time to close the door on immigration.

Many Americans wanted immigrants out of the country. Some American-born workers thought that immigrants would take away their jobs. Few of the new immigrants from Eastern and Southern Europe spoke English. As a result, they did not blend into American society as easily as some earlier immigrants had. These complaints led to restrictions on immigration to the United States.

The Immigration Act of 1917 required immigrants to be able to read and write in some language. In 1924 Congress passed the Johnson-Reed Act. The new law said that the amount of new immigrants could not exceed two percent of the number of people from that country who were already living in the United States in 1890. It also stopped the immigration of Asians. These immigration laws were not changed for more than 40 years.

◀ The Statue of Liberty

> **How do you think the Johnson-Reed Act affected the United States?**
>
> _____
>
> _____

Lesson 3

(?) **Essential Question** **How did the growth of cities affect the United States?**

_____

_____

_____

Go back to **Show As You Go!** on pages 62–63. ≪

networks   There's More Online!
● Games ● Assessment

Map and Globe Skill

Use Cartograms

Population can be shown on a map in different ways. One way is with a special kind of map called a **cartogram**. A cartogram shows information that can be measured in numbers. For example, to compare population numbers for different places, a cartogram changes the size of these places. You can compare populations by looking at the sizes of places.

TRY IT

- **Which state on the cartogram had the largest population in 1900? Which state had the smallest population?**

APPLY IT

- **Draw a cartogram to compare the population of largest and smallest states in population today. Don't forget to include a legend and a title for your cartogram.**

LEARN IT

- **Identify what is being shown in a cartogram. This cartogram shows the United States population in 1900.**

- **Read the map key to learn what each box represents. How many people lived in Georgia in 1900?**

- **Ohio is larger than California on the cartogram. What does that tell you?**

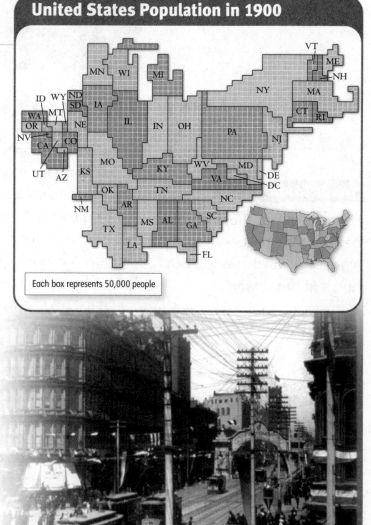

United States Population in 1900

Each box represents 50,000 people

A Changing Society

? Essential Question

How did people promote change and reform in the United States?
What do you think?

_____

_____

_____

_____

_____

_____

Words To Know

Have you heard these words before? Make a guess about what each word means. Then find it in the Lesson.

progressives

_____

muckraker

_____

suffrage

_____

prohibition

_____

Suffragists marching in New York City in 1913

The Rise Of Progressivism

As industrialization spread, social conditions worsened in many places. Challenges against greed, dishonesty, and mistreatment of people led to efforts for change.

By the early 1900s, industry had made a few Americans very wealthy. However, millions of Americans worked long hours in dangerous conditions for low wages. Even young children worked 12 or 14 hours a day.

Some people were concerned by the growing gap between the rich and poor. These people called themselves **progressives**. Progressives believed in using new and creative ideas for social progress and change.

During the Progressive Era, many people tried to help the poor by changing the law. Many of their reforms were aimed at helping the struggling working class. They worked hard for laws that protected workers, limited the power of big business, and shortened the hours that children could work.

The Power of the Press

In 1903 journalist Ida Tarbell wrote a book about John D. Rockefeller and his Standard Oil Company. She showed how Rockefeller had taken unfair advantage of his competitors. Tarbell accused Rockefeller of forming trusts to get rid of competition.

Tarbell was a progressive and a **muckraker**. Muckrakers were writers who dug up dirt, or "muck," about dangerous working conditions or dishonest businesses and politicians.

Several chapters from her book were published as articles in a magazine read by people across the country. Not long after Tarbell's articles appeared, Congress forced Standard Oil to break up into several smaller companies.

> **What did progressives want to accomplish?**
>
> _____
>
> _____

Bain Collection, Library of Congress, LC-USZ62-34985

DID YOU KNOW?
On March 25, 1911, a fire broke out in the Triangle Factory in New York City. Nearly 500 people, mostly immigrants, worked there. Because the owners had locked the factory doors, the workers inside were trapped and 146 people died. Afterward, people were angry and demanded changes.

The Right To Vote

During this period of reform in the United States, many women progressives saw an opportunity to fight for women's rights. Many focused on gaining **suffrage**, or the right to vote, for women.

The Seneca Falls Convention

Many women had been fighting for equal rights since the mid-1800s. In the summer of 1848, Elizabeth Cady Stanton and Lucretia Mott planned the Seneca Falls Convention in Seneca Falls, New York. They wrote a document called the Declaration of Sentiments. The document demanded an end to laws that discriminated against women. It also called for companies to allow women to hold the same jobs as men. The declaration also included woman suffrage.

The Struggle Continues

As the 1800s progressed, the women's rights movement became more vocal. In 1869 Stanton and Susan B. Anthony founded the National Woman Suffrage Association. They called for an amendment to the U.S. Constitution to give women the right to vote in national elections.

▲ Lucretia Mott helped write the Declartion of Sentiments.

Library of Congress LC-USZ62-42559

Mobilizing Groups

Susan B. Anthony helped found the National Woman Suffrage Association. This group brought people together to fight for woman suffrage. Mobilizing groups is one way to organize people. Movements have been used throughout history to call attention to unfair treatment and bring about change. Movements have improved education for children, working conditions and wages for workers, and civil rights for African Americans, Native Americans, and others. Is there a movement you want to join?

In 1890 the National Woman Suffrage Association became the National American Woman Suffrage Association. It was led by Ann Howard Shaw and Carrie Chapman Catt.

Women won voting rights in the West first. In 1869 Wyoming gave women the right to vote. By 1919, women could vote in some elections in most of the 48 states. However, women were still not allowed to vote in national elections.

The Nineteenth Amendment

In 1917 and 1918, four more states gave women full voting rights. The U.S. Congress began debating whether or not to give women the right to vote in national elections. In 1919 Congress voted in favor of the Nineteenth Amendment. This amendment guaranteed woman suffrage. On August 26, 1920, the states approved this amendment, which guaranteed every adult woman the right to vote in a national election and a voice in the government of the United States.

How did women gain the right to vote?

_____

_____

Elizabeth Cady Stanton and Susan B. Anthony (right) and the Seneca Falls Convention (below)

Other Progressive Reforms

In the early 1900s, progressive reforms touched many different parts of society. Some reforms were more successful than others.

Prohibition

During the Progressive Era, many people became involved in the Temperance Movement. This movement supported **prohibition**, or laws that would ban the production and sale of alcohol.

The Temperance Movement led to the ratifying of the Eighteenth Amendment in 1919. This amendment banned the making, selling, and drinking of alcohol. The era that followed was called Prohibition.

Even with two-thirds of Congress and three-fourths of the states approving it, many people did not like Prohibition. They began fighting against it soon after it was ratified. In 1933 the Twenty-first Amendment ended Prohibition.

The Growth of Education

In 1900 only 5 percent of America's youth graduated from high school. Only 2 percent completed college. Instead of attending school, children and young people often were part of the labor force.

Under the Constitution, public education is the responsibility of state governments. States established public school systems, courses of study, and means of funding. As cities grew, so did school systems. As labor laws were gradually passed, more students attended school. Reformers pushed for better education opportunities for all students, including girls and minorities.

Schools were also established for Native Americans on reservations. Some Native Americans attended boarding schools off the reservation. These schools focused on making Native Americans more like European Americans by removing their traditional Native American language and religion.

Can a minority opinion influence the law in a democracy? Support your answer.

_____

_____

_____

▼ New York City police poured alcohol down sewers during Prohibition.

Public Libraries

Another way to educate people was by giving the public access to books. In 1876 the American Library Association met in Philadelphia with the idea of creating public libraries. Libraries became a part of the Progressive movement's goal of improving education.

Steelmaker Andrew Carnegie believed that everyone should have access to a library. Between 1886 and 1919, he donated more than $40 million for the construction of libraries in cities and towns.

▲ Boarding schools for Native Americans discouraged students from keeping their traditional ways.

Higher Education

Many colleges and state universities also developed during this time of growth and reform. The Morrill Act of 1862 granted federal lands to state control. Income from these lands helped pay for colleges. The aim of these schools, called land-grant colleges, was to teach agriculture and mechanics.

Some private colleges, such as Howard University and the Hampton Institute, opened specifically to educate African Americans. These colleges increased career opportunities for African Americans. Still, African Americans faced discrimination and lower pay.

▲ African American students learn about cotton at this school near Tuskegee, Alabama.

Was Prohibition a good idea? Why or why not?

_____

_____

Lesson 5

? **Essential Question** **How did people promote change and reform in the United States?**

_____

_____

_____

Go back to _Show As You Go!_ on pages 62–63.

(t)Library of Congress LC-US262-72450; (b)Library of Congress Prints and Photographs Division [LC-US262-78481]

Essential Question

How do new ideas affect a society?
What do you think?

_____

_____

_____

_____

_____

_____

_____

_____

Words To Know

Look at the words below. Tell a partner what you already know about these words.

patronage

_____

initiative

_____

referendum

_____

recall

_____

Theodore Roosevelt giving a speech in 1912.

Attempts At Labor Reform

Another important social movement involved labor reform. The growth of industry created social problems beyond the dangers inside of factories. Poor housing, poor food, scarce health care, and a lack of education ruined many lives.

The labor union movement had few successes. In some cases, violence turned the public against unions. Some reformers tried to meet the needs of people in distress.

Child Labor

With so many American families struggling to meet their basic needs, some were forced to send their children to work. The idea of children working difficult, dangerous jobs for long hours was not new in the United States. With the growth of industry, the number of child laborers grew rapidly. Hundreds of thousands of children worked in factories, mines, and mills.

Some states passed laws limiting child labor as early as 1837. However, laws were rarely enforced. Reform movements pressed for child labor laws in the 1880s. By 1899, a total of 44 states had some form of child labor law.

How did labor reformers make progress in their causes?

_____

_____

_____

_____

Labor Laws

During the late 1800s, labor unions formed across the country and worked for reform. For many years, the government and the courts sided with business owners in disagreements between employers and workers. Finally, the government began to recognize the workers' right to organize. Unions became increasingly important in elections. States began to pass labor laws, though success was mixed. It was not until the mid-1930s that broad labor protection laws were passed.

Children working hard shucking oysters at ▶ a cannery in Louisiana.

Library of Congress, Prints and Photographs Division (LC-USZ62-12875)

Reforming Politics

Many progressives felt that American politics needed reform. Many politicians had enough power to break laws that were not in their own individual interests. At the time, state leaders often gave government jobs to people who had done favors for them or their political party. This was called **patronage**. It meant that people often got jobs for which they were not qualified because they had donated money to or were friends with politicians.

As a way to stop patronage, Wisconsin governor Robert La Follette started the merit system. Under his plan, people needed to pass a test in order to get a government job. Jobs were given to the people scoring highest on the test. These tests were able to identify qualified employees. Other states soon began using La Follette's idea.

City Government

City governments needed reform, too. Many were run by dishonest political bosses. Political bosses were elected officials who were dishonest in how they controlled the government. They broke the law by not following election rules. Some election officials took money from political bosses to allow people to vote who were not citizens.

Other politicians, such as New York City's political boss George Plunkitt, used their power to get rich. Some accepted kickbacks. This is how a kickback works: A city is taking bids from contractors to build a new bridge. A city official makes sure the job goes to a certain contractor. In return, the contractor gives, or "kicks back," part of the city's contract money to the official.

How is the commission system similar to the council-manager system of government?

_____

_____

_____

_____

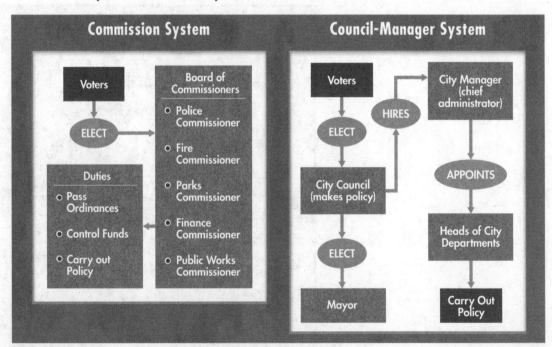

Progressives thought it was time to get rid of political bosses. To prevent a mayor from having too much power, some cities changed to a city commission system. These cities were now governed by a group of elected commissioners. Each of the commissioners was in charge of a different department.

Other cities chose a council-manager system. In this system, the elected city council hires a city manager to run the city. In each system, experts were in charge of operating the city.

▲ A volunteer collects petition signatures on Earth Day.

Initiative
Voters propose new laws or amendments.

Referendum
Voters approve or reject a state or local law.

Recall
Voters vote to remove an official from office.

Lawmaking

Other changes came in the way that laws were made. In Oregon the legislature approved what became known as the Oregon System. Under this process, if enough voters sign a petition, or request, they can introduce a bill and force the legislature to vote on an issue. This is called an **initiative**. Voters can also call for a **referendum**. This allows citizens to vote directly on a proposed law.

Both the initiative and the referendum make it possible for ordinary citizens to vote directly on laws. Today, 24 states and thousands of local governments have initiative and referendum procedures.

Electing Officials

In 18 states, voters have the right to remove elected officials from office. This is done through a **recall** election.

In a recall, voters decide during a special election whether or not to remove the official. If a majority of voters approve the recall, the official is removed from office. The person taking over the position can be reelected in the next election. Most states also have recall procedures for local elections.

Progressives also improved representative democracy when they influenced the way senators are elected. The Constitution originally stated that senators should be chosen by each state's legislature. In 1913 the Seventeenth Amendment changed this by giving people the power to elect senators.

Why might a group of citizens want to call for a referendum?

_____

_____

Progressive Presidents

Even before the Progressive movement swept the nation, Grover Cleveland worked for political reforms during his two terms as President. He fought against patronage and corruption. He also vetoed a bill that would have required new immigrants to pass a literacy test. The only requirements for immigrants, Cleveland felt, should be that they were in good health and willing to work hard.

Cleveland tried, but didn't succeed, in reducing tariffs, or taxes on imported goods. Tariffs protect American businesses, but they make prices higher.

During the early 1900s, progressive ideas were important to several other Presidents as well. One of the most famous progressive Presidents was Theodore "Teddy" Roosevelt.

Theodore Roosevelt

As President, Theodore Roosevelt saw a need for reforms in business and government. He called his program the "Square Deal." Roosevelt wanted governments and business to deal fairly with people. He said:

> **"This country will not be a . . . good place for any of us to live in unless we make it a . . . good place for all of us to live in."**

He thought the federal government should regulate businesses and make rules for them to follow. Roosevelt was sometimes called "the trust-buster" because he fought hard against monopolies. As you learned earlier, a monopoly is total control of a type of industry by one person or one company. Not everyone agreed with Roosevelt. Some people thought that regulating big business would be bad for the economy.

Roosevelt, who loved the outdoors, also pushed for laws to conserve, or protect, America's natural resources. He created 5 national parks and 51 wildlife refuges, or areas set aside to protect animals.

DID YOU KNOW?

Like his friend, Theodore Roosevelt, **John Muir** loved the outdoors and wanted to protect natural places. He wrote many essays and books about Yosemite Valley in California. He founded the Sierra Club, an important conservation organization. His work led to the creation of many national parks.

▼ **Yosemite National Park**

William Howard Taft

William Howard Taft succeeded Roosevelt as President. He also fought against trusts. Under Taft's administration, Congress passed the Sixteenth Amendment, which gave the federal government the right to tax income.

Many progressives felt that taxes hurt consumers and limited competition. Therefore, progressives felt that Taft betrayed their cause when he approved high taxes.

Woodrow Wilson

Woodrow Wilson became President in 1912. He also saw the need for reform. One of his first acts as President was to lower tariffs on imported goods. This lowered prices on goods sold in the United States and expanded trade.

Wilson also put the banking system under public control. He signed the Federal Reserve Act into law. Under this law, banks had to keep a portion of their money in regional banks. This money would provide protection in case banks unexpectedly lost large amounts of money. The law also created a Federal Reserve Board to oversee banks.

Like Roosevelt, Wilson wanted to regulate business. In 1914 he approved the creation of the Federal Trade Commission. This agency enforces antitrust laws and prevents companies from illegally suppressing competition.

Wilson fought monopolies too. He worked to protect labor unions and made peaceful strikes, picketing, and boycotts legal. Under Wilson, Congress also passed laws that limited child labor and helped federal employees who were injured on the job.

> Why was Theodore Roosevelt called the "trust-buster"?
>
> _____
>
> _____

Lesson 6

? Essential Question   How do new ideas affect a society?

_____

_____

_____

Go back to *Show As You Go!* on pages 62–63.

Read each definition to help you unscramble the words below.

1. eerhodtsmea _____
   a person who claimed land on the Great Plains.

2. mtceuom _____
   travel back and forth regularly.

3. vpoytre _____
   being poor

4. lsmu _____
   rundown neighborhood

5. lcaett vdire _____
   large movement of cattle

6. nresvertoai _____
   territory set aside for Native Americans

7. fregasfu _____
   the right to vote

8. mloyonpo _____
   total control of a type of industry

Big Idea Project

Here is your chance to be an actor! You will create a skit about the travels people made and the challenges they faced along the way.

Read the list below to help you create your skit.

Our skit...   Yes it does!

shows how people traveled across the United States and the challenges or success they faced along the way. ☐

has a speaking part for each person in the group. ☐

shows that we worked together as a team. ☐

shows that we have practiced and are ready to perform for our class. ☐

. . . .

Think about the Big Idea

BIG IDEA Location affects how people live.

What did you learn in this unit that helps you understand the BIG IDEA?

_____

_____

_____

_____

_____

Read the passage "Marjorie Kinnan Rawlings" before answering Numbers 1 through 9.

Marjorie Kinnan Rawlings

by Nadia Shepard

Marjorie Kinnan Rawlings always loved to write, even as a little girl. When she was only 11 years old, she had one of her stories published in a large newspaper. She also won a writing contest when she was 11. But it wasn't until she moved to Florida in 1928 that she really began to find her voice as a writer. She moved to Cross Creek, near Gainesville, where she decided to grow oranges and pursue her writing. The rural setting of Cross Creek gave her so much inspiration that within the next several years she wrote five books. Her first book was called *South Moon Under*.

Rawlings's most famous book is called *The Yearling*. It's about a young boy in rural Florida who adopts an orphaned fawn. It was so popular when it was published in 1938 that it was eventually made into a movie in 1946. You can still read this book today! She also published *Golden Apples, Cross Creek*, and a cookbook. You can visit her house and farm which are now National Historic Landmarks.

1 When did Rawlings start writing?

Ⓐ when she was old

Ⓑ when she was young

Ⓒ when she was 16

Ⓓ when she was 38

2 What is the main idea of this passage?

Ⓕ Rawlings loved oranges.

Ⓖ Rawlings was a terrible writer.

Ⓗ Rawlings's books are still worth reading.

Ⓘ Rawlings knew everything about writing.

3 What did Rawlings do AFTER she moved to Florida but BEFORE she wrote *The Yearling*?

Ⓐ She adopted a fawn.

Ⓑ She won a writing contest.

Ⓒ She decided to stop writing.

Ⓓ She wrote *South Moon Under*.

4 Read this sentence from the story.

> **She also won a writing contest when she was 11.**

Why does the author include this detail in the story?

Ⓕ to show Rawlings's love of Cross Creek

Ⓖ to show that Rawlings was a good writer

Ⓗ to show what Rawlings planned to write next

Ⓘ to explain why Rawlings didn't write very much

5 Read this sentence from the story.

> **The rural setting of Cross Creek gave her so much inspiration that within the next several years she wrote five books.**

What does the word *inspiration* mean?

Ⓐ a kind of sickness

Ⓑ a feeling of creativity

Ⓒ a large sum of money

Ⓓ a kind of dance

6 According to the passage, which of the following was Rawlings's most famous book?

Ⓕ *Cross Creek*

Ⓖ *The Yearling*

Ⓗ her cookbook

Ⓘ *South Moon Under*

7 Where did Rawlings's book *Cross Creek* get its name?

Ⓐ from a creek in Georgia

Ⓑ from a Native American word

Ⓒ from the place where she lived

Ⓓ from the name of the town where she was born

8 Why did the author MOST LIKELY write this article?

Ⓕ She doesn't like Rawlings.

Ⓖ She thinks that Rawlings's books are boring.

Ⓗ She thinks that everyone should write a book.

Ⓘ She thinks that more people should read Rawlings's books.

9 As a young girl, what did Rawlings love to do?

Ⓐ read

Ⓑ write

Ⓒ ride horses

Ⓓ grow oranges

UNIT

4 A New Century

What causes a society to grow? It's not just economics and inventions. War can help a society grow as well. In this unit, you will read about the United States' entry into World War I and its effects on the nation. You will also read about the decade after the war with many social and political changes. As you read, think about how culture influences how we live.

Times Square, New York City, in 1938

Miscellaneous Items in High Demand, Library of Congress, LC-USZ62-23866

networks

connected.mcgraw-hill.com
- Skill Builders
- Vocabulary Flashcards

112

Show as You Go! After you read each lesson in this unit, choose a new person, place, or invention that is related to the topic of the lesson. Describe it below. You will use your notes here to help you complete a project at the end of this unit.

Fold page here

Lesson 1

_____

_____

_____

_____

Lesson 2

_____

_____

_____

_____

Lesson 3

_____

_____

_____

_____

Lesson 4

_____

_____

_____

_____

Common Core Standards
RI.5.1: Quote accurately from a text when explaining what the text says explicitly and when drawing inferences from the text.

Make Generalizations

When you read, sometimes it helps to make a generalization. A generalization is a broad statement that shows how different facts, people, or events have something in common. Being able to make generalizations will help you uncover similarities that you might otherwise not notice. Generalizations can also help you make sense of new information you will learn later.

ⒸLEARN IT

- Identify text clues with similarities or relationships.

- Apply what you already know about the topic.

- Make a generalization that is true about all of your text clues and what you know.

- Read the passage below. Think about a generalization you could make.

Causes of the Great Depression

Industries made too many goods. New inventions in machinery increased production. However, workers wages did not grow fast enough to allow them to purchase all of the goods they wanted.

As sales slowed down, manufacturers cut back on how many goods they made. This meant that companies were making less money. As a result, employers cut wages and laid off workers. With lower incomes, many Americans could no longer afford to buy consumer goods.

Text Clue
Workers couldn't afford to buy goods.

Text Clue
People lost their jobs.

TRY IT

Copy and complete the generalization chart below. Then make a generalization about the causes of the Great Depression.

Text Clues	What You Know	Generalization

How did you figure out how to make a generalization?

APPLY IT

- **Review the steps to make generalizations in Learn It.**
- **Read the paragraph below. Then make a generalization about why countries go to war using a generalizations chart.**

At first, World War I was contained to Europe. Germany used submarines, called U-boats, to sink merchant ships. In 1915 the Germans sank the Lusitania, a British ship with 128 Americans on board. This act angered Americans.

In January 1917, a German military leader named Arthur Zimmermann sent a telegram to Mexico, proposing an alliance against the United States. American warships began to protect merchant ships crossing the Atlantic Ocean. When the

Germans sank eight American ships, President Woodrow Wilson asked Congress to declare war on the Central Powers.

▲ Arthur Zimmermann

Words to Know

The list below shows some important words you will learn in this unit. Their definitions can be found on the next page. Read the words.

annex (A • neks)

Spanish-American War (SPAN • ish A • MAR • i • can WOR)

nationalism (nash • nel • iz • em)

alliance (a • LIE • ans)

Great Migration (grayt my • GRAY • shen)

mass production (MAS Pro • DUK • shen)

stock exchange (stok iks • chanj)

public works (pub • lik WERKS)

FOLDABLES®

The Foldable on the next page will help you learn Foldable these important words. Follow the steps below to make your Foldable.

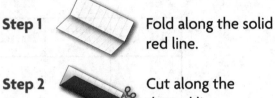

Step 1 Fold along the solid red line.

Step 2 Cut along the dotted lines.

Step 3 Read the words and their definitions.

Step 4 Complete the activities on each tab.

Step 5 Look at the back of your Foldable. Choose ONE of these activities for each word to help you remember its meaning:

- Draw a picture of the word.

- Write a description of the word.

- Write how the word is related to something you know.

To **annex** is to make a country or territory part of another country.	Underline the part of annex that is also a girl's name. _____ _____
The **Spanish-American War** was the war between the United States and Spain in 1898 in which the United States gained control of Puerto Rico, Guam, and the Philippines.	Define the Spanish-American War.
Nationalism means loyalty to one's country.	Name an instance when you showed nationalism.
An **alliance** is an agreement between nations to support and protect each other.	Write the plural of *alliance*.
The **Great Migration** is the movement of African Americans from the South to the North.	Use The Great Migration in a sentence.
Mass production is the process of making large numbers of one product quickly.	An artist making a one-of-a-kind item is the opposite of mass production. Name some products made this way.
A **stock exchange** is a place where shares in companies are bought and sold through an organized system.	Circle the type of item traded at a stock exchange. _____ _____
Public works are projects such as highways, parks, and libraries built with public funds for public use.	Name a public work you have been to.

annex

annex

✂ CUT HERE

Spanish-American War

Spanish-American War

nationalism

nationalism

alliance

alliance

Great Migration

Great Migration

mass production

mass production

stock exchange

stock exchange

public works

public works

Primary Sources

Paintings

Artists often create paintings of historical events and people. Paintings can show what life was like in the past. Paintings can be either primary or secondary sources. Paintings made by witnesses of a place or event are primary sources. Paintings that are based on primary sources to recreate an event or place are secondary sources.

DBQ Document-Based Questions

The painting on this page is from the 1800s and shows a settler's blockhouse. Study the painting and answer the questions below.

1. **What information would you need to know to determine if this painting is a primary source?**

   _____

   _____

2. **Describe what is happening in the painting.**

   _____

   _____

3. **What does this painting tell you about earlier life?**

   _____

   _____

networks
There's More Online!
● Skill Builders
● Resource Library

New States and Territories

❓ Essential Question

How did the United States gain power by 1900?

What do you think?

_____

_____

_____

_____

_____

_____

_____

Words To Know

Write a definition of each word in your own words.

annex

_____

Spanish-American War

_____

buffalo soldiers

_____

In 1896 the discovery of gold in the Klondike region of Alaska drew thousands of people.

Alaska and Hawaii

By the 1890s, the borders of the United States stretched from the Atlantic Ocean to the Pacific Ocean and from Canada to Mexico. Eventually the land would be divided into 48 states. Some Americans wanted the United States to look for more land outside its borders.

The first places Americans turned their attention to were the huge, icy expanse of Alaska and the sunny islands of Hawaii.

Alaska Purchased

In the 1860s, Russia owned the vast wilderness of Alaska. It was home to the Inuit and some Russian fur traders. By 1867, the fur supply was nearly gone. Russia offered to sell the territory to the United States. Secretary of State William Seward agreed to pay $7.2 million for 500,000 square miles. That's an area one-fifth the size of the rest of the United States.

Many people disagreed with Seward's decision. They said Russian America, as it was called, was a large lump of ice, crowded with walruses. But Seward was determined. He insisted that the land contained vast natural resources. In 1896 prospectors proved him right. They found a huge field of gold in a region called the Klondike. Suddenly thousands of people rushed to make their home in "Seward's Icebox." Alaska became a state in 1959.

Hawaii Overthrown

In 1778 British explorer James Cook was the first European to land in Hawaii during his third voyage to the Pacific. On the island, he found a highly developed society. Cook was killed in a struggle there, but even after his death, Europeans remembered the beautiful islands.

Missionaries arrived in the 1820s to convert the islanders to Christianity. Immigrants from the United States discovered they could make a fortune growing sugarcane and pineapples. In 1893 American businessmen overthrew Hawaiian Queen Liliuokalani. Judge Sanford P. Dole became president of Hawaii the next year. In 1898 the United States wanted to build a naval base in the Pacific Ocean. Officials decided that Pearl Harbor in Hawaii was the best location, and Congress voted to **annex** , or take over, the islands. Hawaii became a state in 1959.

▲ Liliuokalani, Queen of Hawaii

Why was Hawaii annexed?

Push for War

In 1898 Cuba and Puerto Rico were the only remaining Spanish colonies in the Americas. Cubans had been fighting for their independence since 1895. Many Americans wanted the United States to help the Cuban rebels. Newspaper owners William Randolph Hearst and Joseph Pulitzer tried to outdo each other with shocking reports of events in Cuba. This helped influence public opinion.

"Remember the *Maine*"

President William McKinley, who had fought in the Civil War as a young man, was not eager for war. He sent the USS *Maine* to Cuba to protect American citizens there.

On February 15, 1898, two explosions sank the *Maine*. The blast killed 266 American sailors. No one ever discovered the cause of the explosions. Newspapers immediately blamed them on the Spanish. "THE WARSHIP MAINE WAS SPLIT IN TWO BY AN ENEMY'S SECRET. . . MACHINE," reported Hearst's *New York Journal*. On April 24, McKinley declared war on Spain.

The War Begins

The **Spanish-American War** became one of the shortest wars in American history. In May the U.S. Navy destroyed a Spanish fleet in the Philippine Islands. In late June, American troops arrived in Cuba.

Are newspapers today more or less influential than in McKinley's day? Think about where you get your news before you answer.

_____

_____

_____

_____

▼ Explosion of the USS *Maine*

◀ While this famous painting shows the Rough Riders on horseback, American troops did not have horses in Cuba.

The American troops were poorly equipped and unorganized. Food supplies often spoiled on the way to Cuba. The cavalry left its horses in Florida because there weren't enough boats to transport them. Their heavy wool uniforms, many of which were left over from the Civil War, were too hot for the tropical climate.

The "Rough Riders"

Despite these problems, U.S. troops quickly overwhelmed the Spanish. Leading the fight was Theodore Roosevelt. Before the war, he had been the secretary of the navy. When war broke out, Roosevelt resigned from his position and formed a group of fighters called the "Rough Riders."

In Cuba the Rough Riders led two important attacks, charging up Kettle Hill and San Juan Hill. They were joined by the **buffalo soldiers** of the 10th Cavalry. Buffalo soldiers were African American troops who had fought in the Plains Wars.

The war in the Caribbean was over in a matter of weeks. In the words of Secretary of State John Hay, the conflict between Spain and the United States was, **"a splendid little war."**

> Why did American troops face difficulties in the first weeks of the Spanish-American War?
>
> _____
>
> _____
>
> _____
>
> _____
>
> _____

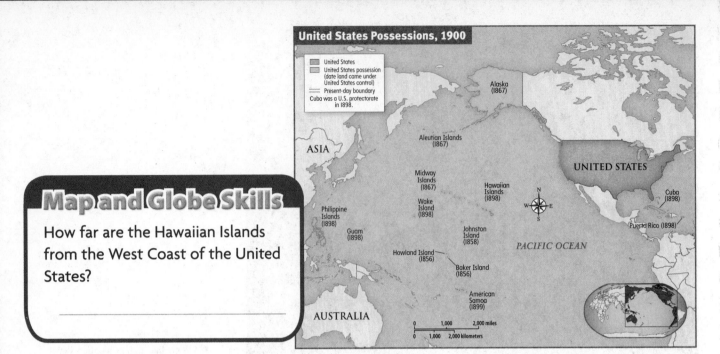

United States Possessions, 1900

Legend:
- United States
- United States possession (date land came under United States control)
- Present-day boundary
- Cuba was a U.S. protectorate in 1898.

ASIA
UNITED STATES

Alaska (1867)
Aleutian Islands (1867)
Midway Islands (1867)
Wake Island (1898)
Hawaiian Islands (1898)
Philippine Islands (1898)
Guam (1898)
Johnston Island (1858)
Howland Island (1856)
Baker Island (1856)
American Samoa (1899)
Cuba (1898)
Puerto Rico (1898)

PACIFIC OCEAN
AUSTRALIA

0   1,000   2,000 miles
0   1,000   2,000 kilometers

Map and Globe Skills

How far are the Hawaiian Islands from the West Coast of the United States?

After the War

In August 1898, the Spanish army decided to surrender. Spain gave up not only Cuba, but Puerto Rico and the island of Guam as well. Spain also sold the Philippines to the United States for $20 million.

In December of 1898, the United States and Spain signed the Treaty of Paris. Under the terms of the treaty, Puerto Rico, Guam, and the Philippines became U.S. territories. Cuba won its independence, though the United States built a naval base at Guantánamo Bay.

The Treaty of Paris was a turning point in American history. The United States had won a war on foregin soil and defeated a European power. For the first time, the United States controlled territories outside its own borders and continent.

Rebellion in the Philippines

In the Philippines, rebels had been fighting the Spanish for years. They wanted to govern themselves, and they felt betrayed when the Americans took control of their island nation.

The rebels went to war again, this time against the new rulers. The war lasted for three years. More than 100,000 American soldiers were sent to the Philippines. More than 4,000 American soldiers died, mostly from disease.

The Filipinos finally won their independence in 1946. Guam and Puerto Rico remain U.S. territories, and the people of those islands are American citizens.

The Roosevelt Corollary

In 1900 President McKinley was reelected, with Theodore Roosevelt as his Vice President. McKinley was assassinated one year later. At 42 years old, Theodore Roosevelt became the youngest person ever to be President.

President Roosevelt wanted to expand the 1823 Monroe Doctrine. The Monroe Doctrine stated that Europeans could not create new colonies in the Western Hemisphere. In return, the United States promised not to interfere with existing European colonies.

At this time, European nations had large amounts of money tied into trade with Latin America. President Roosevelt feared that if any of the Latin American countries became weak or had problems, Europeans would step in to protect their economic interests.

In a speech in 1904, Roosevelt strengthened the role of the United States. He said that the Americas were not open to European influence. He also said the United States had the right and responsibility to protect and maintain order in the Americas. This statement became known as the Roosevelt Corollary.

How was the Spanish-American war a turning point in American history?

_____

_____

_____

_____

▼ U.S. soldiers were sent to the Philippines to fight rebels.

The Panama Canal

President Roosevelt could never resist a challenge. In 1902 he approved one of the biggest construction projects ever attempted. Over the next 12 years, thousands of workers would carve out 240 million cubic yards of earth, separating North America and South America. The result was the Panama Canal.

Central American Shortcut

European explorers in the Americas eagerly searched for the Northwest Passage, a water passage from the Atlantic to the Pacific Ocean. They were never able to find this passage. Ships had to travel all the way around South America to reach the Pacific Ocean.

By the end of the Spanish-American War, American businesses needed a cheaper, easier way to ship products between the two oceans. A canal across Panama would cut the trip from the Atlantic Ocean to the Pacific Ocean by 7,000 miles. This passage would increase global trade for the United States. France began building a canal in 1880. The project failed. Twenty years later, the United States offered to complete the canal.

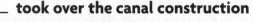

Construction of the canal took more than eight years. Many people came to Panama from the West Indies to work on it. The money they earned allowed them to move with their families to the United States.

Read the statements below. Put the letter that represents the appropriate country next to its matching statement.

a. France   b. the United States   c. Panama

_____ **owned land convenient for the passage**

_____ **quit building a canal**

_____ **took over the canal construction**

In 1900 Panama was a province of Colombia. Colombia wanted more money than President Roosevelt was willing to spend for the right to build the canal. In 1903 he sent the Navy to help Panama gain independence from Colombia. The United States then bought a 10-mile-wide strip of land across Panama. It was called the Canal Zone.

Building the Canal

Before work on the canal could begin, the Canal Zone had to be made safe for workers. Malaria and yellow fever killed thousands of people every year. Doctors had learned that mosquitoes spread those diseases quickly from person to person. An army doctor named William Gorgas came up with a solution. He told workers to drain swamps, spread oil and insecticide over standing water, and cut grassy areas where the mosquitoes laid their eggs.

By 1906, yellow fever had been eliminated and the number of malaria cases was greatly reduced. Finally, in August 1914, the first ship made the 48-mile voyage through the canal from the Atlantic Ocean to the Pacific Ocean.

How did the Panama Canal increase trade for the United States?

_____

_____

_____

Lesson 1

(?) **Essential Question**   **How did the United States gain power by 1900?**

_____

_____

_____

Go back to _Show As You Go!_ on pages 112–113. «

networks   **There's More Online!**
● Games ● Assessment

World War I

Why do nations go to war? What do you think?

_____

_____

_____

_____

_____

_____

Words To Know

Tell your partner what you know about each word.

Nationalism

_____

alliance

_____

convoys

_____

trench warfare

_____

Treaty of Versailles

_____

League of Nations

Woodrow Wilson

The World At War

In 1914 Europe exploded into war. At first the United States tried to stay out of the fight. When American ships were attacked, the country entered World War I.

During the early 1900s, many people had great patriotism, or a feeling of pride in their country. **Nationalism** is loyalty to one's country. However, some people with strong feelings of nationalism felt that their country was not only good, but it was also superior to all other countries.

128

The War Begins

In 1908 Austria-Hungary annexed Bosnia. This angered many ethnic Serbs who lived in that area. The Serbs wanted Bosnia to remain part of Serbia. Many feared that Austria-Hungary would take over Serbia next.

Archduke Franz Ferdinand was heir to the throne of Austria-Hungary. In June 1914, he and his wife were traveling to Bosnia. During the visit, they were assassinated by a Serb rebel.

At that time, most countries in Europe belonged to **alliances**, or agreements between nations to support and protect each other. Countries in each alliance promised to help each other if attacked.

Due to alliances, other European nations were drawn into the conflict between Serbia and Austria-Hugary. Austria-Hungary allied with Germany and declared war on Serbia. Russia was an ally of Serbia. On one side were the Allied Powers—Serbia, Russia, France, and Great Britain. On the other side were the Central Powers—Austria-Hungary, Germany, the Ottoman Empire, and Bulgaria. World War I had begun.

How can forming alliances be both positive and negative?

_____

_____

_____

_____

_____

Map and Globe Skills

Where was Germany located in relation to the Allied Powers?

_____

_____

Europe, 1914

- Allied Powers
- Central Powers
- Neutral nation

ICELAND

NORWAY

ATLANTIC OCEAN

North Sea

SWEDEN

DENMARK

RUSSIA

GREAT BRITAIN

NETH. GERMANY

BELG. LUX.

FRANCE

SWITZ.

AUSTRIA-HUNGARY

ROMANIA

SERBIA BULGARIA

PORTUGAL

ITALY

OTTOMAN EMPIRE

SPAIN

ALBANIA GREECE

MOROCCO (FRANCE) ALGERIA (FRANCE) TUNISIA (FRANCE)

Mediterranean Sea

0   500   1,000 miles

0   500   1,000 kilometers

Fighting The War

The United States tried to stay out of the war. Many Americans felt that the war was Europe's problem. However, the country had strong economic ties with the Allies. Pressure began to build for the United States to enter the war.

Fighting at Sea

At the start of the war, trade with the Allies soared. Many American factories converted to create goods for the Allies, such as weapons and steel. Germany wanted to keep these supplies from reaching the Allies. It used submarines, called U-boats, to sink merchant ships. In 1915 the Germans sank the *Lusitania*, a British ship with 128 Americans on board. This act angered Americans.

> **What do you think the U in U-boats stands for?**
>
> _____
>
> _____

▼ Some women served as nurses for the Red Cross.

In 1917 Germany declared all-out submarine warfare on ships carrying supplies to Allied ports. British Prime Minister David Lloyd George suggested the use of **convoys** to protect Allied ships and move supplies to his country. A convoy is a group of vehicles that travel together to provide better protection.

MOTHERLESS FATHERLESS STARVING

HOW MUCH
TO SAVE THESE LITTLE LIVES?

WAR FUND WEEK
ONE HUNDRED MILLION DOLLARS
MAY 20ᵗʰ–27ᵗʰ

The United States Enters the War

Then, in January 1917, a German military leader named Arthur Zimmermann sent a telegram to Mexico, proposing an alliance against the United States. In return Germany would help Mexico reclaim land in the United States. Americans were outraged.

American warships began to protect ships bound for Europe. German U-boats then sank eight more American ships. The United States declared war on the Central Powers on April 6. In his speech urging Congress to declare war, President Woodrow Wilson said:

"The world must be made safe for democracy."

Deadly Modern Warfare

When American soldiers reached Europe in June, they faced deadly challenges. Machine guns and tanks caused devastation across battlefields. Poison gas killed anyone who breathed it.

Both sides used airplanes to watch enemy troops and to bomb targets. Fighter pilots such as Germany's Baron Manfred von Richthofen, known as the Red Baron, fought duels in the sky called dogfights.

Both sides built long ditches, or trenches. Thousands of soldiers were killed or wounded as they tried to move between trenches. This kind of fighting is called **trench warfare**.

The Home Front

Because the fighting was happening in Europe, it took a lot of time and money for the United States to get all of the troops and resources in place. To raise money, the government issued war bonds. It also raised taxes on individuals and businesses.

Millions of men left their jobs and joined the armed forces. Women and minorities worked in these jobs during the war. Many more factories shifted production to make goods for the war, such as tanks and airplanes.

Due to food shortages in Europe, the United States needed to produce enough food for itself and for the Allies as well. The government asked farmers to produce more food. It also asked the public to consume less food.

Expressing Your Opinion

When should a country go to war? In a democracy, citizens have the right to express their opinions on issues such as declaring war.

Before voicing your opinion, be sure you know the facts. You can find good sources for information about important issues in newspapers or books and on television or the Internet. Listen to what other people say. Keep your mind open. Look for facts that can be supported by evidence. Then express your opinion, such as by writing a letter to a newspaper or to a government leader.

Write About It Write your opinion about an issue being debated in your community.

A ration is the amount of a good a person can buy when the good is scarce. What goods do you think were rationed during the war?

_____

_____

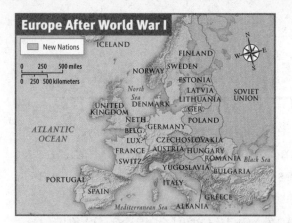

Europe After World War I

New Nations

0 250 500 miles
0 250 500 kilometers

ICELAND
FINLAND
NORWAY SWEDEN
ESTONIA
North LATVIA
Sea LITHUANIA SOVIET UNION
UNITED KINGDOM DENMARK
NETH. GER.
BELG. GERMANY POLAND
ATLANTIC OCEAN LUX. CZECHOSLOVAKIA
FRANCE AUSTRIA-HUNGARY
SWITZ. ROMANIA Black Sea
YUGOSLAVIA BULGARIA
PORTUGAL ITALY
SPAIN GREECE
Mediterranean Sea ALBANIA

Making Peace

By the time American troops arrived in Europe, the Central Powers were weakened. They had lost many troops and were running low on ammunition, food, and other resources. President Wilson began planning for "peace without victory." He felt that if peace was not handled carefully, the world would soon be at war again. His plan was called the Fourteen Points.

The War Ends

World War I ended on November 11, 1918. Over 8 million soldiers died during the war. Later, a peace treaty, the **Treaty of Versailles**, was signed. It treated Germany harshly. The Allies blamed Germany for starting the war. Germany was forced to pay the costs of fighting the war. This ruined the German economy and would lead to another war.

Wilson wanted to prevent future wars. He proposed an organization in which nations could solve their problems peacefully. He called this organization the **League of Nations**. The U.S. Senate, however, refused to allow the country to join the League. Some feared that the United States might be drawn into the political problems of countries far from U.S. borders. The United States, one of the most powerful nations in the world, did not join the League of Nations. Later, this would be one factor that caused the organization to fail.

Map and Globe Skills

What new countries came into existence after World War I?

_____

_____

Should the Treaty of Versailles have treated Germany so harshly?

_____

_____

_____

Lesson 2

(?) Essential Question Why do nations go to war?

_____

_____

Go back to *Show As You Go!* on pages 112–113.

networks

There's More Online!
● Games ● Assessment

Map and Globe Skill

Compare Maps at Different Scales

All maps are drawn to scale. A **map scale** uses a unit of measurement, such as an inch, to show distance on Earth. A map scale explains the size of the area on a map.

A **small-scale map**, such as Map A, shows a large area, but cannot include many details. A **large-scale map**, such as Map B, shows a smaller area with more details.

LEARN IT

- If you want to find out which countries were involved in World War I in Europe, you would use a small-scale map, or Map A. It shows a large area.

- If you want to see a close-up of France, you would need the large-scale map, or Map B. It shows more details, such as the major cities and rivers of France.

- Compare the scales of both maps.

TRY IT

- Which map scale represents a small distance? Which represents a large distance?

- Use the map scale on Map B. How far is Toulouse from Paris?

APPLY IT

- Compare a map of the United States with a map of your state.

- Compare the map scales. Is the state map a large-scale or a small-scale map?

Map A

Europe, 1914

Map B

France, 1914

The Roaring Twenties

Library of Congress Prints & Photographs Division [LC-USZ62-50219]

? Essential Question

How did political and social changes affect Americans during the 1920s?

What do you think?

_____

_____

_____

_____

_____

_____

Words To Know

Define these terms in your own words.

Great Migration

_____

bohemian

_____

expatriate

_____

mass production

_____

Some people were able to afford luxury items during the 1920s.

A Changing Culture

The decade after World War I brought social and political changes that had lasting effects on the country. This era is known as the "Jazz Age" or the "Roaring Twenties."

Americans felt a great sense of relief after World War I. They had a renewed spirit and wanted to enjoy themselves. Jazz music became very popular. Music clubs opened across the country, where people met to talk, listen to music, and dance.

Some women began having shorter hair and wearing shorter skirts. They were called "flappers." A flapper was a young woman who dressed in the new styles, wore make-up, and listened to jazz music.

The Great Migration

During the early 1900s, over 1 million African Americans left the South. They wanted to escape the racial violence and Jim Crow laws that took away their rights. Also, beetles had ruined the cotton crop, causing many people to lose their jobs.

Many African Americans moved to the North and the Midwest. They found jobs in steel mills and automobile plants. They faced discrimination in the North as well, but life there was generally safer and jobs could be found. Later, African Americans also moved west.

This mass movement of African Americans from the South is called the **Great Migration**. During the Great Migration, Chicago's African American population doubled, Cleveland's tripled, and Detroit's became six times larger.

African Americans who moved north brought their culture with them. Midwest cities, including Chicago, St. Louis, and Detroit, became centers for African American music such as jazz and blues.

> Underline the names of three cities where the African American population increased during the Great Migration.

> **Why did African Americans leave the South in the early 1900s?**
>
> _____
>
> _____

▼ An African American family during the Great Migration

The Harlem Renaissance

Why was the Harlem Renaissance important?

_____

_____

_____

_____

During the Great Migration, many African Americans found their way to Harlem, a neighborhood in New York City. Among them were a number of artists, singers, dancers, actors, and writers.

Harlem became alive with energy. It was a time of great creativity and cultural pride. This time is known as the Harlem Renaissance. Artists shared their ideas and used their work to express positive images of African American culture.

Soon, the ideas of the Harlem Renaissance spread to the rest of the country. White Americans began traveling to visit Harlem's nightclubs. African American writers began to be recognized by major publishers. Radio helped songs by African Americans become popular across the country and around the world.

Zora Neale Hurston, 1891–1960, an American author and anthropologist. She was well known for her folklore and short stories.

Louis Armstrong was born in New Orleans, the birthplace of jazz. He found his way to Chicago and later to New York City. Armstrong not only played the trumpet, but he also used his voice like an instrument. Once during a recording session, he dropped his lyrics on the floor. Instead of singing the words, he improvised and made up nonsense syllables—and "scat singing" was born.

Composer and pianist **Duke Ellington** moved to New York from Washington, D.C., in 1923. While playing at the famous Cotton Club, he developed a distinctive style that brought him worldwide fame.

Write a fan letter to the artist on these two pages whose talent most impresses you. Explain why.

_____

_____

_____

_____

_____

_____

_____

Langston Hughes wrote poetry, essays, books, and plays. He inspired many other African American writers. In one of his poems he wrote:

"Listen, America—
I live here, too,
I want freedom
Just as you."

Modern Forms Of Art

During the 1920s, American artists and writers explored what it meant to be "modern." They lived artistic and **bohemian**, or nontraditional, lifestyles. They focused on freedom of expression.

Composers

Popular music of this time blended old elements from classical music with the rhythm and harmonies found in jazz. George and Ira Gershwin used this style to compose and write Broadway shows and movie scores.

Another popular composer was Aaron Copeland. He was determined to see worldwide acceptance of American classical music. In many of his film scores, he combined elements of classical, jazz, and folk music to create a distinctly American sound.

Modern American Art

American artists displayed a wide range of styles. Georgia O'Keeffe was an abstract painter. Abstract art does not show real objects, but uses lines, shapes, and colors to suggest an idea or feeling.

Edward Hopper and Andrew Wyeth were realistic painters. Hopper's paintings focused on isolation in the modern world. Wyeth's paintings showed scenes from real life.

American Literature

Writers of the 1920s varied greatly in style and in subject matter. Authors Carl Sandburg and Willa Cather used common speech to describe daily life in the Midwest. John Steinbeck wrote about the problems faced by the poor.

▼ Movie theaters became popular in the 1920s (below). Edward Hopper painted realistic paintings (right).

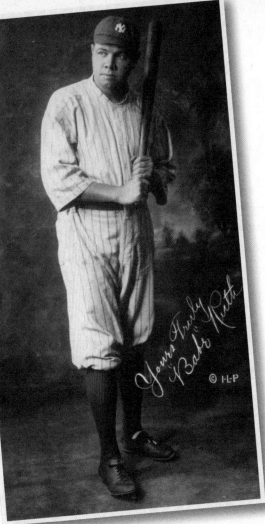

▲ In the 1920s, Americans became more interested in celebrities such as aviator Charles Lindbergh (left) and baseball star Babe Ruth (right).

Some writers were dissatisfied with life after the war. Many of these writers left the United States and moved to Europe. They were called **expatriates**. An expatriate is someone who leaves his or her native country and lives somewhere else for a while. Novelist and expatriate F. Scott Fitzgerald captured the mood of the times in his writings. He gave the twenties the nickname "the Jazz Age."

Celebrity Sweeps America

With the war over, many Americans turned their attention to celebrities. Details of these people, their lives, and their amazing feats were lead stories in the news.

Americans came to love sports, especially baseball. They listened to games on the radio or went to the ballpark. Baseball players such as Babe Ruth drew huge crowds. The most popular players were asked to endorse products in advertisements.

A world-wide aviation contest in the 1920s promised $25,000 to the first person to complete a transatlantic flight, or a flight across the Atlantic Ocean. The 30-hour journey was difficult. Many pilots attempted the flight. In 1927 Charles Lindbergh became a celebrity when he was the first to complete the nonstop flight from New York to Paris.

A year later, Amelia Earhart became the first woman to complete a transatlantic flight. She set many flying records and wrote books about her experiences. When she attempted to fly around the world, Earhart disappeared over the Pacific Ocean. Her plane was never found.

Describe the mood of Americans during the 1920s.

_____

_____

_____

_____

New Technologies

Several important changes took place in the 1920s. Many items we use every day were introduced during this time.

Automobiles and Airplanes

During the 1920s, the automobile became affordable to millions of families. The increasing number of cars created a need for highways, gas stations, motels, and roadside diners. The oil industry grew rapidly because of the need for gasoline and motor oil.

To meet the demand for cars, a system known as **mass production** was used. Mass production means making a large number of products quickly. Automaker Henry Ford used an assembly line to mass produce his cars. On an assembly line, a product is built as it moves past workers. Each person does one job, such as tightening a bolt. By 1925, one Ford came off the assembly line every 10 to 15 seconds.

The airline industry also grew. During World War I, factories in the United States built airplanes for the war. After the war, these companies continued to expand. By 1919, the post office used airplanes to deliver mail across the country. In 1926 the government started giving federal money to build airports. Charles Lindbergh also brought attention to the industry with his transatlantic flight. By 1928 there were 48 airlines across the country.

> Name some positives and negatives about assembly lines.
>
> _____
>
> _____
>
> _____
>
> _____

Library of Congress Prints & Photographs Division [LC-USZ62-50219]

Assembly-line workers in a ▶ Ford factory at Dearborn, Michigan.

Family Around the Oil Heater (left). Vogue Car, 1920 (right).

A Society of Consumers

Modern household goods such as vacuum cleaners, electric stoves, and refrigerators were also mass produced in the 1920s. New ways of reaching a wide audience were developed as well. One important new form of media was the radio. Most American homes had radios.

Magazine and radio advertisements persuaded people to buy new items. Many people who could not afford the items bought on credit. Consumers borrowed money to pay for goods, then paid it back over time. Some people, however, were unable to pay back the money they had borrowed. That would lead to economic problems by the end of the 1920s.

How did new media help business leaders like Henry Ford?

_____

_____

_____

_____

Lesson 3

(?) Essential Question **How did political and social changes affect Americans during the 1920s?**

_____

_____

_____

Go back to *Show As You Go!* on pages 112–113.

networks **There's More Online!**
● Games ● Assessment

Hard Times

Essential Question

How do economic changes affect Americans? List two ways.

_____

_____

_____

_____

_____

_____

_____

Words To Know

Write the definition of each word in your own words.

nativism

_____

stock exchange

_____

speculation

_____

The Works Progress Administration (WPA) payed artists to paint murals, such as this one in San Francisco.

Issues With Immigration

During the 1920s, urban Americans celebrated the new "modern" culture, but not everyone agreed that the new trends were a good thing. Some Americans believed traditional values were under attack.

The 1920s were exciting for many Americans. However, many groups faced harsh discrimination at this time.

During the first two decades of the 1900s, many immigrants came to the United States from Eastern and Southern Europe. Some Americans did not accept these newcomers. They believed in **nativism**, the idea that people born in the United States were superior to immigrants.

These anti-immigrant feelings led to a revival of the Ku Klux Klan. The Klan had nearly disappeared in the South in the 1880s, but now it grew strong again. Klan members discriminated against anyone who wasn't white, of English decent, and a Protestant. This included people who were Jewish, Native American, Catholic, or of Asian, African, Arab, Greek, or Italian heritage. By 1924, the Klan had grown to 4 million members.

Highsmith (Carol M.) Archive, Library of Congress, LC-DIG-highsm-13275

Immigration Limits

As a result of the growing negative feelings toward immigration, Congress passed the Emergency Quota Act in 1921. This law set a limit on the total number of new immigrants allowed to enter the United States. It also set a maximum number on how many people were allowed to enter the United States from each country.

Congress passed more anti-immigration laws in 1924. The National Origins Act reduced the number of immigrants allowed from Southern and Eastern European countries. The Asian Exclusion Act completely excluded people from Japan, India, and East Asia. An 1882 law already prevented Chinese immigrants from entering the country.

Describe challenges immigrants faced during the 1920s.

_____

_____

_____

_____

Immigrants waited in long lines after arriving at Ellis Island.

An Unbalanced Economy

Many people in the United States made money in the 1920s. However, by the end of the decade, the economy was weakening.

Boom and Crash

Many people purchased stocks hoping to get rich. A stock is a share in the ownership of a company. During the late 1920s, the values of stocks on the New York Stock Exchange were higher than ever. A **stock exchange** is an organized system for buying and selling stocks.

Investors bought stocks thinking they would be able to make a profit in a short amount of time. This practice is called **speculation**. Some borrowed money to buy stocks.

The stock market would only continue to do well as long as there were new people to put money into the system. Then, in late September 1929, many professional investors saw this as a problem. They sold their stocks fearing that the market boom would end. This caused stock prices to fall. Brokers who had lent money began demanding repayment.

Prices continued to fall. On October 24, 1929, a day known as "Black Thursday," panicked traders sold almost 13 million shares. Five days later, the market crashed. This event began the Great Depression, a period of severe economic hardship in the 1930s.

Economic Issues

There were other warning signs of economic trouble. Farmers had grown more crops during World War I to send food to Europe. After the war, Europeans again farmed for themselves. They also had to pay to rebuild their countries after the war, so they had less money to buy American crops.

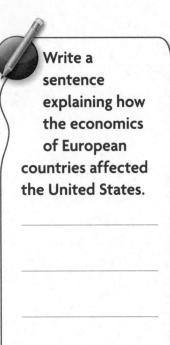

Write a sentence explaining how the economics of European countries affected the United States.

_____

_____

_____

_____

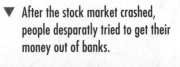

▼ After the stock market crashed, people desparatly tried to get their money out of banks.

Library of Congress Prints & Photographs Division [LC-USZ62-130861]

Many American farmers had borrowed money to buy new land and equipment. They now had more crops than they could sell. As a result, they could not pay their debts.

There were also issues with overproduction, or making too many goods. New technology had increased production, but workers' wages did not grow enough to let them buy all of these goods. This caused sales to slow. As a result, employers had to cut wages and lay off workers. With lower incomes, people could no longer afford to buy consumer goods.

Another issue was the growing gap between the rich and poor. In 1929 nearly 33 percent of the nation's wealth was owned by less than 1 percent of the people. At the same time, nearly 75 percent of American families were living in, or near, poverty.

For much of the 1920s, the economy was fueled by borrowed money. Many small banks failed when people could not pay their loans. Large banks suffered great losses in the stock market crash. Thousands of banks were forced to close. Millions of people lost their money.

The Depression Spreads

In 1930 Congress raised tariffs on imports, which raised the prices of those goods. This made American goods less expensive than foreign imports. However, it also meant that sales of European goods slowed. In return many European countries raised tariffs on American goods. The result was a sharp decrease in international trade. Factories closed and unemployment rose worldwide.

> How did the use of credit lead to the stock market crash?
>
> _____
>
> _____
>
> _____

The Great Depression

Gross National Product, or GNP, is the total number of goods and services produced by a nation's factories. As GNP falls, unemployment tends to go up. Study the graphs below to answer questions about the economy from 1915 to 1945.

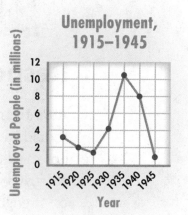

Unemployment, 1915–1945

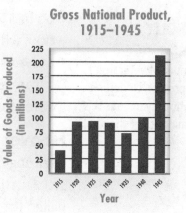

Gross National Product, 1915–1945

> During what year were the most people out of work? When was the GNP the lowest?
>
> _____
>
> Explain the connection between GNP and unemployment.
>
> _____

Many families who were forced out of their homes by poverty moved into crude tent and shack cities called "Hoovervilles." ▶

Farm Security Administration/Office of War Information Black-and-White Negatives, Library of Congress, LC-USF33-006579-M5

Response To Crisis

After the market crashed, many people felt that the government should have worked to solve the crisis. President Herbert Hoover did not think that the government should fund relief programs to help struggling Americans. He believed the government should only focus on strengthening the economy.

By 1932, more than one in four workers were jobless. Those who had lost their homes built shelters out of boxes and scrap wood, which were sometimes grouped together. Some called these "Hoovervilles" because of the President's failure to help.

Farmers were in trouble, too. Crop prices that had already been low fell even lower, causing some farmers to lose their farms.

Hoover Responds

Realizing that something had to be done, Hoover asked businesses to stop cutting wages and to resume the production of goods. He also called for more charity, believing this would pull the nation out of hard times.

Eventually Hoover realized the federal government had to do more. He authorized spending on **public works** projects, such as the construction of highways, parks, and libraries, to create new jobs.

The "Bonus Army"

In 1932 over 15,000 World War I veterans marched to Washington and camped out in Hoovervilles. They were known as the "Bonus Army." They each had been scheduled to receive a $1,000 bonus payment in 1945. However, they were asking for it early. Congress and the President turned them down.

Most of the veterans left, but about 2,000 promised to stay until the bonuses were paid. The U.S. Army was called in to help remove the protestors. A riot broke out. Armed guards used tear gas and clubs against the Bonus Army, and many people were injured. Cameras photographed the conflict, and the nation was deeply troubled by the sight of the U.S. Army acting against its own veterans.

A New Deal

By 1932, the nation faced the worst economic crisis in its history. Franklin D. Roosevelt won the Presidency that year by promising Americans a "New Deal." He planned on using the power of the government to create jobs.

By the time Roosevelt took office, most of the nation's banks had closed. Nearly 25 percent of workers were unemployed. During Roosevelt's first 100 days in office, Congress passed 15 laws that set up new agencies. They came to be called "alphabet" agencies because of their initials. Some government programs hired workers to build roads, dams, parks, and buildings across the country. Other programs regulated farming, labor, business, banking, and the stock market.

The TVA

One of the boldest programs launched by President Roosevelt was the Tennessee Valley Authority (TVA). The TVA built dams to control floods, conserved forests, and brought electricity to rural areas along the Tennessee River. Dams built by the TVA ended the region's disastrous floods and generated affordable electricity using hydroelectric power. This was the first time that thousands of farms and homes in some Southern states had access to electricity.

Major New Deal Programs

Program	Purpose
Tennessee Valley Authority (TVA)*	Provides electrical power to more than 8 million customers
Civilian Conservation Corps (CCC)	Employed people to work planting trees, fighting forest fires, and building reservoirs
Federal Deposit and Insurance Corporation (FDIC)*	Insures bank deposits and protects people's money
Social Security (SS)*	Provides unemployment insurance, disability insurance, and pensions for those who have retired
Securities and Exchange Commission (SEC)*	Regulates and polices the stock market
National Recovery Administration (NRA)	Set prices, established minimum wages, limited length of shifts, limited the number of shifts at factories, and guaranteed the right to form unions
Agricultural Adjustment Act (AAA)	Controlled prices of farm products by paying some farmers to stop farming or to destroy their crops or livestock
Works Progress Administration (WPA)	Constructed public works (highways, buildings, parks, and bridges) and paid artists to create murals, sculptures, and plays

* Still in existence today

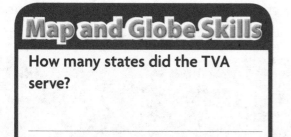

Map and Globe Skills

How many states did the TVA serve?

_____

_____

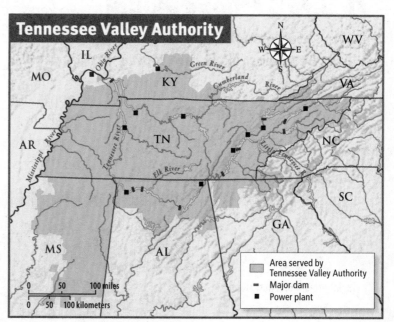

Tennessee Valley Authority

Area served by Tennessee Valley Authority
– Major dam
■ Power plant

Life During The Depression

Life during the Depression was difficult. Many people lost their jobs and couldn't buy food. Many people stood in bread lines or ate at soup kitchens offering free food.

The Dust Bowl

A natural disaster added to the nation's economic problems. For several years beginning in 1930, a severe drought dried out land in the Great Plains. High winds blew away millions of acres of soil. This area came to be known as the Dust Bowl. Many farm families were forced to leave their land and sought jobs in California. They became known as "Okies," because many of them came from Oklahoma.

A Second New Deal

Roosevelt started the Second New Deal in 1935. Congress passed the Revenue Act, which raised taxes on big corporations and the rich. The Works Progress Admininstration, or WPA, put people to work building highways, libraries, schools, and hospitals. It also employed artists, writers, and musicians.

In the mid-1930s, labor unions grew stronger. Congress passed the National Labor Relations Act, which gave unions the right to strike and to bargain. The Fair Labor Standards Act of 1938 guaranteed workers a minimum wage of 40 cents an hour. This law also banned child labor.

Not everyone approved of the New Deal. Some accused Roosevelt of spending too much government money and trying to destroy free enterprise. Some New Deal programs, such as the National Industry Recovery Act and the Agricultural Adjustment Act, were found to be unconstitutional by the Supreme Court.

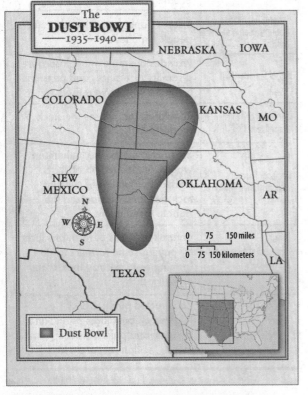

The
DUST BOWL
1935–1940

NEBRASKA   IOWA

COLORADO   KANSAS   MO

NEW
MEXICO
N
W   E
S

OKLAHOMA   AR

0   75   150 miles
0   75   150 kilometers   LA

TEXAS

Dust Bowl

Map and Globe Skills

Why would people living in the Dust Bowl most likely have moved west?

The aftermath of a dust storm ▶

U.S. Department of Agriculture, U.S. Department of Agriculture

Minorities and Women

While few African American men worked in New Deal programs, they did make some political gains. President Roosevelt appointed several African Americans to federal jobs.

Native Americans made more gains than other groups at this time. Congress passed several bills to employ Native Americans, to improve life on reservations, and to restore traditional tribal governments.

Two women played major roles in the government. President Roosevelt's wife, Eleanor, traveled the country and reported conditions to him. Frances Perkins became the first woman to serve in the cabinet. As the secretary of labor, she worked on programs for Social Security and unemployment. Social Security helped people after they retire. Unemployment insurance paid people who were jobless for a certain period of time.

The Roosevelt Recession

In the summer of 1937, the economy seemed to be stable. Roosevelt cut his relief and job programs. The economy fell immediately. This is called the Roosevelt Recession. The economy wouldn't be fully restored until another world war put people back to work.

▲ During the Great Depression, people lined up for meals at soup kitchens.

DID YOU KNOW?
Track star **Jesse Owens** won four gold medals at the 1936 Olympics. He became a hero for struggling African Americans during the Great Depression.

Why were some people against the New Deal?

_____

_____

Lesson 4

(?) **Essential Question** How do economic changes affect Americans?

_____

_____

Go back to *Show As You Go!* on pages 112–113.

(t)Bettmann/Corbis; (b)Library of Congress Prints & Photographs Division [LC-USZ62-27663]

Follow the steps below to complete the vocabulary activity.

1. Place four related words from this unit in the circle. Write a title for this set of words.

_____

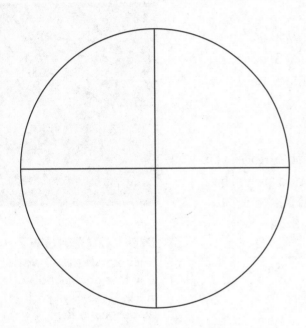

2. How is each word related to your title? Could other words from this unit have been placed in the circle? If so, explain.

_____

_____

_____

_____

3. Replace one or two words with different words and create a new title for that circle.

_____

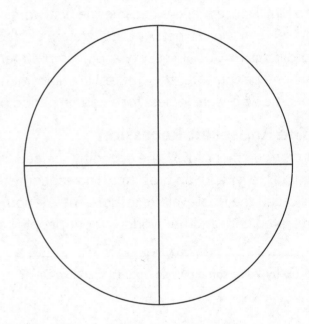

4. Explain the connections between words and how this impacted your new title. Be sure to use details in your explanation.

_____

_____

_____

_____

Minorities and Women

While few African American men worked in New Deal programs, they did make some political gains. President Roosevelt appointed several African Americans to federal jobs.

Native Americans made more gains than other groups at this time. Congress passed several bills to employ Native Americans, to improve life on reservations, and to restore traditional tribal governments.

Two women played major roles in the government. President Roosevelt's wife, Eleanor, traveled the country and reported conditions to him. Frances Perkins became the first woman to serve in the cabinet. As the secretary of labor, she worked on programs for Social Security and unemployment. Social Security helped people after they retire. Unemployment insurance paid people who were jobless for a certain period of time.

▲ During the Great Depression, people lined up for meals at soup kitchens.

The Roosevelt Recession

In the summer of 1937, the economy seemed to be stable. Roosevelt cut his relief and job programs. The economy fell immediately. This is called the Roosevelt Recession. The economy wouldn't be fully restored until another world war put people back to work.

> **DID YOU KNOW?**
> Track star **Jesse Owens** won four gold medals at the 1936 Olympics. He became a hero for struggling African Americans during the Great Depression.

Why were some people against the New Deal?

_____

_____

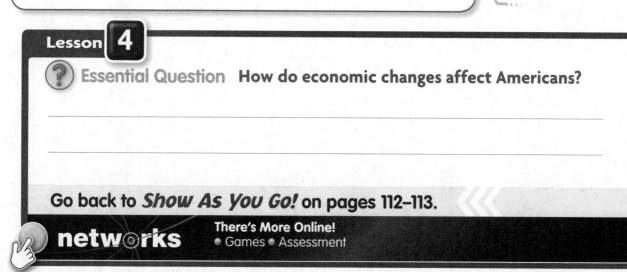

Lesson 4

(?) **Essential Question** How do economic changes affect Americans?

_____

_____

Go back to *Show As You Go!* on pages 112–113.

networks **There's More Online!**
● Games ● Assessment

(t)Bettmann/Corbis; (b)Library of Congress Prints & Photographs Division [LC-USZ62-27663]

UNIT 4 Wrap Up

networks **There's More Online!**
● Games ● Assessment

Follow the steps below to complete the vocabulary activity.

1. Place four related words from this unit in the circle. Write a title for this set of words.

3. Replace one or two words with different words and create a new title for that circle.

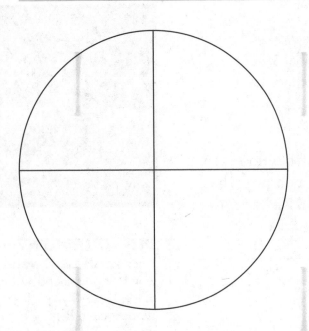

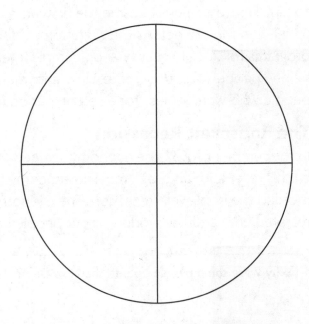

2. How is each word related to your title? Could other words from this unit have been placed in the circle? If so, explain.

4. Explain the connections between words and how this impacted your new title. Be sure to use details in your explanation.

Unit Project

Use the information you learned in this unit to create a board game about a family going through a difficult time. Your game should focus on the potential hardships that settlers faced. Brainstorm how the elements you want to include in your game will work together. Make a game board and a list of rules for the game.

Your board game should include...   **Yes, it does!**

a game board made of cardboard or thick poster board ☐

a story that focuses on potential hardships faced by settlers along the overland trails ☐

game pieces and a method for moving on the board, such as dice or a spinner ☐

clear and easy rules that explain how to play the game ☐

Think about the Big Idea

BIG IDEA Culture influences the way people live.

What did you learn in this unit that helps you understand the BIG IDEA?

_____

_____

_____

Read the essay about a trip to the Kennedy Space Center before answering Number 1 through 7.

My Trip to Kennedy Space Center

by Oscar Sanchez

My family and I went to the Kennedy Space Center last spring. And I had a blast! Kennedy Space Center has been the site of many "firsts" in space. In 1961 the first American rocketed into space from Cape Canaveral (that's the location of the space center). In 1969 the first men to go to the moon blasted off from there. I learned that the National Aeronautics and Space Administration (or NASA for short) was created in 1958. Its creation was part of the space race. The space race was a competition between our nation and the Soviet Union to see which country could get to the moon first.

We went on a bus tour around the whole space center. The tour stops at the Launch Complex 39 Observation Gantry. It is a big observation deck that you can walk onto and look out. You get to see the launch pad and almost the entire complex. It is so cool! Next on the bus tour was the Apollo/Saturn V Center. It has some great displays. I liked the spacesuits the best. Next we saw the rocket display and the capsules. That was really cool too! The space center also shows a film that recreates a launch that is very realistic. Next on the tour was the International Space Station Center. Here visitors can walk through capsules. You can also visit the Astronaut Hall of Fame. It includes a history of the space program and information about the astronauts who have launched from Kennedy Space Center. I learned so much about the space program during our visit!

1 What is the author's MAIN purpose for writing **"My Trip to Kennedy Space Center"**?

Ⓐ to tell where NASA is located

Ⓑ to tell about the moon landing

Ⓒ to tell the reasons for the space race

Ⓓ to tell about their trip to the Kennedy Space Center

2 Where is the Kennedy Space Center located?

Ⓕ on the moon

Ⓖ on Cape Canaveral

Ⓗ on Launch Complex 39

Ⓘ on Apollo/Saturn V Center

3 Read the sentences from the essay.

> **In 1961 the first American rocketed into space from Cape Canaveral (that's the location of the space center). In 1969 the first men to go to the moon blasted off from there.**

What does the phrase "blasted off" mean in this sentence?

Ⓐ created

Ⓑ destroyed

Ⓒ launched

Ⓓ saved

4 What happened AFTER Oscar went to the International Space Station Center?

Ⓕ He went to the Apollo/Saturn V Center.

Ⓖ He went to the Astronaut Hall of Fame.

Ⓗ He watched a film that recreates a launch.

Ⓘ He went to the Launch Complex 39 Observation Gantry.

5 Read the sentence from the essay.

> **It is a big observation deck that you can walk onto and look out.**

What does the word *observation* mean?

Ⓐ the act of looking aside

Ⓑ the act of being noticed

Ⓒ the act of noticing

Ⓓ the act of walking

6 What do you think Oscar's opinion of the film was?

Ⓕ Oscar disliked the film.

Ⓖ Oscar had not seen a launch before.

Ⓗ Oscar thought the film was well made.

Ⓘ Oscar thought the film was the best stop on the tour.

7 Read the sentences from the essay.

> **Next on the bus tour was the Apollo/Saturn V Center. It has some great displays. I liked the spacesuits the best. Next we saw the rocket display and the capsules. That was really cool too! The space center also shows a film that recreates a launch that is very realistic. Next on the tour was the International Space Station Center.**

Which overall text structure did the author use in his essay?

Ⓐ chronology

Ⓑ comparison

Ⓒ cause and effect

Ⓓ problem and solution

UNIT 5

World War II and the Early Cold War

The United States did not want to enter another war. But, after they were attacked, they had no choice. Many minorities picked up the pieces back on the home front whilst many people entered World War II. In this unit, you will read about the United States' entry into World War II and how it led to the Cold War. You will also read about the new way of life in the 1950s. As you read, think about how conflict causes change.

American troops liberating a city in France.

networks

connected.mcgraw-hill.com
- Skill Builders
- Resource Library

Show As You Go! After you read each lesson in this unit, record important details about one important event of World War II and the early Cold War. You will use your notes to help you complete a project at the end of the unit.

Lesson 1 Why did the U.S. Enter the War?

_____

_____

Lesson 2 What new opportunities opened up for minorities?

_____

_____

Lesson 3 What was the turning point of the War?

_____

_____

Lesson 4 How was Europe divided after the War?

_____

_____

Lesson 5 What was the Cold War?

_____

_____

Lesson 6 How did life change in the 1950s?

_____

_____

Fold page here

Reading Skill

Common Core Standards
RI.5.2 Determine two or more main ideas of a text and explain how they are supported by key details; summarize the text.

Summarize

Summarizing is a good way to remember what you read. After you read a paragraph or section in your textbook, make a summary of it. A summary is a brief statement about the topic of a passage. Since a summary leaves out minor details, it should be short.

LEARN IT

- Find key details that tell more about a subject.

- Leave out details that are not important.

- Restate the important points briefly in a summary.

- Read the paragraph below and think about how you would summarize it.

Topic
Japan Attacks Pearl Harbor

Key Detail
Many ships and planes were destroyed.

Key Detail
2,400 Americans were killed.

Unimportant Detail
The Japanese used their six largest aircraft carriers.

JAPAN ATTACKS PEARL HARBOR

On December 7, 1941, the Japanese attacked Pearl Harbor. The Japanese had a massive fleet of ships that included their six largest aircraft carriers. Japanese planes and submarines targeted U.S. ships in the harbor with bombs and torpedoes. Their bombers also destroyed many planes on the ground. The attack was devastating. The United States lost eight of its battleships. Many other ships were sunk or seriously damaged. About 200 planes were destroyed, and more than 2,400 Americans were killed. The United States was fortunate that its aircraft carriers were not at Pearl Harbor. They were spared and ready to fight against the Japanese navy.

TRY IT

Copy and complete the summary chart below. Fill in the top box with pieces of information from the passage on page R10. Add one important detail of your own. Then write a summary based on the information you gathered.

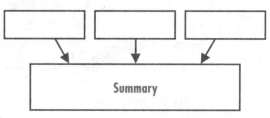

What is the difference between a summary and a main idea?

APPLY IT

- Review the steps for summarizing in Learn It.
- Read the paragraph below. Then summarize the passage by using a summary chart.

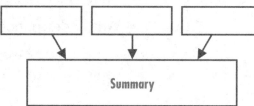

Americans took part in the war effort in many ways. More than 15 million people served in the military. At home, men and women built planes and ships and grew food. Children helped in many ways, including by collecting scrap metal to be recycled. To save supplies and food for the armed forces, people took part in rationing. Rationing is limiting how much of goods people can buy. To replace the food they could not buy, people grew their own vegetables. They called these plots of land "Victory Gardens."

Words to Know

Common Core Standards
RI.5.4 Determine the meaning of general academic and domain-specific words and phrases in a text relevant to a *grade 5 topic or subject area.*

The list below shows some important words you will learn in this unit. Their definitions can be found on the next page. Read the words.

communism (KOM · you · niz · em)

internment camp (in · TERN · ment kamp)

casualty (KA · zhool · tee)

liberate (LI · buh · rayte)

holocaust (HAH · low · kost)

containment (kan · TAYN · mint)

Cold War (KOLD wohr)

espionage (es · pee · an · aj)

FOLDABLES®

The **Foldable** on the next page will help you learn these important words. Follow the steps below to make your Foldable.

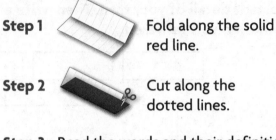

Step 1   Fold along the solid red line.

Step 2   Cut along the dotted lines.

Step 3   Read the words and their definitions.

Step 4   Complete the activities on each tab.

Step 5   Look at the back of your Foldable. Choose ONE of these activities for each word to help you remember its meaning:

- Draw a picture of the word.

- Write a description of the word.

- Write how the word is related to something you know.

Communism is a political system in which business, property, and goods are owned by the government.	(Circle) the key words in the definition of *Communism*. Write those words here. _____ _____
An **internment camp** is a special camp, usually during war time, where people were forced to live and give up their jobs, their businesses, and their homes.	What is the root word of *internment* in the term internment camp.
A **casualty** is a soldier or other person killed, wounded, sick, or missing.	Write the plural form of *casualty*.
To **liberate** means to free an area or person.	Use the word *liberate* in a sentence.
The **Holocaust** was the genocide of a large number of Jews during World War II.	(Circle) two words in the definition of the *Holocaust* that help you understand the meaning.
Containment is the policy or process of preventing the expansion of hostile power or ideology.	Explain the purpose of *containment*.
The **Cold War** was a war fought with ideas, words, money, and sometimes force between the United States and the Soviet Union.	Define the *Cold War* in your own words.
Espionage is spying to gather government secrets.	A person skilled in *espionage* does what for a living?

Communism	Communism
internment camp	internment camp
casualty	casualty
liberate	liberate
Holocaust	Holocaust
containment	containment
Cold War	Cold War
espionage	espionage

CUT HERE

Primary Sources

Diaries

A diary is one type of primary source. While a diary entry can contain many different types of information, most diary entries are records of a person's day-to-day experiences. Through diaries, we can learn much about what it was like to live long ago. We can even learn more about important events through the eyes of those who lived at that time.

Journal – May 13, 1942

Everyone in United States is helping the war effort in any way they can. In town, I've seen them helping by donating to scrap drives. In a scrap drive, the government collects any pieces of metal, such as pots and pans, that people can spare. This metal will then be melted down and reused to make tanks or airplanes. People are also planting gardens to produce food for the war effort. Any area of land is a possible garden—backyards, schoolyards, city parks, and empty lots. The government is encouraging people to grow these "victory gardens" with posters and announcements on the radio. Just the other day, city officials in Charleston announced that the city had over 10,000 victory gardens.

Circle the definition of a scrap drive.

Underline two ways the government advertised the need for victory gardens.

Primary Source

Thursday, the 30th a small snow in the night . . . on Monday last John Bardwell . . . had orders from Shays . . . to have [his company] ready to march. . . .

Monday, the 4th cool towards night snowed . . . John Bardwell marched 40 men with him. . . .

Wednesday, the 6th . . . towards Night orders came . . . for the Militia to be in readiness to march tomorrow to Worcester

Thursday, the 7th . . . Our Militia seemed eager to go . . . I made a speech to them persuading them to be quiet & rest the Matter with [the government]

Friday, the 8th we hear that [General] Shays . . . has took possession of Worcester . . . and has taken [three judges prisoner]

—from the diary of Justus Forward

(bkgd) McGraw-Hill Education

networks There's More Online! ● Skill Builders ● Resource Library

World War II Begins

National Archives and Records Administration (NWDNS-242-GAP-286B(4)

? Essential Question

How did World War II begin?

List two causes.

_____

_____

_____

_____

_____

_____

_____

Words To Know

Identify the part of speech of each word.

_____ **fascism**

_____ **communism**

_____ **isolationism**

Germany invaded France in 1940.

Changes In Europe

By the end of the 1930s, the world was at the edge of war. Germany, Italy, and Japan threatened world peace. Soon, that threat turned into a real conflict, and the world was plunged into a second world war.

President Woodrow Wilson had hoped that World War I would be "the war to end all wars." Within 20 years, though, a new and terrible conflict began.

The Rise of Fascism

Many Italians felt that the Treaty of Versailles did not reward them for helping win World War I. In 1922 Italians chose Benito Mussolini as their leader. He believed in a political system called **fascism**. Fascism is marked by strong national pride and a strong ruler with almost complete power. It also includes racism, or the belief that one race is better or worse than another race.

Hitler Controls Germany

The Treaty of Versailles forced Germany to pay large sums of money to other countries. These payments hurt Germany's economy.

A fascist leader named Adolf Hitler became the leader of the Nazi Party in Germany. In 1933 he became chancellor, or political leader, of Germany. Hitler then made himself dictator. A dictator is a ruler who has complete power and gives people few freedoms.

Tensions Rise in Japan

Dictators also came to power in Asia. In the late 1800s, Japan became one of the strongest countries in Asia. However, Japan did not have many of the natural resources it needed for its factories. By the late 1920s, Japan's economy was failing. Like Italy and Germany, Japan wanted to expand its economy and power.

In 1932 military leaders took control of the government. In 1936 Japan, Germany, and Italy signed a treaty of friendship. They called themselves the Axis countries.

The War Begins

Hitler said that the German people were part of a "master race" called Aryans. He claimed that Germany had a right to expand its territory. With the alliance with Italy and Japan in place, Hitler began to expand German power throughout Europe.

Who were the leaders of the Axis powers?

_____

_____

_____

_____

┌ **DID YOU KNOW?**
Michinomiya **Hirohito** was emperor of Japan during World War II. He had developed an interest in western food and clothing after taking a trip to Europe as a teenager. This angered some traditional Japanese leaders.
└ ....

Ingram Publishing

Germany Expands

In 1938 Hitler sent troops into Austria. This act broke the Treaty of Versailles, but nothing was done about it. Other European countries wanted to avoid war. That same year, Germany conquered Czechoslovakia. In 1939 Hitler created a secret alliance with the leader of the United Soviet Socialist Republics (USSR), Joseph Stalin. The Soviet government operated under the system of **communism**. Under communism, the government controls the economy and people have limited rights to own property.

> How was the German expansion like the American Western expansion? How was it different?
>
> _____
>
> _____

War Breaks Out

One week later, on September 1, 1939, Germany attacked Poland. Two days later, Britain and France, who called themselves the Allies, declared war on Germany. Still, Poland was defeated in just a few weeks. German forces continued to advance.

In April of 1940, Hitler conquered Denmark and Norway. In May, Hitler attacked Belgium and the Netherlands. By June, German troops entered Paris and France quickly fell. Germany now held most of Europe.

▼ Germany bombed London during the war.

Allies in Europe 1944–1945

National Archives and Records Administration (NWDNS-306-NT-3173V)

Axis power
Axis-occupied area, Jan. 1945
Allied power
Neutral power

Map and Globe Skills

Which countries north of Germany were occupied by the Axis powers?

_____

_____

Great Britain was the only country left fighting Germany. Germany attacked British supply ships with submarines. It also bombed cities and airfields for months, trying to destroy the British air force.

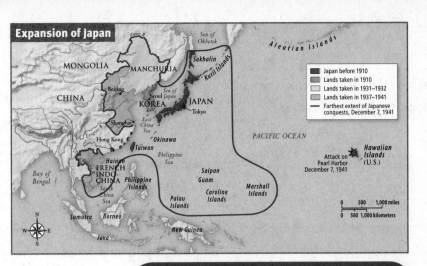

Invading the Soviet Union

In June of 1941, Germany invaded the Soviet Union. German forces quickly surrounded the city of Leningrad, in the north. As a result, the Soviet Union joined the Allies against Germany.

By November, the German advance had stalled. Bad weather slowed German tanks and trucks. Soldiers grew cold. Then the Soviets attacked. Within a month, they had pushed the Germans back along the entire front.

Japan Expands

Japan was a small nation with few natural resources. Its new leaders wanted the nation to expand to boost the country's economy. Their first step was to take control of the northeastern part of China in 1931.

Japan was a member of the League of Nations, which had been formed after World War I. The League ordered Japan to leave China. Instead, the Japanese pulled out of the League and seized more of China. In 1933 the Chinese government was forced to accept Japan's control of these areas. By 1937, Japan had invaded other parts of China, and the Chinese government had to flee.

Japan then turned its attention to European colonies in Asia with important reources. Colonies are lands controlled by another country. European countries had to concentrate on fighting Germany. As a result, they were not be able to defend their colonies.

> **Map and Globe Skills**
>
> Which lands did Japan take in 1910?
>
> _____
>
> _____

> **What were the causes of World War II?**
>
> _____
>
> _____

165

America Enters The War

Why did Roosevelt think it was important to help Britain?

_____

_____

While the situations in Europe and Asia grew more tense in the 1930s, the United States struggled with the Great Depression. Most Americans worried more about their jobs and families than about faraway problems. As a result, the nation followed a policy of **isolationism**. Isolationism means not becoming involved in issues concerning other countries.

When war broke out in 1939, President Franklin D. Roosevelt quickly announced that the United States would be neutral. However, Roosevelt allowed American businesses to sell weapons to the countries fighting Germany.

Moving to Help the Allies

Meanwhile, German submarines continued to sink British ships. Britain did not have enough money to pay cash for new ships. In 1941 Congress passed a law that allowed Britain to buy military goods on credit. Britain used the law to buy American ships and weapons.

In August 1941, British Prime Minister Winston Churchhill met with President Roosevelt. Together they drafted the Atlantic Charter. The charter set goals for a postwar world. They agreed that all peoples should choose their own government.

Pearl Harbor, Hawaii, taken by surprise, during the Japanese aerial attack.

National Archives and Records Administration (NWDNS-80-G-19948)

Problems with Japan

Japan bought large amounts of oil and steel and other resources from the United States. In response to Japan's attack on China, President Roosevelt put a partial block on trade with Japan in these resources. This hurt Japan's economy and angered Japanese leaders.

Japan and the United States held talks to settle their differences, but they did not produce a solution. Japan's leaders began planning an attack against the United States.

Pearl Harbor

The U.S. Navy had a large base at Pearl Harbor, Hawaii. The Japanese believed that a surprise attack would weaken the American navy. This would open the way for them to expand further.

On December 7, 1941, the Japanese attacked Pearl Harbor. Japanese planes and submarines targeted U.S. ships in the harbor with bombs and torpedoes. Their bombers also destroyed many planes on the ground.

The attack was devastating. The United States lost eight of its battleships. Many other ships were sunk or seriously damaged. About 200 planes were destroyed, and more than 2,400 Americans were killed.

Primary Source

Yesterday, December 7, 1941—a date which will live in infamy—the United States of America was suddenly and deliberately attacked by the naval and air forces of the Empire of Japan. . . . No matter how long it may take us . . . the American people . . . will win through to absolute victory.

—from President Franklin D. Roosevelt's address to Congress, 1941

Why did the United States enter World War II?

_____

_____

Lesson **1**

(?) Essential Question   How did World War II begin?

_____

_____

_____

Go back to _Show As You Go!_ on pages 154–155.

The Home Front

 Essential Question

How did the United States prepare for World War II?

What do you think?

_____

_____

_____

_____

_____

_____

▲ Women working on an assembly line during the war.

Ingram Publishing

Words To Know

Write a number to show how much you know about the meaning of each word.

1 = I have no idea!

2 = I know a little.

3 = I know a lot.

_____ **mobilize**

_____ **civil defense**

_____ **ration**

_____ **internment camp**

Preparing For War

While the armed forces fought overseas, Americans helped at home. Millions of people went to work in factories to make the supplies and weapons the soldiers needed. Everyone pitched in to help.

Winning the war required the nation to **mobilize**, or assemble for action. Mobilizing includes getting the people needed to serve in the armed forces and to work in the nation's factories and farms. It also means shifting to a wartime economy.

The Wartime Economy

Factories switched from producing consumer goods to making military equipment. Instead of making cars, automakers now made tanks and planes. Clothing factories made uniforms and parachutes. Increased demand for goods and the production of them for the war finally helped end the Great Depression.

The government raised money for the war by placing an additional income tax on American workers. It also sold war bonds. Movie stars encouraged Americans to buy these bonds.

Americans took part in the war effort in many ways. More than 15 million served in the military. At home, men and women built planes and ships and grew food. Children helped in many ways, including collecting scrap metal to be recycled.

People took part in **civil defense** actions. Civil defense aims at protecting the homeland. For example, people turned off lights at night to create blackouts. Blackouts prevented enemy planes from seeing important targets lit up.

People took part in **rationing** to save supplies and food for the armed forces. To ration is to limit how much of a good people can buy. People had to decide what to buy, or not buy, with the limited ration stamps they received. When people decide on one item over another, the item they do not choose is their opportunity cost.

> Highlight the paragraph that summarizes the changes factories made.

DID YOU KNOW?

Norfolk, Virginia, had one of the nation's largest naval bases. Early in the war, German submarines patrolled the area. They could see ships in the waters off Norfolk at night if the city lights were turned on. By organizing blackouts, the people of Norfolk saved American ships—and lives.

SERVICE ON THE HOME FRONT
★ CITIZENS DEFENSE CORPS
★ CITIZENS SERVICE CORPS
★ AMERICAN UNITY
★ SALVAGE PROGRAMS
★ VICTORY GARDENS

There's a job for every Pennsylvanian in these CIVILIAN DEFENSE EFFORTS
PENNSYLVANIA STATE COUNCIL OF DEFENSE
CAPITOL BUILDING.   HARRISBURG, PENNA.

> How did the United States supply its armed foces?
>
> _____
>
> _____
>
> _____
>
> _____

Women And Minorities

▼ "Rosie the Riveter"(top) encouraged women to work for the war effort. Women did construction during World War II (bottom).

The war created new opportunities for women. Members of minority groups, such as African Americans, Latinos, and Native Americans, took part in the war effort as well.

Women and the War

For the first time, women served in large numbers in the armed forces. About 350,000 women worked in non-combat roles.

Special military units, such as the Women's Army Auxiliary Corps (WAAC), were set up for women to work in the army. The WAAC was an auxiliary corps, which meant that it was not part of the regular army. A year later, the army created the Women's Army Corps (WAC), which was part of the regular army. Over 150,000 women served in the WAC.

The Women Accepted for Volunteer Emergency Services (WAVES) was an all-female division of the United States Navy. Many of these women worked as nurses and and had other important jobs in the navy.

In 1941 the United Service Organizations (USO) was created. The USO is a nonprofit organization that provides recreation and entertainment for the military. The USO hired popular entertainers and other civilians to entertain the troops. Many women and men performed on stage for the troops.

Women in the Workforce

The government encouraged women to get jobs outside the home. It made posters with a character named "Rosie the Riveter" to show that women were needed for factory jobs. A riveter is a worker who joins together pieces of metal to make planes and other machines.

Women made up more than one-third of all workers. Other women tended to farms while their sons and husbands fought in the war.

Describe the positive and negative changes the war caused for women.

_____

_____

(t)National Archives and Records Administration (NWDNS-179-WP-1563); (b)National Archives and Records Administration (NWDNS-86-WWT-85-16

Women were not treated fairly at work. On average, they were paid less than men, sometimes very much less. Some people believed that working in a job outside the home was not proper for women. Government messages said this action was only was only necessary during wartime. After the war, when men came back home, many women were let go from their jobs.

Many women enjoyed the opportunity to work outside the home, though. If they lost their jobs to men, they found other jobs and continued working after the war.

Minority Groups in the War

Members of minority groups had suffered badly during the Great Depression. The booming wartime economy gave them a chance to have better lives.

Nearly a million African Americans joined the armed forces. They served in units that were segregated. Segregated means that they were separated from white soldiers. Some of these units became famous. Tuskegee Airmen trained in Alabama. They were led by Benjamin O. Davis, the highest-ranking African American in the U.S. Army at the time. The Tuskegee Airmen flew many combat missions in Europe.

Latinos did not have to serve in segregated units. Twelve Latinos won the Medal of Honor, the highest military honor. Native Americans served in the armed forces as well. The U.S. Marines used several Navajo to speak in "code" over radios so that enemy soldiers could not understand them. The code the Navajo used was their language.

Members of minority groups also played important roles at home. Hundreds of thousands of African Americans left the South for the cities of the North and West, where they worked in factories. When they were not paid the same as white workers, leaders threatened to organize a protest. In response, President Roosevelt set up a new office called the Fair Employment Practices Commission. It aimed to make sure that African Americans received equal pay.

Many Native Americans left reservations to work in factories as well. Large numbers of Mexicans came to the United States during the war. They came under a special program called the Bracero Program. They planted and harvested crops to keep farms working.

Tuskegee Airmen (below) and Navajo speaking in "code" over radios (right)

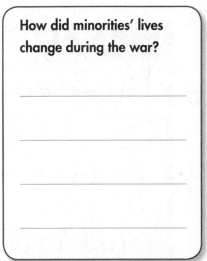

How did minorities' lives change during the war?

_____

_____

_____

_____

(t)National Archives and Records Administration [07428]; (b)National Archives and Records Administration (NWDNS-208-MO-18H-2205l)

Japanese Internment

Many Asian Americans took part in the war effort as well. Chinese, Korean, and Philippine Americans joined the armed forces to fight for more than just the United States. Japan controlled the lands their families had come from, and they hoped to end that control. Many Japanese Americans faced a difficult time during the war, however.

▼ Japanese Americans arriving at an internment camp in Owens Valley, California, in 1942

Japanese Americans in Camps

After Pearl Harbor, some Americans wrongly feared that Japanese Americans would secretly help Japan. In February 1942, President Roosevelt issued an order that forced all Japanese Americans living on the West Coast to leave their homes.

More than 100,000 people had to give up their jobs, their businesses, and their homes. They were gathered together and then sent to special camps, called **internment camps**, built mostly in desert areas. Many Japanese Americans lost everything they owned.

Life in the camps was difficult. Police patrolled the camps to prevent escape. Families could stay together, but they lived in large buildings that they had to share with many other families. The last of these camps was not closed until 1946.

At Work and in the Army

Japanese Americans in other parts of the country were not sent to camps. More than 30,000 Japanese Americans served in the armed forces. They fought well and won dozens of medals, including the Medal of Honor.

Library of Congress Prints and Photographs Division [LC-DIG-ppprs-00329]

Lesson 2

(?) Essential Question How did the United States prepare for World War II?

_____

_____

_____

Go back to *Show As You Go!* on pages 154–155.

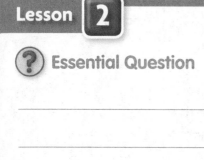

netw❂rks   **There's More Online!**
● Games ● Assessment

Map and Globe Skills

Use a Historical Map

As you read Unit 5, you will learn about many of the battles in Europe and the Pacific during World War II. You can see the location of major battles by looking at a **historical map**. This kind of map shows where events from the past took place. Historical maps can show how the population of an area changed over time, where battles occurred, or how landforms have changed.

 LEARN IT

- Look at the map title and dates to find the map topic. Most historical maps have dates.
- Look at the map key to find out the meaning of symbols or shading on the map.

TRY IT

- When did the Battle of the Bulge take place?

_____

- In what country was the Battle of the Kasserine Pass?

_____

APPLY IT

- As you read the rest of this unit, look for other historical maps.
- Compare the information that is given in those maps with the information that you read in each lesson.

Major Battles of World War II

Key:
- Axis control before war
- Axis control, Nov. 1942
- Allies
- Neutral nation
- Battle

ICELAND

FINLAND

NORWAY
North Sea
Leningrad Jan. 1944

DEN.
Baltic Sea
GER.

SOVIET UNION

UNITED KINGDOM

GERMANY
POLAND
Stalingrad Feb. 1943

D-Day June 1944
BELG.
Battle of the Bulge Jan. 1945
RUTHENIA

ATLANTIC OCEAN
FRANCE
AUSTRIA
SLOV.
HUNGARY
ROMANIA
Black Sea

YUGOSLAVIA
BULGARIA

ITALY
Sicily Aug. 1943
GREECE

Kasserine Pass Feb. 1943
ALBANIA (ITALY)
Mediterranean Sea

MOROCCO
ALGERIA
TUNISIA

0   250   500 miles
0 250 500 kilometers

LIBYA (ITALY)
EGYPT

Lesson

3

The Road to Victory

? Essential Question

How did the Allies fight the Axis powers in World War II? What do you think?

_____

_____

_____

_____

_____

_____

Words To Know

Write the definition of each word in your words.

casualty

_____

liberate

_____

kamikaze

_____

Ingram Publishing

Turning Points

By the time the United States joined the Allies fighting against the Axis, the Allies were in trouble. The Allies remained determined to win.

Britain was battered every day by German bombs. The Soviets had lost much of their western lands to Germany.

Battles in North Africa

The British and Americans fought the Germans and Italians in North Africa. In the middle of 1942, the British defeated the Germans near a town called El Alamein. They forced German troops to retreat, or move backward. By May of 1943, the Allies had won. The Germans who remained there surrendered. Hitler's army had been defeated in North Africa.

Fighting in Italy and in the Air

In July 1943, American and British troops landed in Sicily, Italy. Within a few weeks, they swept Italian and German troops off the island and moved on to the mainland of Italy. At the same time, the Italians removed Benito Mussolini from power. The new government surrendered to the Allies.

Germany was now fighting alone in Italy. The Allies made some gains, but with many **casualties**, or soldiers killed, wounded, or missing. By January 1944, the fighting had slowed.

Stalingrad

At the same time, the Soviets were fighting the Germans in the east. By the fall of 1942, German troops had captured the city of Stalingrad. Then the Soviets began a siege, or a long fight in which one army surrounds another and denies it supplies. After months of fighting, bitter cold, and hunger, about 90,000 German soldiers surrendered.

The Germans tried another attack the following spring. Hitler then called off his attack. He had to move some of the troops from that battle to meet the new threat from the Allies in Italy.

How did Italy exit the war?

_____

_____

Adolf Hitler and Benito Mussolini in Munich, Germany in 1940 ▶

National Archives and Records Administration (NWDNS-242-EB-7-38)

Victory In Europe

Throughout 1943, the Americans poured military forces, equipment, and supplies into Britain. They were preparing for a huge invasion of German occupied France.

D-Day

On June 6, 1944, the invasion began. This day became known as D-Day. The attack was the largest single invasion in history. Over 100,000 soldiers were carried by ships to the beaches of Normandy, in northern France. They faced fierce gunfire from German defenses, and over 9,000 Allied soldiers lost their lives.

D-Day marked the beginning of the end for Germany. The Allied soldiers broke through German lines. By late June, nearly a million Allied soldiers were in northern France. The troops defeated German defenses and moved east and south. By the end of August, they had **liberated**, or freed, Paris from German control.

After the success of D-Day, Allied forces had Germany surrounded on three sides. The Soviets came in from the east. The British and Americans attacked from the south through Italy and the from west across France.

> Highlight the date of D-Day. Circle the landform where the battle began.

National Archives and Records Administration

American troops march inland with supplies after the victorious D-Day invasion

Winning the War

In December 1944, the Germans unleashed one last surprise attack against the Allies in Belgium. German troops took advantage of a hole in the Allies' lines and quickly poured in. This fight became known as the Battle of the Bulge. With the arrival of new supplies, however, the Allies pushed the Germans back. The battle resulted in over 100,000 casualties.

Hitler saw his troops being pushed back in from all directions. The Americans in Italy had made great advances. American and British troops from the west crossed the Rhine River in March. German defenders fell back, and the Allies advanced quickly. By April, Soviet troops were approaching Berlin, the German capital, from the east.

Many German leaders fled the city. Hitler chose to stay, but he hid from daily bombings in a set of fortified underground rooms. On April 30, 1945, defeated but determined to avoid capture, Hitler killed himself. A few days later, on May 7, the Germans surrendered.

On May 8, Americans and other Allies celebrated V-E Day. The letters stood for "Victory in Europe." The long, hard war in Europe was finally over.

A New President

Before the Americans could enjoy this victory, however, they suffered a blow. Franklin Roosevelt had been President since 1933. On April 12, 1945, he complained of a terrific pain in the back of his head. Suddenly, he was dead. Vice President Harry Truman took office as President. He told reporters:

> "When they told me yesterday what had happened, I felt like the moon, the stars, and all the planets had fallen on me."

Truman knew ending the war would be difficult. He

▲ Field Marshall Wilhelm Keitel, signing the ratified surrender terms for the German Army.

Highlight text from a primary source.

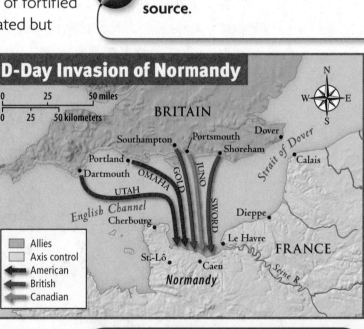

D-Day Invasion of Normandy

Legend:
- Allies
- Axis control
- American
- British
- Canadian

BRITAIN · Southampton · Portsmouth · Dover · Shoreham · Calais · Portland · Dartmouth · OMAHA · GOLD · JUNO · SWORD · Strait of Dover · UTAH · English Channel · Cherbourg · Dieppe · Le Havre · St.-Lô · Caen · FRANCE · Normandy · Seine R.

Map and Globe Skills

From which cities did American troops depart on D-Day?

_____

_____

The Pacific Front

The war in Europe had ended. War-weary Americans could not rest, though. Fighting raged on in the Pacific.

Early Japanese Victories

The Japanese had captured several key spots when the war began. These sites included the American islands of Guam and Wake, along with British Singapore. The Japanese also invaded the Philippines.

In April 1942, the Americans launched an attack on Japan. Bombers flying from an American aircraft carrier dropped bombs on Tokyo, the Japanese capital.

In June, Japan sent ships to attack Midway Island. American planes sank all four of the aircraft carriers Japan sent to the fight. This was a major turning point of the war in the Pacific. The badly damaged Japanese navy was now much less powerful.

Island Hopping

The Americans now launched a strategy called "island hopping." This meant attacking one island from the air, landing troops, and then gaining control of it. The United States then used these islands as bases. Next, American ships carried planes and troops to the next island and did the same thing there.

The fighting at each of these island invasions was bitter. Slowly but surely, though, American forces moved north and west through the Pacific. These efforts eventually led to one of the largest naval battles in history.

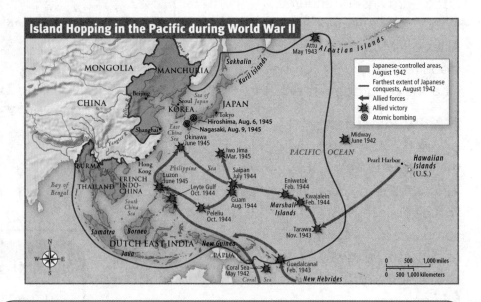

Island Hopping in the Pacific during World War II

What two cities were destroyed by atomic bombs?

_____

_____

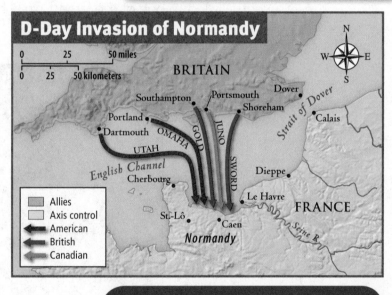

American dive-bomber used during the Battle of Midway.

In October 1944, the fleets of the United States and Japan clashed in the Battle of Leyte Gulf, near the Philippines. The battle raged for three days. In the end, the Americans lost 7 ships, the Japanese lost 26 ships. Leyte Gulf was the last large naval battle of the Pacific. The United States now controlled the seas.

Kamikaze Pilots

As the fight continued, the Japanese tried new, desperate ideas. Some Japanese pilots agreed to fly **kamikaze** missions. Kamikaze missions were suicide attacks. Pilots flew planes into American ships, hoping to sink them.

Two More Islands

The next year, the Americans launched attacks on two more islands. First, in February, came the assault on Iwo Jima, south of Japan.

Though the island is small, it was difficult to capture. The Japanese were heavily armed with vast bunkers. The battle was the first on the Japanese home islands. Japanese troops fought for a month before being defeated. Nearly 18,000 Japanese and 7,000 Americans lost their lives in this terrible fighting.

The next stop was Okinawa, a larger island southwest of Japan. American troops needed almost two months to win the battle.

While ground troops gained these victories, American flyers played a role as well. They were stationed at bases on islands that marines and soldiers had captured. From there, they were able to fly over Japanese cities to bomb factories, ports, and key buildings.

▼ American troops planting the American flag on Iwo Jima, Japan.

Why was the Battle of Midway on important victory?

_____

_____

_____

Victory In The Pacific

The victories on Iwo Jima and Okinawa brought U.S. forces to Japan's doorstep. The next step would be to invade the country. However, American leaders feared that such an attack would cost too many lives.

The Manhattan Project

Many years before, scientist Albert Einstein told President Roosevelt that the Germans were working on a new, powerful weapon. It would harness the power of atoms, the basic bits of matter that make up every object. He said that such a bomb would be more powerful than any other weapon that existed at the time.

Roosevelt ordered American scientists to develop such a weapon. This top secret operation was called the Manhattan Project. Roosevelt wanted the atomic bomb in case it was needed against Germany.

Dropping the Bomb

By 1945, American scientists had made two bombs. President Truman had an important decision to make. If the United States invaded Japan, many American soldiers would die. However, using the atomic bomb would kill Japanese civilians. President Truman decided to use the bombs. He hoped this would end the war quickly, avoiding many more casualites.

▼ Japanese City of Hiroshima during the Atomic Bomb Drop

USAF

Write a sentence about a time you had to make a difficult decision. How did you come to your decision?

_____

_____

National Archives and Records Administration (NWDNS-80-G-377094)

Americans celebrating the end of World War II.

On August 6, a bomber called the Enola Gay dropped the first atomic bomb on the city of Hiroshima. The force of the explosion and the fires that followed wiped out about sixty percent of the city. About 70,000 people died. Three days later, a second bomb destroyed about 30 percent of Nagasaki. This bomb killed about 40,000 people.

The same day that the bomb was dropped on Hiroshima, the Soviet Union declared war on Japan. The destruction of the bombs and the threat of the Soviets now joining the fight against Japan convinced Japan's government to surrender. On August 14, the Japanese announced their surrender. It was called V-J Day, or "Victory in Japan" Day.

How did the war with Japan end?

_____

_____

_____

_____

Lesson 3

? **Essential Question** **How did the Allies fight the Axis Powers in World War II?**

_____

_____

_____

Go back to *Show As You Go!* on pages 154–155. ◀◀

netw⦿rks **There's More Online!** ● Games ● Assessment

After the War

? **Essential Question**

What was it like after the War?
What do you think?

_____

_____

_____

_____

_____

_____

_____

_____

Words To Know

Write the plural form of the two singular nouns below. Leave the other words as they are.

Holocaust

_____

genocide

_____

anti-semitism

_____

United Nations

_____

▲ Lots of damage was caused during the war.

National Archives and Records Adminstration (NWDNS-306-NT-901(72))

The Holocaust

World War II devastated Europe. The fighting destroyed cities and killed millions of people. However, not all of the dead were soldiers.

Among the civilians who died were millions of European Jews. The Nazis killed them in an effort to wipe out the Jewish population of Europe. This mass killing is called the **Holocaust**.

The Holocaust was an example of **genocide**. Genocide is the planned killing of a specific group of people. Nazis killed more than 6 million Jews in the Holocaust. They also killed another 4 million people who were not Jewish.

As Hitler rose to power, he often blamed Jews for Germany's troubles. His speeches against Jews increased a powerful feeling called **anti-Semitism**. Anti-Semitism is discrimination against the Jewish people.

Once in power, Hitler passed laws that took away the rights of Jews. Eventually, he forced Jews into concentration camps. Hitler tried to keep the camps a secret by building them in remote areas.

Conditions in the camps were brutal, with no freedom and little food. Many died from illness or starvation. Then the Nazis began killing Jews, including women and children, in camps specifically built for mass executions.

Remembering the Holocaust

Many people work to keep the memory of the Holocaust alive. They believe that reminding people of this horror will help prevent it from happening again.

In 1993 the U.S. Holocaust Memorial Museum opened in Washington, D.C. Millions of people have visited the museum. Exhibits describe Hitler's policies and the suffering in the camps. Some exhibits relate the heroic actions of people, both Jews and non-Jews, who resisted the Holocaust or helped some people escape.

Children being released from a concentration camp.

Why is it important for people to remember the Holocaust?

_____

_____

Cost Of The War

More than 60 nations took part in World War II. More than 110 million people served in the armed forces of those nations.

The Human Cost

World War II claimed more lives than any other war in history. More than 40 million people died during the war. Over half of the deaths were civilians who died from bombings, disease, starvation, or the Holocaust.

The World War II Memorial is located in Washington, D.C. It pays tribute to the millions of men and women who served in the United States armed forces during the war.

The Axis on Trial

The Allies wanted to punish leaders of Germany and Japan who committed violent and inhumane acts during the war. In August 1945, the Allies set up the International Military Tribunal (IMT) to put those leaders on trial.

The International Military Tribunal held trials in Nuremberg, Germany, and Tokyo, Japan. In all, 22 German leaders and 25 Japanese leaders stood trial. The trials continued through April 1949. Those trials included lower ranking members of the government and the military as well.

CASUALTIES OF WAR

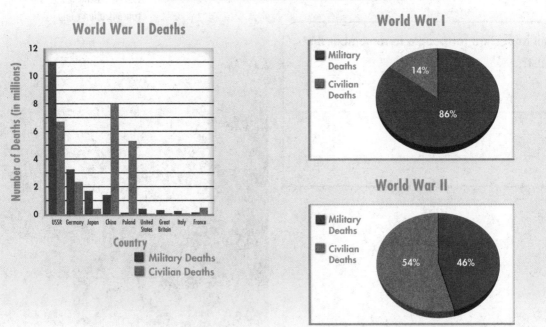

What do the charts tell you about World War II?

Germany After the War

Much of Europe was in ruins. Homes, factories, bridges, roads, and cities needed to be rebuilt. Many people had been forced to leave their homes and wanted to return. Some had been moved far from where they lived. Much work needed to be done.

Germany was treated harshly by the Treaty of Versailles that ended World War I. This caused problems for Germans after that war and helped lead to the rise of Hitler and the Nazi party. The Allies did not want anything like that to happen again. They wanted to rebuild Europe and the world in order to create a lasting peace.

▲ Marines unloading Japanese POW from a submarine returned from a war patrol.

After Germany surrendered, it remained occupied by Allied forces and was divided. American, British, and French troops stayed in the western part of Germany and in Western and Southern Europe. Soviet troops stayed in eastern Germany and Eastern Europe.

Soviet leader Joseph Stalin wanted complete control of these areas. He made sure they had communist governments like his. Germany was divided. The eastern parts of Germany and Europe had communist governments. The western parts had democratic governments. Western Germany quickly became an ally for the United States.

Rebuilding Japan

After the war in the Pacific, American soldiers occupied Japan. General Douglas MacArthur headed the temporary government.

MacArthur worked with Japanese leaders to write a new constitution. It allowed the emperor to remain Japan's traditional leader. However, he would have no real power. Elected officials would run the government. The new constitution gave Japan's people freedom they had not previously enjoyed.

Americans also worked with the Japanese people to rebuild their country. As the country rebounded, its economy grew. Japan's people exercised their rights and chose their own leaders. By 1952, Japan's new leaders had taken full control of their country again.

That same year, the United States and Japan signed a treaty making them allies. Today, Japan remains one of America's strongest allies in Asia.

> How were the western and eastern parts of Europe different after the war?
>
> _____
>
> _____

Plans For The Future

After World War I, many nations joined the League of Nations. Leaders had hoped that it would prevent war from arising again. The League failed, but the terrible cost of World War II convinced leaders to try again.

Eleanor Roosevelt

The United Nations

Before World War II ended, President Roosevelt had pushed for a new organization. Shortly after his death in 1945, representatives from 50 nations met in San Francisco to organize the **United Nations** (UN). The UN headquarters was built in 1950 in New York.

President Truman appointed former First Lady Eleanor Roosevelt to serve as a representative for the United States at the UN. The UN then created the Commission on Human Rights. Eleanor Roosevelt became the head of that commission.

In 1948 Roosevelt and the Commission wrote the Universal Declaration of Human Rights. This document stated that everyone in any society had rights that could not be taken away. The Declaration includes four freedoms: freedom of speech, freedom of belief, freedom from fear, and freedom from want.

The UN has not prevented all wars, but it has settled some conflicts. Through diplomacy, or the act of holding negotiations between nations, the UN has helped nations talk about issues with other nations.

Lesson 4

? **Essential Question** **What was life like after the War?**

_____

_____

_____

Go back to *Show As You Go!* on pages 154–155.

networks
There's More Online!
● Games ● Assessment

Chart and Graph Skills

Use a Double Bar Graph

A **double bar graph** compares information. It shows information in two sets of bars on the same graph. Look at the double bar graph on this page as you follow the steps.

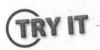

TRY IT

- **How many military deaths did Japan have?**

- **Which country had the most military and civilian deaths combined?**

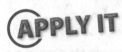

APPLY IT

- **Make a double bar graph showing the number of boys and the number of girls in each class in your school.**

LEARN IT

- **A double bar graph uses bars side by side to compare information.**
- **The title shows the topic of the double bar graph.**
- **The bars use different colors to show each set of information clearly.**
- **The labels on each side of the graph tell you how to understand the information.**

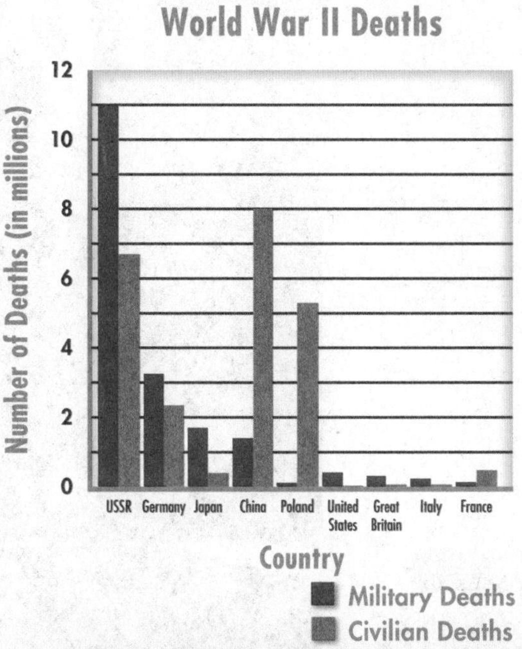
World War II Deaths
Number of Deaths (in millions)
0
2
4
6
8
10
12
USSR
Germany
Japan
China
Poland
United States
Great Britain
Italy
France
Country
Military Deaths
Civilian Deaths

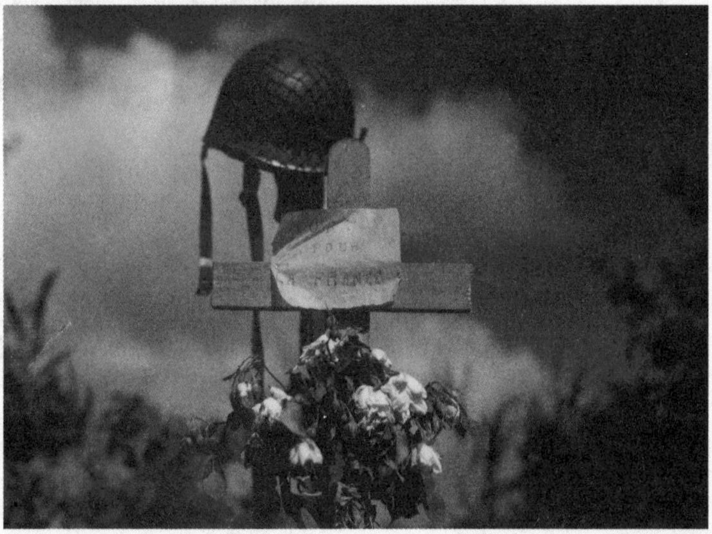

National Archives and Records Administration (NWDNS-111-SC-190597)

Lesson

5

The Cold War Begins

? Essential Question

How did the Cold War affect the World from 1945 to 1960?
What do you think?

_____

_____

_____

_____

_____

_____

_____

Words To Know

Circle the words with suffixes.

containment

Cold War

stalemate

demilitarized zone

An atomic bomb test in Nevada in the 1950s.

Photo courtesy of National Nuclear Security Administration/Nevada Site Office/DOE

A Divided Europe

Even before World War II ended, tensions arose between the United States and the Soviet Union. The countries had been allies during the war, but now they became bitter enemies.

In February 1945—with the war in Europe almost over—Roosevelt, Churchill, and Stalin met in Yalta, a Soviet city on the Black Sea. They came to discuss the postwar world. The United States and Britain feared Soviet control in Eastern Europe would lead to the spread of communism.

The Yalta Conference

During the Yalta conference, the three leaders agreed to divide Germany into four zones. Great Britain, the United States, the Soviet Union, and France would each control one zone. The same four countries would also divide the capital of Berlin, even though it was in the Soviet zone of Germany.

Stalin insisted that the Soviet Union keep the territories in Eastern Europe it had occupied during the war. He agreed to allow free elections in Eastern Europe and to cooperate in the planning of the United Nations.

Distrust soon grew between the West and the Soviet Union, however. Stalin did not keep his promise to allow free elections in Eastern Europe. Instead Soviet leaders set up communist governments. Europe was soon split into two—communist Eastern Europe and democratic Western Europe.

Churchill believed the division between East and West was permanent. In 1946 he stated in a speech that "an iron curtain" had descended across Europe. "Behind the Iron Curtain" became a phrase used to describe communist-controlled countries.

Circle the former Axis power.
Underline three Allies.

How did distrust grow between the Soviets and the West?

_____

_____

Churchill, Roosevelt, and Stalin at Yalta ▶

The Division of Germany, 1945

Allied Occupation Zones, 1945–1949
- American
- British
- French
- Soviet
- Present-day Germany

Map and Globe Skills

In what zone in the divided Germany was Berlin located?

_____

_____

Fighting Communism

The United States and the Soviet Union had different ideologies, or systems of beliefs. The United States is a democratic nation founded on the principles of capitalism. Capitalism is an economic system in which land and businesses are owned and controlled by individual people instead of by the government. The Soviet Union was a country ruled by dictatorship and communism.

President Harry Truman feared that, if the Soviet Union expanded, communism would spread and destroy capitalism and democracty. Many people believed communism would spread from one country to another.

An advisor to Truman, George Kennan, suggested a way to prevent the spread of communism. He wanted to use forceful steps against the Soviets. His ideas led to **containment**, a policy of preventing the expansion of a hostile power or ideology.

The Truman Doctrine

The United States used the containment policy for the first time in 1947. Civil war raged in Greece, as Communists attempted to overthrow the government. At the same time, the Soviet Union pressured Turkey to let them build naval bases there. Stalin wanted access to the Mediterranean Sea. In a speech to Congress, Truman declared that the United States, as "leader of the free world," must support democracy worldwide and fight against the spread of communism. This policy came to be known as the Truman Doctrine.

Truman asked Congress for money to help Greece and Turkey fight communists. The Truman Doctrine gave immediate help to the Greek government and eased the Soviet Union's demand in Turkey.

◀ President Truman signed the Foreign Aid Assistance Act, which provided aid to Greece and Turkey.

The Marshall Plan

That same year Secretary of State George C. Marshall suggested a plan to help rebuild the economies of European countries. Under this plan, the United States provided large amounts of aid to Europe. The effort took time, but European economies improved.

Crisis in Berlin

President Truman believed that a reunited Germany was important to the future of Europe. Stalin feared that reuniting Germany would threaten the Soviet Union. Still, on June 7, 1948, the United States, Great Britain, and France announced a plan to reunite their sections of Germany, forming a new West German Republic. This plan also included their portions of Berlin. In response, Stalin ordered a blockade of supplies to West Berlin's 2.2 million people. Stalin thought this would force the West out of Berlin.

The Berlin Airlift

Truman feared another war. Rather than using military force to end the blockade, he organized a large airlift to save the city. For 10 months, American and British planes delivered food, fuel, and other supplies to the people of West Berlin.

Stalin realized that the West would not give up. In May 1949, he ended the blockade. Despite the airlift's success, Berlin and Germany remained divided. By the end of that year there were two German states. The Federal Republic of Germany (West Germany) was allied with the United States. The German Democratic Republic (East Germany) was a communist state allied with the Soviet Union.

Why did Western nations want to contain the spread of communism?

_____

_____

The Cold War Deepens

The United States and the Soviet Union were the world's two "superpowers," or the nations with the most military strength. They were locked in what was called the **Cold War**. The Cold War was fought with ideas, words, money, and sometimes force. The countries never fought each other directly. Still, each side began building up its military forces and weapons in order to frighten the other.

In 1949 a number of nations, including the United States, Great Britain, and France, created the North Atlantic Treaty Organization, or NATO. Member nations agreed to fight the spread of communism. The Soviet Union responded by forming an alliance, called the Warsaw Pact, with six countries in Eastern Europe.

President Truman's advisors in the National Security Council felt that the United States could not rely on other nations to contain the Soviet Union. They said that the United States should begin spending more money on the military, security measures, and civilian defense programs. They considered the Soviet Union a real threat to them, and thought the survival of the free world was at stake.

Map and Globe Skills

Which alliance did Italy join?

_____

_____

Nuclear Weapons

During the 1950s, the United States and the Soviet Union continued to develop more powerful atomic bombs, called nuclear weapons. They also built up large numbers of other weapons. This buildup was called the arms race. Both nations spent enormous amounts of money on weapons.

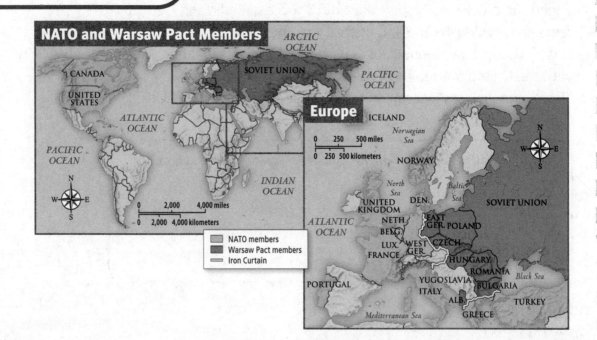

NATO and Warsaw Pact Members

Europe

NATO members
Warsaw Pact members
Iron Curtain

Each nation felt that having the strongest weapons was the best way to prevent an attack and protect its people. Some American families, fearful of an attack from the Soviet Union, built bomb shelters in their backyards. Fear of a nuclear attack was part of daily life in the 1950s. During school hours, students practiced air-raid drills by crouching underneath classroom desks.

Communist China

Events in China added to the worries. In 1949 Communists under the leadership of Mao Zedong won a civil war in China. Under Mao, the People's Republic of China soon became a powerful ally of the Soviet Union. Once the United States lost China as an important ally in Asia, it saw Japan as a key ally in fighting communism. This is the reason the United States encouraged the rapid recovery of Japan's industrial economy.

Why did the U.S. government want Japan's economy to succeed?

_____

_____

Soldiers loading a missile onto a military airplane.

The Korean War

At the end of World War II, the allies divided Korea at the 38th parallel of latitude. South Korea became a democratic republic, with a government backed by the United States. North Korea was controlled by Communists.

On June 25, 1950, North Korean troops attacked South Korea. By September, the North Korean army had taken over much of South Korea. President Truman reacted quickly, believing the invasion was backed by the Soviet Union. The United Nations (UN) sent troops led by American general Douglas MacArthur, a hero of World War II. The UN forces landed in the middle of the Korean peninsula and took control of the region, pushing the North Korean army back across the 38th parallel.

The Korean War

The circle graph below shows the number of U.S. troops that fought in the Korean War. The bar graph shows 10 states that lost the most soldiers. Use the graphs to answer the questions below.

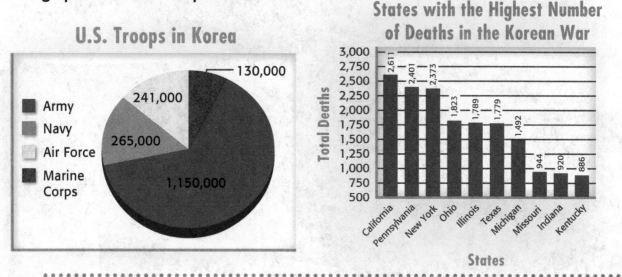

U.S. Troops in Korea

- Army
- Navy
- Air Force
- Marine Corps

130,000
241,000
265,000
1,150,000

States with the Highest Number of Deaths in the Korean War

Total Deaths

California 2,611
Pennsylvania 2,401
New York 2,373
Ohio 1,823
Illinois 1,789
Texas 1,779
Michigan 1,492
Missouri 944
Indiana 920
Kentucky 886

States

Think about the Korean War

1. Which state had the most troop deaths?

2. Which branch of the military had the most troops serving in the Korean War?

Taking the Offensive

South Korea now was safely under the control of UN forces. General MacArthur urged President Truman to order an invasion of North Korea. He convinced the President that neither China nor the Soviet Union would enter the war.

Truman wanted to create a unified democratic Korea. He received UN approval. General MacArthur moved UN troops into North Korea, pushing toward the Chinese border. The Chinese government felt threatened by this action. It sent hundreds of thousands of Chinese troops into North Korea. UN troops fought back. The war became a **stalemate**, a situation in which neither side is able to gain much ground or achieve victory.

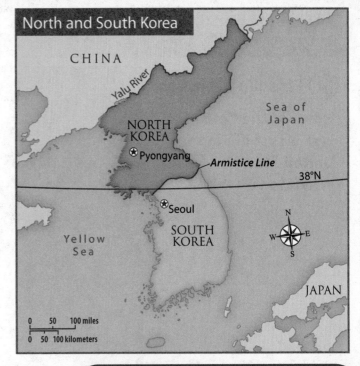

North and South Korea

The Conflict Ends

In July 1953, during the Presidency of Dwight D. Eisenhower, the two sides agreed to a truce, or an agreement to end fighting. It set up a **demilitarized zone**, or an area free from armies and fighting. The fighting ended with no victory for either side and almost no change in borders. More than 36,000 U.S. and UN soldiers had been killed, and more than 103,000 were wounded. Nearly 2 million Koreans and Chinese had died. However, by fighting China, the United States proved to the Soviet Union that it was prepared to fight to prevent the spread of communism.

Map and Globe Skills

What line divides North and South Korea?

_____

_____

Lesson 5

(?) Essential Question   How did the Cold War affect the World from 1945 to 1960?

_____

_____

_____

Go back to *Show As You Go!* on pages 154–155.

networks   There's More Online!
● Games ● Assessment

Television became the main source of news and entertainment for most Americans in the 1950s.

Library of Congress Prints and Photographs Division [LC-DIG-ppmsca-03125]

Essential Question

How did the Cold War affect life in the United States? What do you think?

_____

_____

_____

_____

_____

_____

Words To Know

Use each word in a sentence.

espionage

_____

censure

_____

suburb

_____

The Red Scare

As the Cold War continued, many Americans believed that communists wanted to invade the United States. This led to investigations of suspected communists in the government and in Hollywood.

The Cold War was a time of fear and confusion in the United States. Many Americans worried that members of the Communist Party, sometimes referred to as Reds, were in the United States. This "Red Scare," as it is called, led to a massive search for communists living in the United States. President Truman was concerned about **espionage**, or spying to gather government secrets. He ordered an investigation into the loyalty of all federal employees.

Investigating Communists

The House Un-American Activities Committee (HUAC) held hearings about suspicions of communists in the United States. Hollywood was of special interest to the committee. HUAC thought filmmakers would use movies to influence people and spread thier ideas. Film companies created blacklists, or lists of individuals whose loyalty was in question. People who had been blacklisted were no longer able to find work in the film industry.

McCarthyism

Some politicians used the Red Scare for political gain. Between 1950 and 1954, many suspected communists were called before Senator Joseph McCarthy's Senate committee. McCarthy's committee never proved a single case. The senator's attacks became known as McCarthyism. In 1954 Congress passed a vote of **censure**, or formal disapproval, against McCarthy for his actions.

How did Joseph McCarthy affect the lives of Americans?

_____

_____

_____

_____

Write It

Imagine you are a Hollywood actor who has been unfairly blacklisted. Describe your feelings toward McCarthyism.

_____

_____

_____

_____

Senator Joseph McCarthy symbolized the fear ▶ of communism in the early 1950s.

If you owned a grocery store at the time of the railroad strike, what impact would it have on your business?

_____

_____

The Post-War Years

Just as the nation had to gear up for war at the beginning of World War II, it now had to transition to a peace-time economy. People had done without many things during the war. Now that the war was over, they wanted more goods, but goods were scarce. Factories needed time to switch back to normal production.

During the war, workers agreed that they would not get an increase in pay. They agreed to this with the understanding that wages would increase after the war. This didn't happen right away. Labor unions organized strikes to demand wage increases.

The most severe strike was held by railroad workers. The nation depended on its railroads. Then railroad workers walked off the job, and the trains stopped running. All transportation and delivery of goods stopped. The striking workers rejected a settlement offered by the railroad companies. President Truman threatened to use the army to run the railroads. Finally, the strikers agreed to settle.

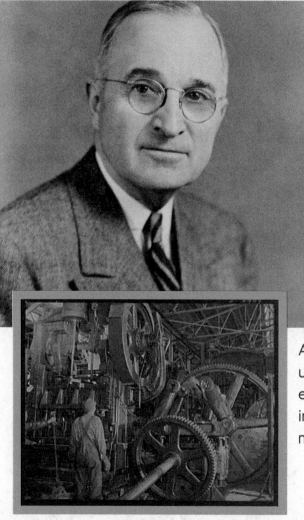

Harry S. Truman (top) and workers for a telephone company (below)

Justice at Home

Truman continued many of Roosevelt's social programs, but he also developed his own. In 1949 Truman presented to Congress his plan which he called the Fair Deal. He said:

> "Every segment of our population and every individual has a right to expect from his government a fair deal."

Truman's program included the Fair Employment Act. This act required employers who signed contracts with federal agencies to not discriminate in hiring based on skin color, creed (beliefs), or nationality.

Truman also disagreed with segregation. The armed services were all segregated. African Americans served in separate units and usually received the worst duties. Truman issued an executive order to desegregate the armed forces in 1948. This order created more opportunities for minorities within the United States military.

Security and Information

In order to be successful in containing the Soviet Union and communism, Truman knew the nation needed reliable information. In 1947 Congress passed the National Security Act (NSA). This act created several agencies to coordinate foreign and military policy. It also created the Central Intelligence Agency (CIA). The CIA coordinated the gathering of intelligence information about the nation's enemies around the world.

The Soviet Union's Sputnik was the world's first man-made satellite.

The Space Race

During this time, the United States continued in the arms race with the Soviet Union. On October 4, 1957, the Soviets launched *Sputnik*, the first man-made **satellite**, into space. A satellite is an object that orbits something else. Congress was concerned that the United States was falling behind the Soviets in new technology. The National Aeronautics and Space Administration (NASA) was created to coordinate missile research and space exploration. The "space race" was on.

Sputnik began a new phase of the Cold War. Satellites were now used for communication and to spy on the other nation. Today, satellites are an important part of everyday life. They transmit television, cell phone, and Global Positioning System (GPS) signals.

How did the United States respond after the Soviets launched *Sputnik*?

_____

_____

▼ The armed forces were desegregated after President Truman signed an executive order in 1948.

(t)NASA, (b)National Archives and Records Administration [NWDNS-342-FH-4A(29278)]

Good Times At Home

Many people began commuting from cities to suburban homes in the 1950s.

Americans sometimes call the 1950s the Eisenhower years. Dwight D. Eisenhower was President from 1953 to 1961. He had served as Supreme Commander of the Allied Forces in Europe during World War II. Like Truman, Eisenhower was strongly against communism.

Changes during these years affected the way many Americans lived and worked. Many troops returned from World War II, got married, and began raising families. As a result, more than 77 million children were born from 1946 to 1964. This period of high birth rate is called the "baby boom."

A New Way of Life

The Servicemen's Readjustment Act, also known as the GI Bill, boosted the American economy. The act provided money to veterans to help them start businesses, buy homes, and attend college. The GI Bill allowed more Americans than ever before to go to college.

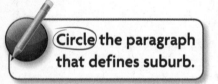

Circle the paragraph that defines suburb.

A new kind of American town, called a **suburb**, developed after World War II. Suburbs are small communities close to larger cities. People moved to suburbs because houses were affordable and there were open spaces for schools and parks. People used cars to commute, or travel to work in the city.

The Federal Aid Highway Act of 1956 built more than 40,000 miles of interstate highways over a 20-year period. Interstate highways connected major American cities. They made transporting goods and people easier. Suburbs were built just off major highways for an easy drive to the city.

Families and children were an important part of life in the suburbs. Women had worked in factories during the war. Now they were being encouraged to stay home so returning troops could find work. The economy was strong and people had money to spend. Many people were living the "American dream."

(l)Steve Allen/Brand X Pictures

Popular Culture

American teens began listening to a new kind of music called rock 'n' roll. This new style grew out of rhythm and blues music and had some elements of country music. Rock 'n' roll was different because the tempo was faster than other music at the time and it used electrical instruments.

By 1957, more than 80 percent of American homes had televisions. Television became the main source of news and entertainment for most people. Popular comedies, such as *I Love Lucy*, and variety shows, such as *The Ed Sullivan Show*, reflected the idea that Americans were enjoying life.

Elivis Presley (left) became rock 'n' roll's first superstar. The Cleaver family was a popular show in the 1950s.

> **What was the purpose of the Federal Aid Highway Act of 1956?**
>
> _____
>
> _____

Lesson 6

(?) Essential Question   How did the Cold War affect life in the United States?

_____

_____

_____

Go back to *Show As You Go!* on pages 154–155.

(b)Library of Congress Prints and Photographs Division [LC-USZ6-2067], (t)Library of Congress, Prints & Photographs Division, NYWT&S Collection [LC-USZ62-113833]

networks   **There's More Online!** ● Games ● Assessment

Fill in the chart with words from the box to tell how and why the U.S. was at war.

Holocaust	communism	genocide	mobilize
fascism	kamikaze	demilitarized zone	stalemated
rationed	censured	espionage	casualties

Neither side in the Cold War gained much ground, or they were _____ for a while. In 1953 it finally ended and a _____ was set up.

A belief in a strong leader, or _____, is different than a belief in a strong government, or _____.

Spying, or _____, was a concern after the Cold War ended. McCarthyism was disapproved of, or _____ .

The _____ was an example of _____, or the planned killing of specific groups of people.

_____ missions were suicide attacks that caused many _____.

People _____, or saved, supplies and food, once the war caused the nation to _____.

Unit Project

Your class will complete the unit project in groups. Each group will be on a different side of the Cold War. You will write, vote on, and discuss your role in the war. You will need to be able to answer these questions: Why are you on that side? What decisions are you making and why? At the end of the experience, you will share with the rest of your class. In your role you will also evaluate others' presentations. As you work, keep these tasks and behaviors in mind.

Task and behaviors to keep in mind...   **Yes I do!**

I know the reasons for the Cold War. ☐

I know what role I am assigned and why it is/was important. ☐

I know how my group will work with other groups. ☐

I participate in the decision-making process. ☐

I listen respectfully during others' presentations. ☐

I share my views and opinions on the decisions. ☐

Think about the Big Idea

BIG IDEA Conflict causes change.

What did you learn in this unit that helps you understand the BIG IDEA?

_____

_____

_____

Read the article "Trading with Other Countries" before answering Numbers 1 through 6.

Trading with Other Countries

by Adam Jones

Buyers and sellers in the United States work together to make goods and provide services. But we cannot make everything we need, so we have to trade with other countries. We trade the goods and services we have for the goods and services we need.

The United States sends its goods and resources to countries all over the world. It also brings in goods and resources from other countries. This system of trade helps the economies of all countries.

States also play an important part in the economy of the United States. For example, Florida trades goods including fruit, phosphates, and machine parts to countries around the world. In return, Florida receives wood from Canada, oil from Africa, and computers and other machines from Japan.

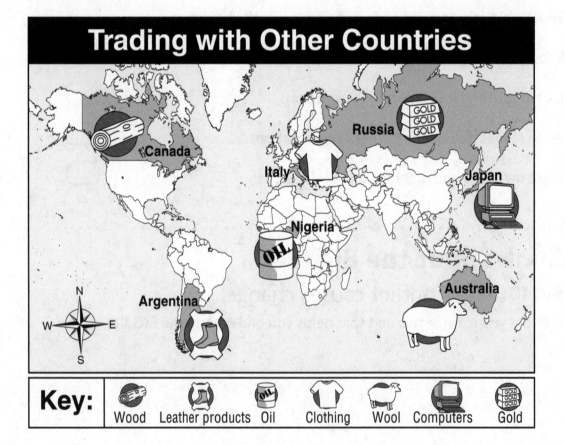

1 By reading the article and looking at the map, you can tell that Canada trades

Ⓐ oil.

Ⓑ clothing.

Ⓒ computers.

Ⓓ wood.

2 Which sentence from the article tells the main idea?

Ⓕ *Florida plays an important part in the economy of the United States.*

Ⓖ *We trade the goods and services we have for the goods and services we need.*

Ⓗ *The United States sends its goods and resources to countries all over the world.*

Ⓘ *Buyers and sellers in the United States work together to make goods and provide services.*

3 How is the system of trade in Florida SIMILAR to the system of trade in the United States?

Ⓐ They both trade goods with countries around the world.

Ⓑ They both trade services with Canada.

Ⓒ They both trade goods with buyers in Japan.

Ⓓ They both trade goods with sellers in Italy.

4 Which of the following is something that all countries of the world have in common?

Ⓕ oil

Ⓖ wool

Ⓗ gold

Ⓘ trade

5 What is the MOST LIKELY reason the author wrote this article?

Ⓐ to explain how Florida produces goods

Ⓑ to explain why the United States trades

Ⓒ to explain what goods Florida trades

Ⓓ to explain how goods are transported during trades

6 Which product does Florida ship to other countries?

Ⓕ oil

Ⓖ phosphates

Ⓗ computers

Ⓘ wool

UNIT 6
The Modern Era

 BIG IDEA Culture influences the way people live.

The United States is a mix of many different cultures. Not only within each state, but immigrants make the diversity unique. During the 1950s, equal rights were finally becoming the new way of life. In this unit you'll read about a bright future. There were still conflicts, but our Presidents fought for our safety and freedom. You will also read about the war on terrorism and today's government and economy. As you read this unit, think about how culture influences the way people live and the way of the new technology.

networks
connected.mcgraw-hill.com
● Skill Builders
● Vocabulary Flashcards

Add the following to the map:

After Lesson 1:
☐ Brown vs. Board
☐ Montgomery Boycott

After Lesson 2:
☐ Equal Rights
☐ Bay of Pigs

After Lesson 3:
☐ Watergate
☐ Jimmy Carter

After Lesson 4:
☐ September 11, 2001

After Lesson 5:
☐ Barack Obama
☐ Trade with Mexico

After Lesson 6:
☐ Computers
☐ Complete the Map Key
☐ Give the map a title

Show As You Go! After you read the following lessons, complete the map of the United States. Use the checklist on page 206 for suggestions of what to add to your map and map key.

Fold page here

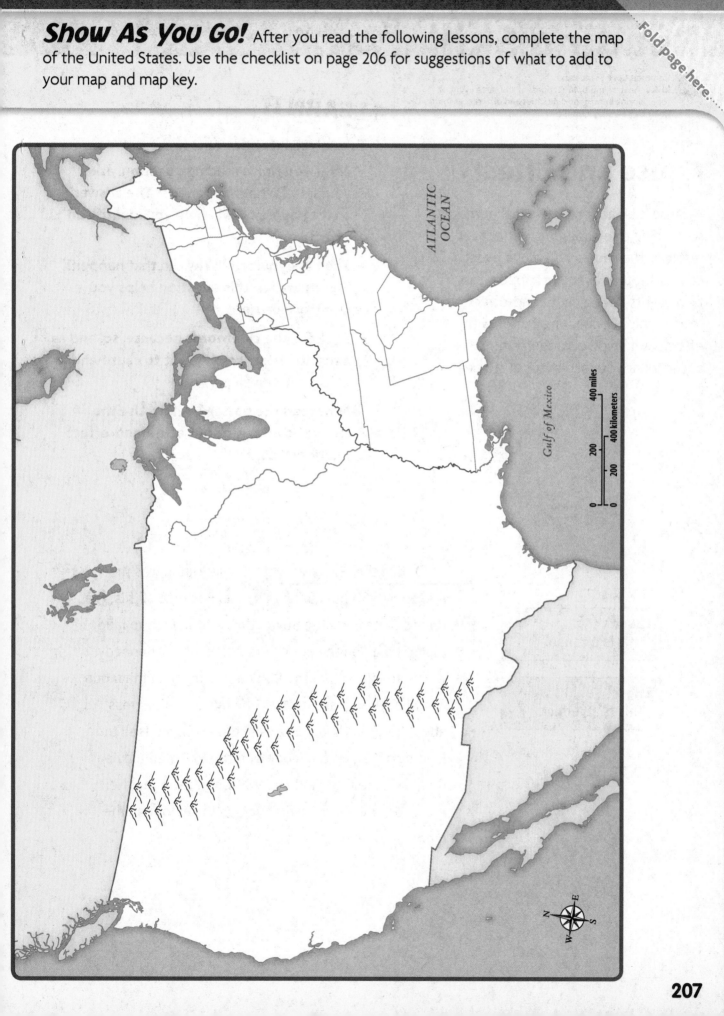

ATLANTIC OCEAN

Gulf of Mexico

400 miles

400 kilometers

200

200

N
E
W
S

Reading Skill

Common Core Standards
RI.5.6 Analyze multiple accounts of the same event or
topic, noting important similarities and differences in the
point of view they represent.

Cause and Effect

A cause is an action or event that makes
something else happen. An effect is the
result of the cause. When one event
causes another event to happen, the
two events have a cause-and-effect
relationship. Connecting causes with
effects will help you understand more
about what you read in social studies.

LEARN IT

To analyze information:

- After you finish reading a section, ask
  yourself, "What happened?" The answer
  to that question will help you identify an
  effect.

- Then ask yourself "Why did that happen?"
  The answer to this question helps you
  identify a cause.

- Look for the clue words because, so, and as
  a result. These words point to cause-and-
  effect relationships.

- Now read the passage below. Use the
  steps above to pick out cause-and-effect
  relationships.

The Space Race

During the Cold War, the Soviet Union was the
first country to put a man in space. Because of this, the
United States and the Soviet Union competed to land
the first man on the moon. President John F. Kennedy
was determined that the first people to reach the moon
would be Americans. In 1961 he talked to Congress
about how the United States should commit itself to
landing a man on the moon before 1970. Kennedy's
dream was realized in July 1969 when astronaut Neil
Armstrong became the first person to set foot on the
moon.

Cause
This is a cause.

Effect
This is an effect.

208

TRY IT

Complete the cause and effect chart below. Then fill in the chart with another cause and effect from the paragraph.

Cause	→	Effect
	→	
	→	
	→	

How did you figure out the causes and effects?

APPLY IT

- Review the steps for understanding cause and effect in Learn It.
- Read the passage below. Then use the chart to list the causes and effects from the passage.

Cause	→	Effect
	→	
	→	
	→	

The Cold War came to a dramatic end in the German city of Berlin. For 28 years, the Berlin Wall had split the city in two. Communist East Berlin lay on one side, capitalist West Berlin on the other. By November 1989, huge protests forced the East German government to open the border. People on both sides attacked the wall with axes and sledgehammers. They shouted, "Germany is free and one." One by one, communist governments fell all across Eastern Europe. In 1991 the Soviet Union broke up into 15 independent countries.

Common Core Standards
RI.4: Determine the meaning of general academic and domain-specific words and phrases in a text relevant to a grade 5 topic or subject area.

The list below shows some important words you will learn in this unit. Their definitions can be found on the next page. Read the words.

integrate (IN • te • grayte)

boycott (BOI • kot)

peace corps (PEECE kor)

inflation (in • FLAY • shen)

terrorism (TER • a • riz • em)

globalization (glo • bal • i • zay • shen)

recession (re • sess • shen)

microchip (MY • kro • chip)

The Foldable on the next page will help you learn these important words. Follow the steps below to make your Foldable.

Step 1 Fold along the solid red line.

Step 2 Cut along the dotted lines.

Step 3 Read the words and their definitions.

Step 4 Complete the activities on each tab.

Step 5 Look at the back of your Foldable. Choose ONE of these activities for each word to help you remember its meaning:

- Draw a picture of the word.
- Write a description of the word.
- Write how the word is related to something you know.

◀ **The Constitutional Convention was held in Independence Hall in Philadelphia.**

	FOLD	
		Use the word *integrate* in a sentence.
To **integrate** is to bring together people of all races.		
A **boycott** is a form of organized protest in which people refuse to do business with a company or nation.		**Find a word in boycott that probably describes about half your classmates and maybe you. Write it below.**
The **Peace Corps** is an agency created by President Kennedy that trains and sends American volunteers overseas to work with people in developing countries.		**Define the Peace Corps in your own words.**
Inflation is a rise in prices of goods and services.		**Draw a box around each syllable in inflation.**
Terrorism is the use of violence by non-governmental groups to achieve political goals.		**Terrorism ends in *–ism*. Write two other words with this ending below.** _____ _____
Globalization is a trend where companies do not consider national boundaries when they decide where to buy and sell goods and services.		**What is the root word in *globalization*?**
A **recession** means no economic growth for six straight months, a general slowing of economic activity, and high unemployment.		**Name another word that begins with *re-*.**
A **microchip** is a tiny computer part that processes information quickly.		**What is the prefix in *microchip*?**

integrate

CUT HERE

boycott

peace corps

inflation

terrorism

globalization

recession

microchip

integrate	
boycott	
peace corps	
inflation	
terrorism	
globalization	
recession	
microchip	

Primary Sources

Photographs

Photographs capture events as they happen and show what people and places looked like at a specific time. Newspapers and Web sites are two places where you can often see photographs. To analyze a photograph, ask yourself questions about it. When was it taken? What are the people in the photo doing? How do they look? What action is taking place in the photo? What objects are shown in the photograph? The answers to these questions will help you understand what life was like when the photo was taken.

DBQ Document-Based Questions

Examine the two photographs on this page. Use them to answer the questions below.

1. Describe what is happening in the top photograph.

_____

2. Describe what is happening in the bottom photograph.

_____

3. Synthesize, or combine, your information about these photos. What do both of these photographs tell you about workers?

_____

_____

(t) Gary John Norman / Getty Images, (b) NASA Kennedy Space Center (NASA-KSC)

networks
(image: pointing hand)
There's More Online!
● Skill Builders
● Resource Library

Lesson 1 The Civil Rights Movement

 Essential Question

How can fighting for equal rights change society?
What do you think?

_____

_____

_____

_____

_____

Words To Know

Write a number on each line to show how much you know about each word.

1 = I have no idea!

2 = I know a little.

3 = I know a lot.

_____ **integrate**

_____ **boycott**

_____ **migrant farm worker**

Separate but not Equal

Barbara Johns went to class in a segregated African American school. The building was shabby and her books were old. Johns knew it wasn't fair. In April 1951, she led 450 students to march out on strike.

Since 1896, segregation had the approval of the United States Supreme Court. The Court ruled in *Plessy* v. *Ferguson* that segregated facilities for African Americans and whites were legal as long as they were of equal quality. In reality, the facilities for African Americans were rarely equal. African Americans were left with run-down schools, hospitals, restaurants, and even cemeteries.

> Why did Barbara Johns lead 450 students on strike?
>
> _____
>
> _____

214

The NAACP

The National Association for the Advancement of Colored People (NAACP) had been fighting segregation for more than 40 years. NAACP lawyers took Barbara Johns' case and four others to court. One of the cases involved Oliver Brown from Topeka, Kansas. His daughter, Linda, walked 21 blocks to an African American school. She could have gone to a white school seven blocks away.

The *Brown* Decision

In 1952 the five cases went to the Supreme Court. They were put together under the heading *Brown* v. *Board of Education of Topeka, Kansas.* Thurgood Marshall led a team of lawyers for the NAACP to overturn the *Plessy* decision. Marshall had already won several court cases forcing states to provide more money to African American schools.

On May 17, 1954, the Court announced its decision. It said that the 1896 *Plessy* v. *Ferguson* decision was wrong. Separate schools are always "unequal." Segregation in public schools was now against the law.

Thurgood Marshall became a United States Supreme Court Justice. He served from 1967 to 1991. ▼

Protests and Marches

Change came slowly after the Court's ruling. By 1960, only 10 percent of public schools in the South were **integrated**. To integrate means to bring together people of all races. In the 1950s, other facilities remained segregated. African Americans had to sit in the backs of buses. Most Southern states also kept African Americans from voting.

Still, *Brown* v. *Board of Education* convinced African Americans that change was possible. In the next decade, people risked their lives challenging unjust laws and traditions. The civil rights movement was born.

The Montgomery Bus Boycott

On December 1, 1955, Rosa Parks finished work at a department store in Montgomery, Alabama, and boarded a bus to go home. When the bus filled up, the driver told Parks to give up her seat to a white passenger. When she refused, Parks was arrested.

In response to Parks's arrest, the local NAACP leader, E. D. Nixon, organized a **boycott** of the Montgomery buses. To boycott means to refuse to do business with or buy goods from a person, group, or country. An English teacher named Jo Ann Robinson printed up 35,000 leaflets to announce the boycott. Dr. Martin Luther King, Jr., who was just 26 years old, began preaching to huge meetings in churches in Alabama.

The boycott lasted nearly 400 days. Proud protesters carpooled or walked to work. "We got our heads up now," said an African American man involved in the boycott, "and we won't ever bow down again—no sir—except before God." Finally, in November 1956, the Supreme Court ruled that segregation on public buses was illegal.

Reading Skill

Cause and Effect

What was the effect of Rosa Parks' refusal to give up her seat?

_____

_____

▼ Civil Rights March

Sit-Ins and Freedom Rides

In February 1960, the civil rights movement took a new path. African American students sat at "whites only" lunch counters until they were arrested. These "sit-ins" soon spread to nine Southern states. The Student Nonviolent Coordinating Committee (SNCC) was formed to organize the protests. That year, at least 3,000 people were arrested during sit-ins.

The following summer, African Americans and whites protested segregated bus stations in an action called the Freedom Rides. They rode interstate buses through the South and then walked together into segregated areas. Both sit-in protesters and Freedom Riders were sometimes beaten and taunted by angry whites.

The protests had mixed results. Some businesses and cities integrated when faced with sit-ins. Most did not. The Freedom Rides were more successful. In September 1961, the government told bus companies that they could not use segregated facilities.

Fannie Lou Hamer, American Civil Rights Leader

Voting Rights

Civil rights supporters also pushed for the right to vote. The Fifteenth Amendment extended that right to African American men in 1870. However, officials in the South found ways to keep African Americans away from the polls. They charged expensive poll taxes or gave tests that few voters could pass. They threatened African American voters with violence or fired them from their jobs.

The SNCC worked to register African American voters. Fannie Lou Hamer did not even know African Americans could vote until SNCC workers told her. Hamer was beaten when she tried to register. She was also fired from her job. Yet little by little, African American voters began to demand their rights.

> **What led to the Freedom Rides?**
>
> _____
>
> _____
>
> _____

Fighting for Change

In April 1963, protesters in Montgomery, Alabama, started a string of sit-ins, boycotts, and demonstrations. The police beat back peaceful marchers with firehoses, nightsticks, and attack dogs. They threw 2,000 protesters in jail. Television news broadcast the violence across the country to a shocked audience.

One Sunday morning, a bomb exploded in an African American church in Birmingham. It killed four young girls. That incident shocked many people and helped convince Birmingham officials to end segregation.

The March on Washington

In August, Dr. King and other leaders staged the largest political protest the nation had ever seen. More than 200,000 people showed up for the protest in Washington, D.C.

Protesters demanded a federal civil rights law that would force state and local governments to end discrimination. From the steps of the Lincoln Memorial, Dr. King addressed the crowd. He spoke of his "dream" for a world free of prejudice. His words brought the audience to tears. By the end of the summer, Dr. King's leadership and the violence in Birmingham had made millions of Americans aware of the injustices in the South.

(t) eLibrary of Congress Prints and Photographs Division (LC-US262-116775); (b) National Archives and Records Administration [542068]

Dr. & Mrs. Martin Luther King, Jr.

▼ Martin Luther King, Jr. in Washington, D.C.

New Laws

The federal government also took action at this time. Congress passed the Civil Rights Act of 1964, making segregation in public places illegal. It also made it illegal to deny someone a job based on race. Later, the Twenty-Fourth Amendment banned poll taxes in federal elections. However, in some parts of the country, like Selma, Alabama, whites blocked entrances to voting places or threatened African Americans who tried to vote.

The Selma March

Selma's sheriff would rather arrest African Americans than let them register to vote. In 1965 Martin Luther King and others organized a march from Selma to the state capital in Montgomery. On March 7, hundreds of marchers were met by the police. Officers brutally beat the marchers and forced them to withdraw. The marchers vowed to try again.

In response President Lyndon B. Johnson sent federal troops to protect them. A few hundred people made the march from Selma to Montgomery. Thousands more marched in Montgomery to the steps of the state capitol to hear Dr. King speak about voting rights.

More New Laws

President Johnson took advantage of the attention given the marchers. He pushed Congress to pass the Voting Rights Act of 1965 into law. Congress also passed the Civil Rights Act of 1968, which banned discrimination in housing.

What was the effect of the Selma March?

_____

_____

I have a dream that one day this nation will rise up and live out the true meaning of its creed: "We hold these truths to be self-evident, that all men are created equal. . . ."

I have a dream that my four little children will one day live in a nation where they will not be judged by the color of their skin but by the content of their character. . . .

This will be the day when all of God's children will be able to sing with a new meaning: "My country, 'tis of thee, sweet land of liberty, of thee I sing. Land where my fathers died, land of the pilgrim's pride, from every mountainside, let freedom ring."

A section from the "I have a dream" speech by Martin Luther King, Jr., August 28, 1963, Washington, D.C.

▲ Civil rights march in Washington, D.C. in 1963.

Equal Rights for All

After 1960 more groups sought equal rights. Protests were organized for improved working conditions and equal pay.

Helping Migrant Workers

One group that protested during the 1960s was **migrant farm workers**. Migrant farm workers travel from farm to farm to plant and harvest crops. These workers faced dirty and dangerous working conditions for little pay.

In 1962 two Mexican Americans, César Chávez and Dolores Huerta, organized a labor union that later became the United Farm Workers, or UFW. The union led strikes and boycotts against farm owners. In time the efforts of the UFW brought higher wages and better working conditions to migrant workers.

César Chávez (right) urged workers to strike (*huelga in Spanish*) for better wages and workers' rights.

Betty Friedan

The Women's Movement

Women gained the right to vote in 1920, but many women still did not have economic equality. In 1960 women were paid less than men for doing the same jobs. In 1966 writer Betty Friedan formed the National Organization for Women (NOW). NOW insisted that the government enforce the Civil Rights Act of 1964, which made it illegal to discriminate against women in the workplace.

In 1972, a congresswoman from Hawaii, Patsy Takemoto Mink, wrote a law giving women equal rights in education. This law, first known as Title IX, expanded women's sports programs in schools. In 2002 the law was renamed in her honor.

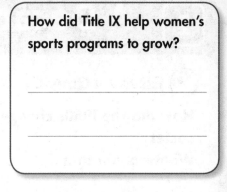

How did Title IX help women's sports programs to grow?

_____

_____

Rights for Native Americans

In 1968 Native Americans organized the American Indian Movement (AIM), to work for equal rights and the improvement of living conditions for Native Americans. It also drew attention to poverty on reservations. After many AIM protests, the Supreme Court ruled that states had to honor treaty agreements. As a result, in the 1970s millions of acres of land were returned to Native Americans in Alaska, Maine, New Mexico, and South Dakota.

People with Disabilities

For years, millions of Americans with disabilities faced discrimination at work and in education, housing, and transportation. In 1990 the Americans with Disabilities Act, or ADA, made it illegal to discriminate against people who are disabled. It also required all levels of government to make public facilities accessible to people with disabilities.

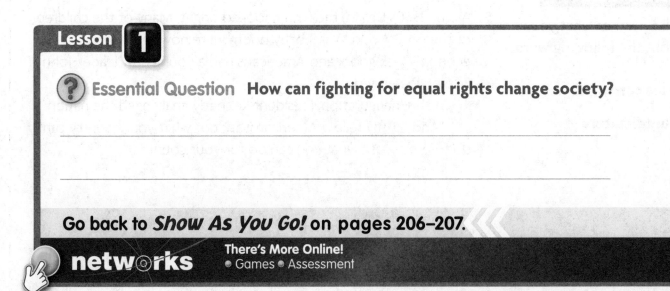

Lesson **1**

(?) Essential Question   How can fighting for equal rights change society?

_____

_____

Go back to *Show As You Go!* on pages 206–207.

networks There's More Online!
● Games ● Assessment

Lesson 2 — A Decade of Change

(?) **Essential Question**

How did the 1960s change society?
What do you think?

_____

_____

_____

_____

_____

_____

_____

_____

Words To Know

Tell a partner what you know about the following words.

Peace corps

counterculture

NASA Headquarters - GReatest Images of NASA (NASA-HQ-GRIN)

Kennedy giving historic speech to Congress in 1961

A New Frontier

As the 1960s began, the future looked bright. Many of the children of the post-World War II baby boom were now teenagers. The economy was good, and Americans had a young new leader, John Fitzgerald Kennedy.

At his inauguration, President Kennedy challenged the nation:

"And so, my fellow Americans: ask not what your country can do for you—ask what you can do for your country."

A Plan for the Nation

Kennedy believed the United States should show the world what a democratic society could offer. His plan was called the "New Frontier." This plan included raising the minimum wage, cutting taxes, guaranteeing equal pay for women, rebuilding the inner cities, and increasing education funding. Kennedy also wanted to assist the elderly with medical costs.

Congress refused to pass his health care program and tax cuts, fearing they would be too costly for the nation. Congress raised the minimum wage and started a program to rebuild urban areas. These helped create jobs and low-income housing. In 1963 Kennedy signed the Clean Air Act, which called for a reduction of air pollution.

The Peace Corps

Kennedy also started the **Peace Corps**. This agency trains American volunteers and sends them to work with people in poor countries. It assists countries in the areas of education, business, technology, agriculture, and the environment. The Peace Corps works to help people outside the United States understand American culture and to help Americans understand the cultures of other nations.

Since its beginning, more than 190,000 Americans have responded to Kennedy's challenge by serving in the Peace Corps. Most volunteers have been young adults.

> **Why did Kennedy create the Peace Corps?**
>
> _____
>
> _____

Donald Uhrbrock/Time & Life Pictures/Getty Images

A Peace Corps volunteer ▶

Cold War Conflicts

In the 1960s, Americans were still involved in the Cold War with the Soviet Union and still worried about communism. They were especially worried about Cuba, an island nation about 90 miles from Florida. In 1959 Fidel Castro had led a successful revolution and set up a communist government there. After Castro took power, many Cubans fled their country to live in the United States.

The CIA had a plan to train Cubans living in the United States to invade Cuba. The idea was that the Cuban people then would rise up and overthrow Castro's government. Kennedy gave his go-ahead for the plan.

The plan, called the Bay of Pigs Invasion, was a complete failure. The invaders were captured, and the incident was a huge embarrassment. Kennedy took all the blame, but the attempted overthrow of the communist nation made relations between Cuba and the United States much worse.

▼ Fidel Castro and Nikita Khrushchev make their way in the midst of a crowd

The Berlin Wall

Between 1949 and 1962, about 2.5 million East Germans escaped to West Germany through West Berlin. Many of these East Germans were highly educated people. For example, one day the entire math department of a university fled the country.

East Germany needed educated workers for its economy and looked for a way to stop these escapes. The leader of the Soviet Union, Nikita Khrushchev, threatened to take West Berlin by force. Kennedy responded by building up the military. He increased spending on defense and on nuclear weapons.

Grafitti on a German Wall

In 1961 Khrushchev ordered a wall built to separate communist East Germany from West Berlin. This wall prevented East Germans from escaping. The Berlin Wall became a symbol of the division between communism and democracy.

Missiles in Cuba

After the Bay of Pigs, Khrushchev thought Kennedy was weak. In early 1962 he placed nuclear missiles in Cuba, aimed right at American cities. In October 1962, Kennedy announced on television that American spy planes had found evidence that the Soviet Union had put long-range missiles in Cuba.

Kennedy responded by ordering the Navy to blockade Cuba in order to prevent more missiles from arriving. A blockade is an action that prevents the passage of people or supplies. Kennedy also demanded that the Soviet Union remove the missiles.

Both the United States and the Soviets had nuclear weapons. Everyone knew that a wrong move could start a new world war.

For thirteen days, the world held its breath. Finally, Khrushchev compromised. He ordered Russian ships to turn back. Soviet missiles were taken apart and removed. In return the United States agreed not to invade Cuba. Secretly, the United States also agreed to remove American missiles in Turkey that were a threat to the Soviet Union.

Kennedy's Last Years in Office

You read in Unit 5 how the Soviet Union was the first country to launch a satellite into space. With Cold War tensions on the rise, the United States and the Soviet Union competed to land the first human on the moon. Kennedy was determined that the first people to reach this goal would be Americans. In 1961 he told Congress to commit to landing a man on the moon before 1970. Kennedy's dream was realized in July 1969, when astronaut Neil Armstrong became the first person to set foot on the moon.

Sadly, Kennedy did not live to see the moon landing. On November 22, 1963, he visited Dallas, Texas. He was riding in a convertible so crowds could see him. Shots were fired, and President Kennedy died. Within a few hours, Lyndon B. Johnson was sworn in as President.

NASA

DID YOU KNOW?
On July 19, 1969, it didn't matter where on Earth you lived. If you had a television, you were probably watching the **first moon landing.** In a fuzzy image on the screen, an astronaut named Neil Armstrong moved in almost slow motion. He climbed carefully down the ladder of the landing vehicle and then stepped onto the moon. His voice crackled through the TV: "That's one small step for a man, one giant leap for mankind."

Why did Kennedy order the U.S. Navy to blockade Cuba?

_____

_____

Be a Leader

Lyndon Johnson was a good leader. He identified problems and worked hard to do something about them. This is what leaders do. Think about what you could do to be a leader in your school or community. Maybe there is a problem in your school or community. Talk to others about it. Find others to help solve a problem, and make sure everyone has a chance to contribute.

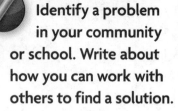

Identify a problem in your community or school. Write about how you can work with others to find a solution.

_____

_____

_____

_____

Fighting Poverty

Although the 1950s had been a time of increased wealth for our country, this wealth did not reach all Americans. By 1965, almost 5 out of every 10 nonwhite Americans were officially considered poor by the government. About 2 out of every 10 white Americans were this poor. During the 1960s, many leaders fought the problems of poverty and discrimination.

The Great Society

In 1964 President Johnson declared a "War on Poverty." His programs were aimed at building what he called the "Great Society." He wanted to provide education, equal rights, and health care to all Americans.

One program Johnson fought for was Medicare, which helps people over the age of 65 pay for medical care. Another program, Medicaid, provided health care for low-income families. Both programs are still in existence.

There were other programs that helped citizens. The Job Corps helped young people develop skills. Head Start provides pre-school programs for poor children. The Elementary and Secondary Education Act (ESEA) provided federal funds to schools to improve education.

Johnson worked hard to pass the civil rights bill that Kennedy had introduced to Congress. As you have read, he signed the Civil Rights Act of 1964 into law. Johnson also worked to get the Voting Rights Act of 1965 passed. This law allowed federal agents to use their power to make sure all citizens were allowed to vote.

Malcolm X and Dr. King's Campaign

Poverty and discrimination drew the attention of many leaders. Malcolm X became a popular leader in the 1960s. He felt that an end to poverty and discrimination was not coming fast enough.

Malcolm X fought against poverty and discrimination

Malcolm X believed that change would come faster if African Americans took control of their own lives. He joined the Nation of Islam. They believed that African Americans should separate from whites and govern themselves.

By 1965, however, Malcolm X had begun to change his ideas. Instead of racial separation, he called for "a society in which there could exist honest white-black brotherhood." He left the Nation of Islam and criticized the organization. Soon afterwards, members of the Nation of Islam assassinated Malcolm X.

With the passage of the Civil Rights Act of 1964 and the Voting Rights Act of 1965, Martin Luther King, Jr. began a new program. He called it "The Poor People's Campaign." Its goal was to end poverty for both blacks and whites. Dr. King said the Poor People's Campaign was the second phase of the civil rights movement.

On May 12, 1968, the Poor People's Campaign arrived in Washington, D.C. Protesters campaigned for an economic bill of rights. The protesters called for a massive government jobs program to rebuild America's cities, housing for the poor, and a guaranteed annual income for the poor. The campaign ended in mid-June. Congress never passed the economic bill of rights.

> **Why do you think Johnson fought for Kennedy's civil rights bill?**
>
> _____
>
> _____

227

The Vietnam War

While people were fighting for equal rights at home, the United States became involved in a war in Vietnam. North Vietnam was a communist nation, supported by the Soviet Union and China. South Vietnam was a republic, backed by the United States. Many worried that if Vietnam fell, other Asian countries would also fall to communism.

The War Begins

In August 1964, President Johnson announced that North Vietnam had fired on American warships in the Gulf of Tonkin. Johnson did not mention that the American warships were helping South Vietnam against North Vietnam. Then the North Vietnamese attacked a military base in South Vietnam, killing 7 Americans and wounding 100. Less than 14 hours after that attack, some 132 American aircraft bombed North Vietnam.

Counterculture

Many believed that the United States should not fight in a war that wasn't a threat to its own safety. Some young people turned their backs on the "establishment," or standard American culture, and joined the **counterculture**. A counterculture has ideas and values that are different from the larger society.

The counterculture consisted mostly of young people called hippies. They had long hair and dressed in loose, colorful clothing. Some of them created their own communities known as communes. They often listened to music that was influenced by that of Asian countries.

Vietnam War protestors Veterans for Peace at the March on the Pentagon.

As the 1960s progressed, differing views about equal rights and the Vietnam War increased tensions between members of the counterculture and the rest of the country.

A Season of Violence

In 1968 the country was filled with protests and violence. The Vietnam War was the first "television war." Every night, footage from the war was on the nightly news. The whole country saw wounded or dead American soldiers nearly every day. People began to doubt if the war could be won. Anti-war protests continued to grow.

Assassinations rocked the nation. In April, Dr. Martin Luther King, Jr., was killed. This event led to riots in several cities. In June, Robert Kennedy, the brother of President Kennedy, was also killed. Today, both Robert Kennedy and Dr. King are remembered for their leadership in the fight for civil rights and their work to end poverty. On the third Monday in January, our nation celebrates the birth of Dr. King.

The War Ends

In 1968 more than 250,000 protesters came to Washington, D.C., to speak out against the war. A new President, Richard Nixon, withdrew some troops, but the war continued.

By 1973, President Nixon ordered U.S. troops to stop fighting in Vietnam, but they continued to help South Vietnamese troops. The war ended in 1975. Vietnam was united under a communist government. Overall, over 57,000 Americans died in the war. Nearly two million Vietnamese were killed as well.

DID YOU KNOW?

In August 1969, more than 400,000 young people gathered on a farm in New York for a music festival called **Woodstock**. Supply shortages and heavy rain caused people to share their food and blankets and bathe in the rain while they listened to popular music. Many hippies attended Woodstock. This concert was one of the many ways hippies changed the way Americans thought, dressed, lived, and the music they listened to.

Lesson 2

? Essential Question How did the 1960s change society?

_____

_____

_____

Go back to *Show As You Go!* on page 206–207.

The Century Ends

? Essential Question

How did events at the end of the century change society?
What do you think?

_____

_____

_____

_____

_____

_____

_____

Words To Know

Look at the words below. Tell a partner what you already know about these words.

détente

inflation

hostages

budget deficit

Philip Hayson/Photolibrary/Getty Images

People celebrating on New Year's Eve 2000

Nixon's Presidency

President Nixon hoped a trip to China would help end the war in Vietnam. He also hoped a visit to the Soviet Union would begin a thaw in Cold War politics.

In 1972 President Richard Nixon tried to reach out to the communist world. He became the first President to visit Communist China and the Soviet Union. Nixon helped bring about **détente**—an easing of tensions between nations.

Détente began with an effort to improve American-Chinese relations. Nixon hoped to strengthen ties with the Chinese and also improve Soviet relations. Since the 1960s, a rift had developed between the Soviet Union and China. Troops of the two nations sometimes clashed at the border. Soon after Nixon's trip to China, he went to the Soviet Union to meet with leaders there. This meeting led to an agreement to limit nuclear weapons, increase trade, and exchange of scientific information.

In 1973 Nixon's presidency was wrecked by scandal. A scandal is a dishonest act that causes public shame to the people involved. Newspapers reported that members of Nixon's staff had ordered a break-in at the Democratic headquarters at the Watergate Hotel in Washington, D.C.

Congress investigated the Watergate Scandal, and many of Nixon's aides went to jail. In July 1974, Nixon resigned from office. Vice President Gerald Ford became President. Early in his presidency, Ford gave Nixon a pardon, meaning Nixon would not be punished for any crimes.

What caused Nixon to visit the People's Republic of China?

_____

_____

▼ Richard M. Nixon
campaign 1968

Carter and Reagan

Jimmy Carter, a governor from Georgia, was elected President in 1976. His presidency faced high **inflation**. Inflation is the rising of prices for goods and services. Economic problems continued throughout Carter's presidency.

Israel and Palestinian Territories

0 25 50 miles
0 25 50 kilometers

LEBANON
SYRIA
Nahariyya
Haifa
Golan Heights
Sea of Galilee
Nazareth
Hadera
Mediterranean Sea
Tel Aviv
West Bank
Ashdod
Ashqelon
Jerusalem
Dead Sea
Gaza Strip
Beersheba
Dimona
ISRAEL
JORDAN
Negev
EGYPT
N W E S
Elat
Gulf of Aqaba

Israel
Palestinian Territories

Map and Globe Skills

What are the names of the Palestinian territories?

_____

_____

Carter and World Events

President Carter had both his greatest success and his greatest failure in the Middle East. His success was that he began the process of making peace between Israel and Arabs. For a long time, most people who lived where Israel is today were Arabs. Some Jews always lived in their homeland, the location of the ancient Kingdom of Israel. Before World War II, many Jews migrated to the region, then called Palestine, to escape harsh anti-Semitism in Europe. Both Arabs and Jews wanted their own state in the region.

The UN voted to divide this area into two states, and in 1948 the Jews established the independent State of Israel. The Arabs did not think Jews had a right to make a state there. Five Arab countries attacked Israel, but Israel won, and other wars followed. The United States has usually supported Israel. Many Arab states are angered by this policy. Despite these problems, Carter helped bring about a peace treaty between Egypt, an Arab nation, and Israel.

Carter's biggest failure in the Middle East also came in 1979. Iranian students and clergy led a revolution against the American-backed government in Iran. The students stormed the U.S. embassy in the capital. They took 52 American **hostages**. A hostage is a person who is held prisoner until certain demands are met.

► Egyptian President Anwar el-Sadat (left), President Carter (center), and Israeli Prime Minister Menachem Begin (right) at the White House after signing a 1979 peace treaty.

Americans blamed Carter for this crisis, and he lost the 1980 election to Ronald Reagan.

Reagan and the Cold War

President Ronald Reagan took a strong stand against communism. He called the Soviet Union an "evil empire." He insisted the United States could help bring about freedom in faraway parts of the world—but only if it had the most powerful military in the world.

▲ Mikhail Gorbachev

Reagan sped up the arms race by spending billions of dollars on new weapons. The Soviet Union tried to keep pace, but it had a weaker economy than the United States. The Soviet government spent so much money on weapons that it had trouble feeding its people. Little by little, hungry Soviets began to protest.

In 1985 the new Soviet leader, Mikhail Gorbachev, saw that it was time for a change. He allowed Russians to speak out against their government. He met with Ronald Reagan, and the two men developed a friendship. In 1987 they signed an agreement to reduce weapons.

No one realized it at the time, but this agreement marked the beginning of the end of the Cold War. With an arms deal in place, Gorbachev felt that Soviet military spending could be reduced. Gorbachev also pulled Soviet troops out of Eastern Europe, where people were beginning to demand change from their own communist governments. He pushed ahead with economic and political reforms that eventually led to the collapse of communism in Eastern Europe and the Soviet Union.

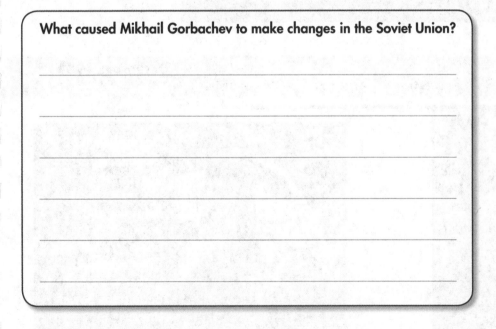

What caused Mikhail Gorbachev to make changes in the Soviet Union?

_____

_____

_____

_____

_____

Communism Ends in Europe

In December 1988, Mikhail Gorbachev stood before the United Nations to describe the "new world order" to come. Gorbachev said that people throughout the world wanted "independence, democracy, and social justice."

The end of the Cold War did not happen overnight. In 1980 a trade union called Solidarity had formed in Poland. It had worked underground for many years. In 1988 Solidarity held a massive strike that forced the government to meet its demands. In June 1989, Poland became the first country behind the iron curtain to hold a democratic election.

The call for democracy spread throughout Eastern Europe. Demonstrators filled the streets of major cities. As a result of public pressure and a relaxation of Soviet control, communist governments continued to topple. Throughout 1989 Gorbachev not only refused to stop the movement, but he encouraged it.

September 1989 Hungary becomes independent. East Germans are allowed to travel through Hungary to reach West Germany.

June 1989   September 1989   December 1989

November 1989 Protesters force the East German government to open the border between East and West Germany. The protesters tear down the Berlin Wall.

December 1989 Communist governments fall in Czechoslovakia, Bulgaria, and Romania. In this photo, crowds in Czechoslovakia gather to protest against the Soviet Union.

The Cold War came to a dramatic end in the German city of Berlin. For 28 years, the Berlin Wall had split the city in two. Communist East Berlin lay on one side, capitalist West Berlin on the other. By November 1989, huge protests forced the East German government to open the border. People on both sides attacked the wall with axes and sledgehammers. They shouted, "Germany is free and one."

More communist governments fell all across Eastern Europe. In 1991 the Soviet Union broke up into 15 independent countries. When George H. W. Bush became President in 1989, the end of the Cold War was in sight. It was time, he said confidently, to "move on into a new era."

> **Why did East Berlin and West Berlin unite?**
>
> _____
>
> _____

May 1990 Boris Yeltsin is elected President of Russia. By August 1991, the former Soviet Union divides into 15 independent countries.

March 1990 Lithuania becomes independent from the Soviet Union.

March 1990   June 1990   December 1990

October 1990 Germany is reunited. This photo shows the celebration in 2009, the 20-year anniversary of the fall of the Berlin Wall.

Bush and Clinton

Early in his term, President Bush dedicated himself to repairing the nation's economy. However, the United States was about to be drawn into a foreign conflict.

The Persian Gulf War

In 1990 Bush faced a major challenge in the Middle East. In August, Iraq invaded its neighbor, Kuwait, to seize oil fields along their shared border. President Bush acted carefully. He organized a **coalition** of 20 countries to force Iraq out of Kuwait. A coalition is a group formed for a common purpose.

Coalition forces began a massive bombing of Iraq in January 1991. Six weeks later, troops invaded Kuwait and Iraq. The fighting lasted just 100 hours. About 10,000 Iraqi soldiers and 200 coalition troops were killed.

On March 3, Iraq signed a cease-fire with the United States. Bush left Iraq's ruler Saddam Hussein in power.

Clinton Becomes President

Despite his success in Iraq, Bush lost the election of 1992. The economy was not doing well and voters wanted a change. They elected Democrat Bill Clinton from Arkansas.

One of Clinton's goals was to reduce the **budget deficit**. A budget deficit is the amount by which spending exceeds income. To do this, he raised taxes for middle and upper-income Americans. During the late 1990s, the economy boomed, and by the end of his term, the deficit was gone.

Clinton also continued peace efforts in the Middle East. In 1993 Clinton attended the signing of the Olso Accords. This agreement between the Palestinian people and Israel established the Palestinian National Authority. The Palestinian National Authority now governed the land under Palestinian control in the Gaza Strip and the West Bank.

Clinton's second term in office was ruined by scandal. He was accused of lying under oath and impeached by the House. The Senate voted to let him stay in office. Clinton was only the second President in history to be impeached.

▼ Bill Clinton

The attacks of September 11, 2001, were carried out by a terrorist group called al-Qaeda. Al-Qaeda was created in 1988 by Osama bin Laden, a wealthy Saudi Arabian, to aid Muslims fighting Soviet troops in Afghanistan. In 1979 the Soviet Union had invaded Afghanistan. The Soviet retreat in 1989 convinced bin Laden that superpowers could be beaten. Al-Qaeda wanted to drive all outsiders from Muslim nations, to destroy Israel, and to unite all Muslims under a strict form of Islam.

Angry that the United States had bases in Saudi Arabia, bin Laden made plans to attack the United States. Bin Laden was helped by the Taliban, a group of radical Muslims that controlled Afghanistan. The Taliban allowed him to use their country to train men and plan attacks.

In 1998 al-Qaeda exploded truck bombs outside American embassies in the African countries of Kenya and Tanzania. More than 200 people died in these two attacks. In 2000 al-Qaeda attacked a U.S. warship, the Cole, near the nation of Yemen. Seventeen American sailors were killed.

Elevated view of firefighters at the Pentagon following the terrorist attack of September 11, 2001

Tech. Sgt. Cedric H. Rudisill/DoD

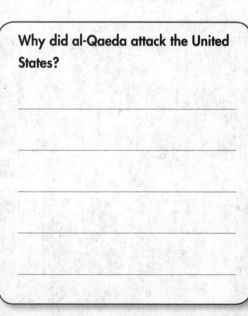

Why did al-Qaeda attack the United States?

_____

_____

_____

_____

_____

The War Begins

President Bush believed that it would take more than just military power to fight terrorism. He and Congress worked together to pass several new laws to protect Americans.

Protecting Americans

With the support of Congress, in November 2002, President Bush created the Department of Homeland Security (DHS). This new department has the job of protecting Americans at home. DHS has over 200,000 employees and is in charge of all agencies responsible for the public's safety. DHS has taken many actions to keep America safe. One of these actions was to increase security at airports around the country.

Shortly after the September 11 terrorist attacks, President Bush issued an order to freeze the money of suspected terrorists. Several other nations issued similar orders.

Congress also passed the Patriot Act. This law gave more power to law enforcement agencies to tap phones, track Internet usage, and search the homes of suspected terrorists. Both houses of Congress passed the bill overwhelmingly.

1. How did the September 11 attacks affect the government?

_____

2. How did they affect the life of a typical American citizen?

_____

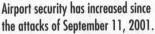

Airport security has increased since the attacks of September 11, 2001.

©H. Mark Weidman Photography/Alamy Stock Photo

Some critics were concerned that people in power could use the Patriot Act against innocent people and organizations. For this reason, the Office for Civil Liberties and Civil Rights was created to listen to these concerns of the American people.

The Afghanistan War

President George W. Bush vowed to find the terrorists who planned the September 11 attacks and defeat them. The President told the Taliban to hand over bin Laden and al-Qaeda members in Afghanistan. When they refused, he sent troops to that country to fight both al-Qaeda and the Taliban. In a speech to Congress, President Bush said:

> "Our war on terrorism begins with al-Qaeda, but it does not end there. It will not end until every terrorist group of global reach has been found, stopped, and defeated."

The United States and its allies formed a coalition to defeat the Taliban. American and allied troops quickly drove the Taliban from power. They also closed down al-Qaeda bases. However, they failed to capture bin Laden.

The United States and its allies worked with Afghan leaders to create a new government. They have also worked to improve the lives of many Afghan people.

Although the Taliban was forced out of power, it did not go away. Taliban leaders vowed to take back control of Afghanistan. By 2009, they had regained control of some parts of the country, particularly in the mountains of southern Afghanistan.

What caused the creation of the Department of Homeland Security?

_____

_____

▲ New recruits of the Afghan National Army line up to receive an issue of new uniforms and equipment.

Southwest Asia

DoD photo by Sgt. Kevin P. Bell, U.S. Army.

Map and Globe Skills

What countries share a boundary with Afghanistan?

_____

_____

DoD photo by Airman 1st Class Kurt Gibbons III, U.S. Air Force

U.S. and Iraqi soldiers fighting in Iraq.

The Iraq War

President Bush was also concerned that weapons of mass destruction, such as nuclear bombs or chemical or **biological weapons** could fall into the hands of terrorists. Biological weapons can spread disease on a large scale. These weapons could kill tens of thousands of people at once.

Road to War

Saddam Hussein was the dictator of Iraq. A dictator is a person with complete power over a country. Hussein was known to have chemical weapons—and to have used them in the past.

Late in 2002, the United States joined the UN in warning Iraq that it had to agree to inspections looking for these deadly weapons. The U.S. Congress voted to authorize the President to use force if Iraq did not cooperate. Early the next year, Bush declared that the time for waiting had ended. He gave Hussein two days to leave the country or fight.

On March 20, 2003, the United States and several of its allies attacked Iraq. Many Americans and others around the world argued about whether or not Iraq should have been invaded. Nevertheless, the war was on.

Ending Hussein's Rule

American troops and their allies quickly moved into Iraq. Within days, they had captured Baghdad, the capital. Hussein was later captured and executed. United States and coalition forces helped the Iraqi people create a new government by holding free elections for the first time. Some American soldiers fanned out to find Hussein's weapons of mass destruction, but none were found.

Iraqis Fighting Iraqis

Iraq has two major groups of people, called Sunnis and Shias. Though both are Muslims, they hold different views about some beliefs of Islam. The Shias are the majority, but the Sunnis have usually held power in the country. Conflict between these two groups followed the defeat of Hussein's government. Some Iraqis were happy to see the dictator gone.

Others did not like foreign troops on Iraqi soil. Some terrorists attacked American troops and other officials in the new Iraq government. Shias sometimes attacked Sunnis, whom they blamed for these attacks. For several years, the fighting was intense.

The Wars Continue

By 2008 American troops and the new Iraqi government had managed to bring more order to the country. The number of attacks against Iraqi and American troops steadily decreased.

In 2010 the war in Afghanistan continued to rage on. There were still tens of thousands of American troops in Iraq and Afghanistan. By 2010, over 5,000 Americans had lost their lives in the fighting in the two countries.

> Why did the fall of Saddam Hussein's government not lead to peace in Iraq?
>
> _____
>
> _____

Lesson 4

? Essential Question How have modern conflicts changed society?

_____

_____

Go back to *Show As You Go!* on page 206–207.

networks There's More Online!
• Games • Assessment

Government and Economy Today

? Essential Question

How do changes in government and the economy affect society?

What do you think?

_____

_____

_____

_____

_____

_____

_____

Words To Know

Write the definition of each word in your own words.

interdependent

_____

globalization

_____

offshoring

_____

recession

_____

The President lives and works at the White House in Washington, D.C.

Digital Vision/Getty Images

The Government Today

The First Amendment guaranteed that the government could not take away the rights to freedom of speech, press, assembly, petition, and religion. This allowed individual, ethnic, and cultural diversity not only to exist, but also to grow.

Since the civil and women's rights movements of the 1960s, the number of women and minorities has increased in every area of our government. Over 58 percent of federal workers are women. Over 32 percent are minorities.

Diversity in Government

In 2009 there were 17 senators and 74 members of the House of Representatives who were female. There were also 19 minorities in the Senate and 113 in the House that year.

When Barack Obama was elected in 2008, he became the first African American President in U.S. history. He received 365 electoral votes, compared to 173 for Senator John McCain. Obama had a close primary battle with Senator Hillary Clinton for the Democratic nomination. He later appointed her Secretary of State.

President Obama was sworn into office on January 20, 2009. At that time, our nation was fighting two wars. The nation's economy was troubled and unemployment was high. He said:

"Today I say to you that the challenges we face are real. They are serious and they are many. They will not be met easily or in a short span of time. But know this America: They will be met."

Why are there more women and minorities in government today than in the 1960s?

_____

_____

_____

_____

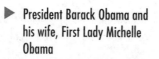

► President Barack Obama and his wife, First Lady Michelle Obama

Aaron Roeth Photography

The Global Economy

More than ever before, countries today are **interdependent**, or connected. This means that countries rely on each other to meet the needs and wants of their people. To meet these needs and wants, businesses use voluntary exchange. Voluntary exchange allows buyers and sellers to exercise their economic freedom by working out their own terms of exchange.

Trade

The basic problem in economics is scarcity. People do not have enough resources to meet all their wants and needs. The same is true of nations. No nation has all of the resources it needs. Trade is one way that nations solve this problem of scarcity.

Nations trade for some goods and services because they would not have them otherwise. For example, the United States buys coffee and bananas from other countries because it does not have the right soil and climate to grow enough of these foods to meet demand. The United States buys industrial diamonds from other countries because it has no deposits of these minerals.

In the same way, other nations buy goods from the United States that they cannot produce themselves. Commercial aircraft built in Washington state are sold to other countries that do not have the factories or the skilled workers needed to build these planes. This kind of specialization improves the lives of people that produce these goods.

©PhotoLink/Photodisc/Getty Images

◀ Globalization has led to an increase in trade for the United States and the rest of the world.

Globalization

In today's economy, companies usually go beyond national boundaries when they buy and sell goods and services. This trend is called **globalization**. Globalization has both lowered prices for consumers and opened new markets for American products.

However, to produce goods and services cheaply, American businesses sometimes move some operations to other countries that have the resources or technology to make products or provide services at a lower cost. This movement of businesses to other countries is called **offshoring**.

Offshoring can lead to a loss of local jobs. However, businesses and consumers benefit from goods that are produced more cheaply in other countries. In return, other countries benefit from goods that are made more cheaply in the United States.

Trade Agreements

Many countries place taxes on trade called tariffs. In order to eliminate tariffs, many parts of the world have signed regional trade agreements. In 1993 three nations—the United States, Canada, and Mexico—signed the North American Free Trade Agreement (NAFTA). NAFTA promised to remove tariffs on goods brought into each country.

Some argue that NAFTA has led to a loss of American jobs. Still, the agreement has increased trade. Today, the United States and Canada are each others' largest trading partners. Mexico is the second-largest trading partner for the United States.

In 2005 the United States and five Central American countries signed the Central American Free Trade Agreement (CAFTA) to increase trade in the region. Certain nations in Southeast Asia also have regional free trade agreements.

Trade with Canada and Mexico

The bar graph shows U.S. exports and imports of goods with Canada. The line graph shows exports and imports of goods with Mexico. Study the graphs. Then answer the questions below.

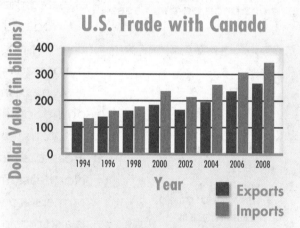

1. What was the value of United States exports to Mexico in 2008?

_____

2. With which country does the United States trade more goods, Canada or Mexico?

_____

The Economy Today

Just like the government, the general workforce has also become more diverse. More women and minorities have become lawyers, doctors, and executives than ever before.

A Diverse Economy

The United States has the largest and most diverse economy in the world. Since the 1900s, our economy has changed and expanded. Factors such as population, transportation, and resources have affected these changes.

Today, the South has expanding cities, growing industries, and diverse populations. The South is also a technology center and a major trading partner with Latin America. With a long history of growing cash crops, agricultural products are still an important piece of the South's economy.

With few mineral resources and poor soil for farming in many areas, the Northeast has long focused on business. Unlike the Northeast, the Midwest has plenty of fertile, or rich, soil. Midwestern farmers grow corn, wheat, soybeans, and other crops. The Midwest is also rich in mineral resources, making the cities there centers of manufacturing.

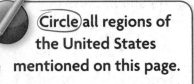

Circle all regions of the United States mentioned on this page.

▼ The South has growing industries, such as textiles, computers, and airplane parts.

▼ The transportation systems of the Northeast move its large population quickly and easily.

◀ Farmers raise fruits and vegetables in the fertile valleys of the West.

The West and Southwest also have expanding cities. Some are centers for technology. Others are centers for trade with Asia. Fish, timber, and mineral resources are also important in the West. The Interior West has growing information technology industries.

Economic Crisis

Our economy sometimes goes through periods of low economic growth. The economic crisis of 2008 started with the collapse of the housing market in 2007. Banks had made risky home loans at a time when home prices turned downward. Banks suffered huge losses, and many had to close.

By the end of 2008, a deep **recession** gripped the nation and the world. A recession is a period of no economic growth for at least six straight months, a general slowing of economic activity, and high unemployment.

By 2009, people who still had jobs worried that they might lose them, so they began saving money. They put more money in checking and savings accounts than in previous years. Many Americans did this by making a personal budget, or a plan for using money for a specific purpose. Personal budgets list the items that are paid each month. They show you how much, and on what, you spend your money. This important tool shows where spending and saving changes can be made.

▲ Many families keep their money in savings or checking accounts.

What effect can a personal budget have on your spending?

_____

_____

Lesson 5

? **Essential Question** **How do changes in government and the economy affect society?**

_____

_____

_____

Go back to *Show As You Go!* on page 206–207.

netw⊙rks **There's More Online!**
● Games ● Assessment

Technology Today

How does technology change society?
What do you think?

_____

_____

_____

_____

_____

_____

_____

Words To Know

Rank the words (1–5) to show how well you understand each term.

_____ **microchip**

_____ **Internet**

_____ **biotechnology**

_____ **nanotechnology**

The International Space Station was launched into orbit in 1998.

©Brand X Pictures/PunchStock

The Personal Computer

The development of the modern computer began in 1946. The first computer weighed over 30 tons and was the size of a small house.

A few years later, in 1959, Robert Noyce designed the first integrated circuit, or **microchip**, on a single chip of silicon. A microchip is a tiny computer part that processes information quickly. The microchip made it possible to build smaller and more powerful computers. Soon, new companies began using microchips. Many were located near Noyce's office in Northern California, and the region became known as Silicon Valley.

The Personal Computer

One of the pioneers in the industry was Bill Gates. His company creates software, or programs that tell computers what to do. Software allows people to do many different things with computers. By 2010, about 80 percent of American households had at least one computer.

Personal computers are now being used in homes, schools, and businesses more than ever before. Some are small enough to fit on your lap or even in your hand.

The Internet

The development of the **Internet**, a system of computer networks, created new uses for computers. People are now able to communicate online with e-mail, social networks, or instant messaging (IM). They find and share information, shop, listen to music, watch movies, play games, and much more.

Laptop computers offer wireless access to the Internet. Cell phones are powerful tools as well. They let friends chat from almost anywhere. Many cell phones can also receive e-mail and connect to the Internet. Americans and people around the world can now work and learn from almost any location.

> **What effect did the microchip have on computers?**
>
> _____
>
> _____

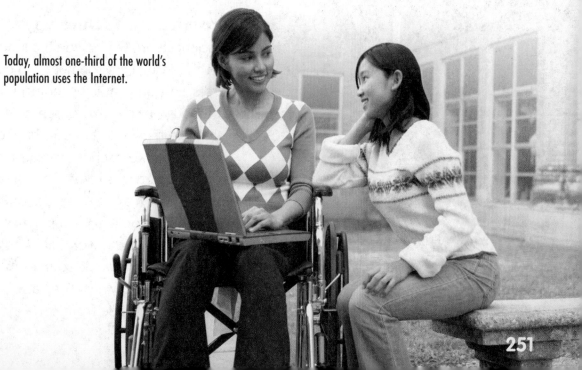

▶ Today, almost one-third of the world's population uses the Internet.

Jack Hollingsworth/Photodisc/Getty Images

Modern Technology

Technology is constantly growing to meet the needs of people. It has made people and businesses more productive. Technology has improved the health of millions of people and has allowed many to live longer lives. It also helps people use clean sources of energy, protecting the Earth.

Business Productivity

Throughout history, technology has helped companies make better and less-expensive products. Businesses are more productive and make a profit more easily when they use technology. For example, you learned earlier how assembly lines made cars cheaper.

Today, computers and the Internet greatly help people working in business and manufacturing. Tasks that once took many people can now be done by one person—with greater speed and accuracy.

Modern communication technology has also helped businesses. Companies today use computers to hold meetings. People can see and talk to each other even if they are continents apart. People can even work on the same product or document at the same time from different locations.

▼ A scientist working in a water treatment laboratory

Biotechnology

Computers have greatly helped scientists in the field of **biotechnology**, or the study of cells, to find ways of improving health in living things. Through biotechnology, researchers have developed new medicines that fight disease and improve people's health. Biotechnology has also been used to make plants and farm animals grow better.

Environmental Technology

Many scientists are working on technologies that will protect the natural environment and conserve its resources. Environmental technologies are products and methods which allow consumers and businesses to decrease the impact that people have on the environment.

One of the most serious threats to our environment is pollution. Pollution is something—such as harmful chemicals—that makes our air, soil, and water dirty. These chemicals often come from burning coal, oil, or natural gas.

People around the world are finding ways to use more clean and renewable sources of energy. These include sunlight and wind. They also include fuels such as ethanol, which is made from corn and other renewable

Modern wind farms use the force of wind to generate activity.

products. One of the most common sources of renewable energy is hydroelectricity. Hydroelectricity is energy made from the movement of water in rivers and oceans.

The fastest growing use of renewable energy is solar energy, or energy made from sunlight. Flat plates called solar panels collect energy from the sun and turn it into electricity. The sun can make over 10,000 times the energy that people currently use.

Scientists will continue to search for more clean, renewable energy sources and uses. Some technologies may produce renewable energy from waste materials. Others will make electric automobiles faster and cheaper.

The Future

No one knows exactly what technologies the future holds. You and your classmates live in a world where technology touches your daily lives. By learning about new technologies, you will be ready for the changes of tomorrow.

> **How has technology affected business production?**
>
> _____
>
> _____

Nanotechnology

One new technology that is already changing our lives is **nanotechnology**. This technology uses atoms—the tiniest parts of matter—to make structures that are about a million times smaller than the head of a pin. Such small structures do amazing things.

Nanotechnolgy is already used today. Putting "nanowhiskers" on fabric helps keep some clothes from getting stained. Soon, paint may be able to change color on command or video wallpaper could replace televisions.

Using nanotechnology, scientists hope to build tiny machines that can enter the body and repair damaged organs. Nanotechnology could also protect troops with lightweight bulletproof uniforms and sensors that can spy on the enemy and detect chemical weapons.

Companies continue to look for ways to apply new technologies. Whatever form new technologies take, they will change our lives.

A nanotechnology probe attacking a cancer cell.

Coney Jay/Stone/Getty Images

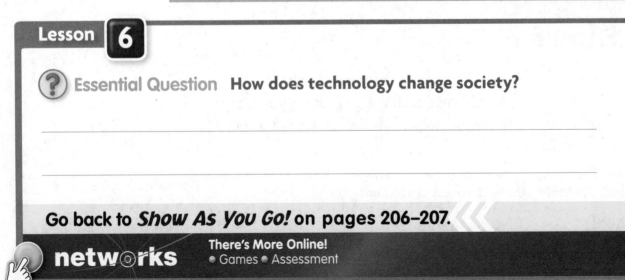

Lesson 6

(?) **Essential Question**   **How does technology change society?**

_____

_____

Go back to *Show As You Go!* on pages 206–207. «

networks   There's More Online!
● Games ● Assessment

Map and Globe Skill

Use GPS

New technologies are helping **geographers,** or people who study geography, make better maps. One system they use to make maps is the **Global Positioning System** (GPS). GPS uses radio signals from satellites to determine the exact location of places on Earth. GPS was originally used by the U.S. military for navigation, map-making, and guiding missiles. Today, many people use GPS devices instead of traditional maps when hiking. Others have a GPS device installed in their car to help them find their way while they are traveling.

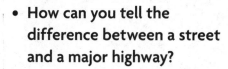 TRY IT

- How would this GPS device help you decide where to cross the river on the map?

_____

- How can you tell the difference between a street and a major highway?

_____

APPLY IT

- Imagine that you are going on a vacation across the country. How might a GPS device be useful when going on vacation?

_____

_____

LEARN IT

- Look at the image. You will notice that it shows different streets and where they intersect.

- Some GPS devices provide street names. Some even give audio directions as you approach your destination.

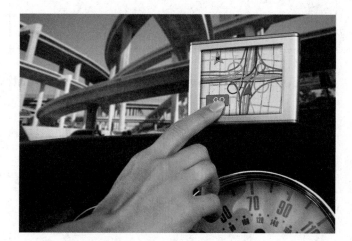

Write the word next to the sentence that best matches the description.

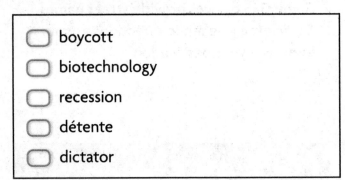

- ⬭ boycott
- ⬭ biotechnology
- ⬭ recession
- ⬭ détente
- ⬭ dictator

1. A person with complete power over a country.

   _____

2. The study of cells to find ways of improving health.

   _____

3. To refuse to do business or have contact with a person, group, company, country, or product.

   _____

4. A period of no economic growth for at least six straight months, a general slowing of economic activity, and high unemployment.

   _____

5. An easing of tension between nations.

   _____

Unit Project

Work with a partner to present a newscast. You and
your partner will be co-anchors of a nightly news
program. Use the internet to research a current
news topic. Before you begin working, look back at
Show As You Go! to review your notes. Also, read
the list below to see what information should be
included in your newscast. As you work, check off
each item as you include it.

Your newscast should...

be based on your research about a current news topic.

be presented and shared with your partner.

include both facts about the topic and an editorial expressing
an opinon about the topic.

be presented like a news anchor.

Think about the Big Idea

BIG IDEA Culture influences the way people live.

What did you learn in this unit that helps you understand the BIG IDEA?

_____

_____

_____

Read the passage "Surprise Attack!" before answering numbers 1 through 6.

Surprise Attack!

December 7, 1941, was a peaceful Sunday in Hawaii. The American naval base was quiet in the soft morning sunshine. Suddenly, the peace was shattered as Japan launched a surprise air attack on the base. The attack destroyed 19 ships, smashed 188 planes on the ground, and killed more than 2,000 people.

1 This passage tells about the surprise attack at

Ⓐ D-Day.

Ⓑ Pearl Harbor.

Ⓒ Stalingrad.

Ⓓ Midway.

2 Which of the following countries was a member of NATO?

Ⓕ Poland

Ⓖ China

Ⓗ France

Ⓘ Soviet Union

3 People had to decide what to buy as they rationed goods during World War II. What is the value of the second- best choice when choosing to buy something?

Ⓐ opportunity cost

Ⓑ price incentive

Ⓒ specializaiton

Ⓓ voluntary exchange

4 Between 1950 and 1954 many suspected communists were called before Senator Joseph McCarthy's Senate committee. The massive search for communists living in the United States was called the

   Ⓕ Fair Deal.

   Ⓖ Red Scare.

   Ⓗ Marshall Plan.

   Ⓘ Eisenhower Years.

5 What was the year of the attack?

   Ⓐ 1941

   Ⓑ 1940

   Ⓒ 1942

   Ⓓ 1939

6 Who attached Hawaii?

   Ⓕ Russia

   Ⓖ France

   Ⓗ Japan

   Ⓘ China

Reference Section

Geography and You

Geography is the study of Earth and the people, plants, and animals that live on it. Most people think of geography as learning about cities, states, and countries, but geography is far more. Geography includes learning about land, such as mountains and plains, and bodies of water, such as oceans, lakes, and rivers.

Geography includes the study of how people adapt to living in a new place. Geography is also about how people move around, how they move goods, and how ideas travel from place to place.

Dictionary of Geographic Terms

1. **BAY** Body of water partly surrounded by land
2. **BEACH** Land covered with sand or pebbles next to an ocean or lake
3. **CANAL** Waterway dug across the land to connect two bodies of water
4. **CANYON** Deep river valley with steep sides
5. **CLIFF** High steep face of rock
6. **COAST** Land next to an ocean

7. **DESERT** A dry environment with few plants and animals
8. **GULF** Body of water partly surrounded by land; larger than a bay
9. **HARBOR** Protected place by an ocean or river where ships can safely stay
10. **HILL** Rounded, raised landform; not as high as a mountain
11. **ISLAND** Land that is surrounded on all sides by water

12 **LAKE** Body of water completely surrounded by land

13 **MESA** Landform that looks like a high, flat table

14 **MOUNTAIN** High landform with steep sides; higher than a hill

15 **OCEAN** Large body of salt water

16 **PENINSULA** Land that has water on all sides but one

17 **PLAIN** Large area of flat land

18 **PLATEAU** High flat area that rises steeply above the surrounding land

19 **PORT** Place where ships load and unload goods

20 **RIVER** Long stream of water that empties into another body of water

21 **VALLEY** Area of low land between hills or mountains

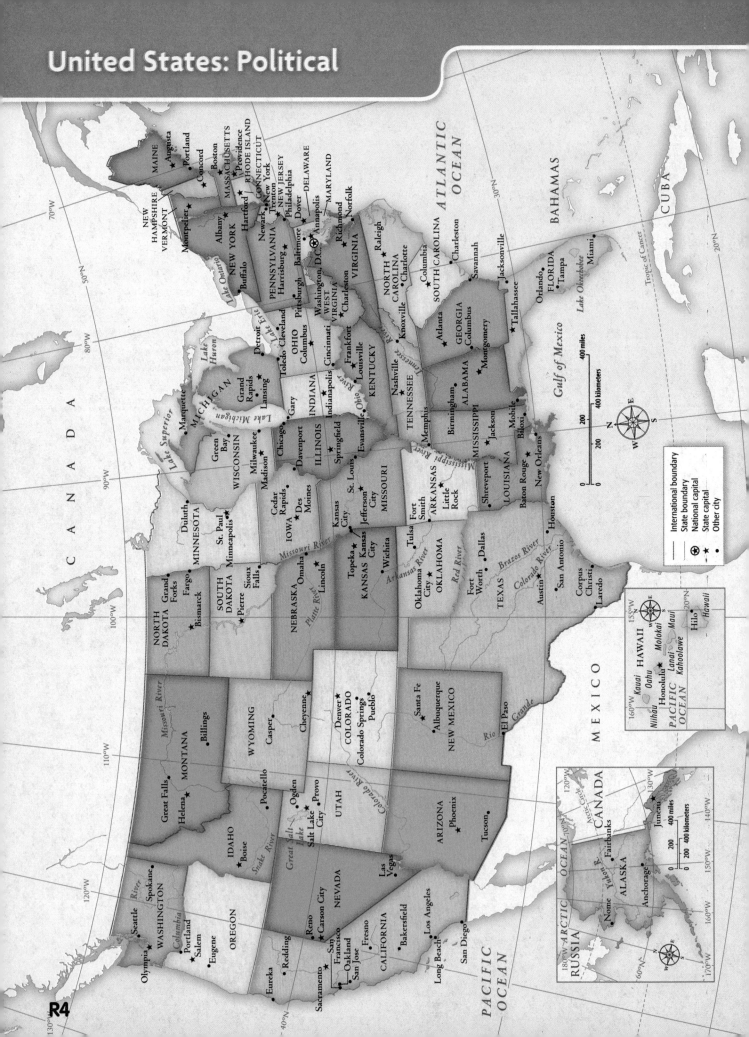

CANADA

MAINE
Augusta ★
Portland ●
Concord ★
NEW HAMPSHIRE
VERMONT
Montpelier ★
Albany ★
NEW YORK
Buffalo ●
MASSACHUSETTS
Boston ★
Providence ★
RHODE ISLAND
Hartford ★
CONNECTICUT
New York ●
Newark ●
NEW JERSEY
Trenton ★
Philadelphia ●
Dover ★
DELAWARE
MARYLAND
Baltimore ●
Annapolis ★
Washington, D.C. ⊛
Richmond ★
Norfolk ●
VIRGINIA
Raleigh ★
NORTH CAROLINA
Charlotte ●
Columbia ★
SOUTH CAROLINA
Charleston ●
Savannah ●
Jacksonville ●
ATLANTIC OCEAN
BAHAMAS
CUBA
Tropic of Cancer

PENNSYLVANIA
Harrisburg ★
Pittsburgh ●
WEST VIRGINIA
Charleston ★
Lake Ontario
Lake Erie
Detroit ●
Cleveland ●
Toledo ●
OHIO
Columbus ★
Cincinnati ●
Frankfort ★
Louisville ●
Knoxville ●
VIRGINIA

Lake Superior
Lake Huron
Marquette ●
MICHIGAN
Grand Rapids ●
Lansing ★
Lake Michigan
Green Bay ●
WISCONSIN
Milwaukee ●
Madison ★
Chicago ●
Gary ●
INDIANA
Indianapolis ★
Springfield ★
ILLINOIS
Evansville ●
Ohio River
KENTUCKY
Nashville ★
TENNESSEE
Memphis ●
Tennessee River
Atlanta ★
GEORGIA
Columbus ●
Montgomery ★
ALABAMA
Birmingham ●
Tallahassee ★
FLORIDA
Orlando ●
Tampa ●
Lake Okeechobee
Miami ●

Duluth ●
MINNESOTA
St. Paul ★
Minneapolis ●
IOWA
Cedar Rapids ●
Des Moines ★
Davenport ●
St. Louis ●
MISSOURI
Jefferson City ★
Kansas City ●
Fort Smith ●
ARKANSAS
Little Rock ★
Shreveport ●
MISSISSIPPI
Jackson ★
LOUISIANA
Baton Rouge ★
Mobile ●
Biloxi ●
New Orleans ●
Gulf of Mexico

NORTH DAKOTA
Grand Forks ●
Fargo ●
Bismarck ★
SOUTH DAKOTA
Pierre ★
Sioux Falls ●
NEBRASKA
Omaha ●
Lincoln ★
Platte River
Missouri River
KANSAS
Topeka ★
Kansas City ●
Wichita ●
OKLAHOMA
Tulsa ●
Oklahoma City ★
Arkansas River
Red River
Fort Worth ●
Dallas ●
TEXAS
Brazos River
Houston ●
San Antonio ●
Austin ★
Corpus Christi ●
Laredo ●
Colorado River
Mississippi River

MONTANA
Great Falls ●
Helena ★
Billings ●
WYOMING
Cheyenne ★
Casper ●
Denver ★
COLORADO
Colorado Springs ●
Pueblo ●
Santa Fe ★
Albuquerque ●
NEW MEXICO
El Paso ●
Rio Grande
MEXICO

IDAHO
Boise ★
Pocatello ●
Snake River
UTAH
Salt Lake City ★
Ogden ●
Provo ●
Great Salt Lake
Colorado River
ARIZONA
Phoenix ★
Tucson ●
NEVADA
Carson City ★
Reno ●
Las Vegas ●

WASHINGTON
Seattle ●
Spokane ●
Olympia ★
Columbia River
OREGON
Portland ●
Salem ★
Eugene ●
Redding ●
Eureka ●
CALIFORNIA
Sacramento ★
San Francisco ●
Oakland ●
San Jose ●
Fresno ●
Bakersfield ●
Los Angeles ●
Long Beach ●
San Diego ●
Las Vegas ●
PACIFIC OCEAN

N
400 miles
400 kilometers
200
200

Legend
International boundary
State boundary
⊛ National capital
★ State capital
● Other city

HAWAII
Kauai
Oahu
Niihau
Honolulu ★
Molokai
Lanai
Maui
Kahoolawe
Hilo ●
Hawaii
PACIFIC OCEAN

ARCTIC OCEAN
RUSSIA
Arctic Circle
CANADA
ALASKA
Nome ●
Fairbanks ●
Yukon R.
Anchorage ●
Juneau ★
400 miles
400 kilometers
200

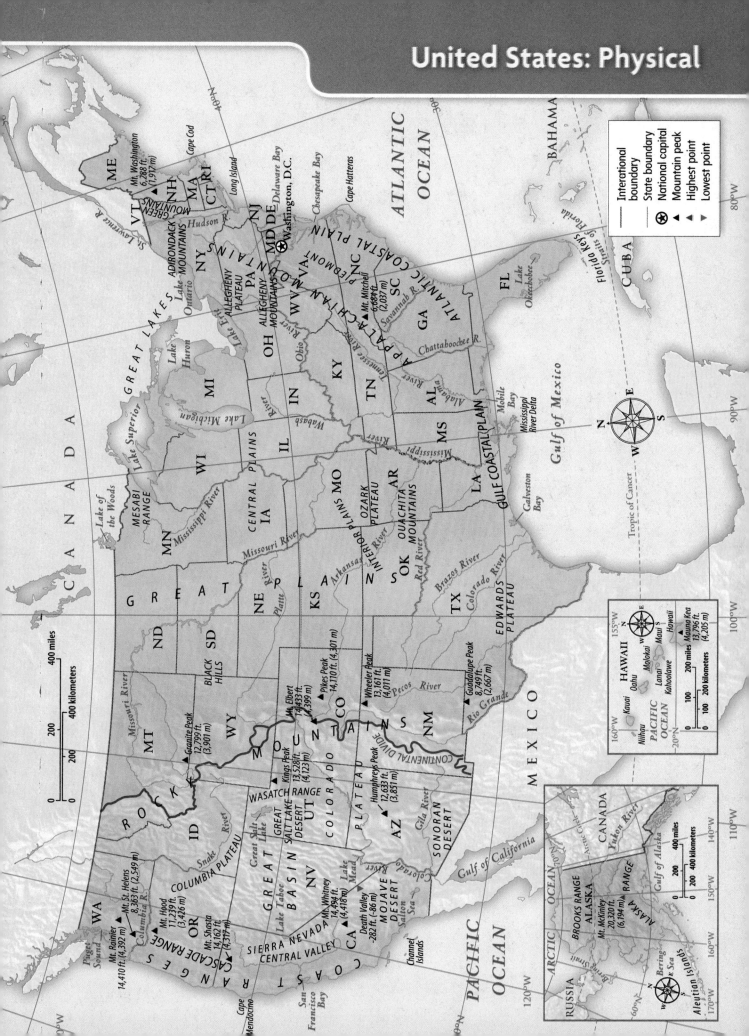

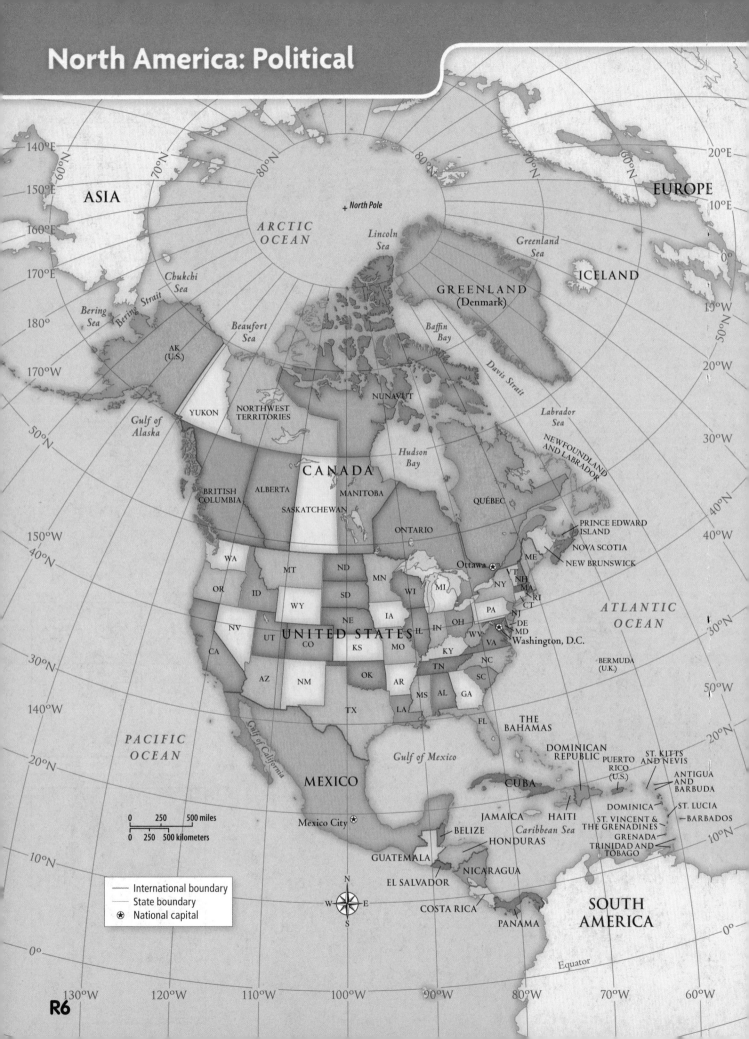

North America: Political

ASIA

ARCTIC
OCEAN

+ North Pole

Lincoln
Sea

Greenland
Sea

EUROPE

ICELAND

GREENLAND
(Denmark)

Baffin
Bay

Chukchi
Sea

Bering
Sea

Bering Strait

Beaufort
Sea

AK
(U.S.)

Davis Strait

NUNAVUT

Labrador
Sea

YUKON

Gulf of
Alaska

NORTHWEST
TERRITORIES

NEWFOUNDLAND
AND LABRADOR

Hudson
Bay

CANADA

QUÉBEC

BRITISH
COLUMBIA

ALBERTA

MANITOBA

SASKATCHEWAN

ONTARIO

PRINCE EDWARD
ISLAND

NOVA SCOTIA

NEW BRUNSWICK

WA

MT

ND

MN

Ottawa ✪

ME

VT
NH
MA
RI
CT

ATLANTIC
OCEAN

OR

ID

SD

WI

MI

NY

OR

WY

NE

IA

PA

NJ
DE
MD

NV

IL

IN

OH

WV

UT

UNITED STATES

CO

KS

MO

VA

Washington, D.C. ✪

CA

KY

BERMUDA
(U.K.)

AZ

NM

OK

AR

TN

NC

SC

MS

AL

GA

TX

LA

FL

THE
BAHAMAS

PACIFIC
OCEAN

Gulf of California

Gulf of Mexico

MEXICO

DOMINICAN
REPUBLIC

PUERTO
RICO
(U.S.)

ST. KITTS
AND NEVIS

ANTIGUA
AND
BARBUDA

CUBA

DOMINICA

ST. LUCIA

Mexico City ✪

JAMAICA

HAITI

Caribbean Sea

ST. VINCENT &
THE GRENADINES

BARBADOS

BELIZE

HONDURAS

GRENADA

TRINIDAD AND
TOBAGO

GUATEMALA

NICARAGUA

EL SALVADOR

SOUTH
AMERICA

COSTA RICA

PANAMA

Equator

0   250   500 miles
0   250   500 kilometers

N
W   E
S

International boundary
State boundary
✪ National capital

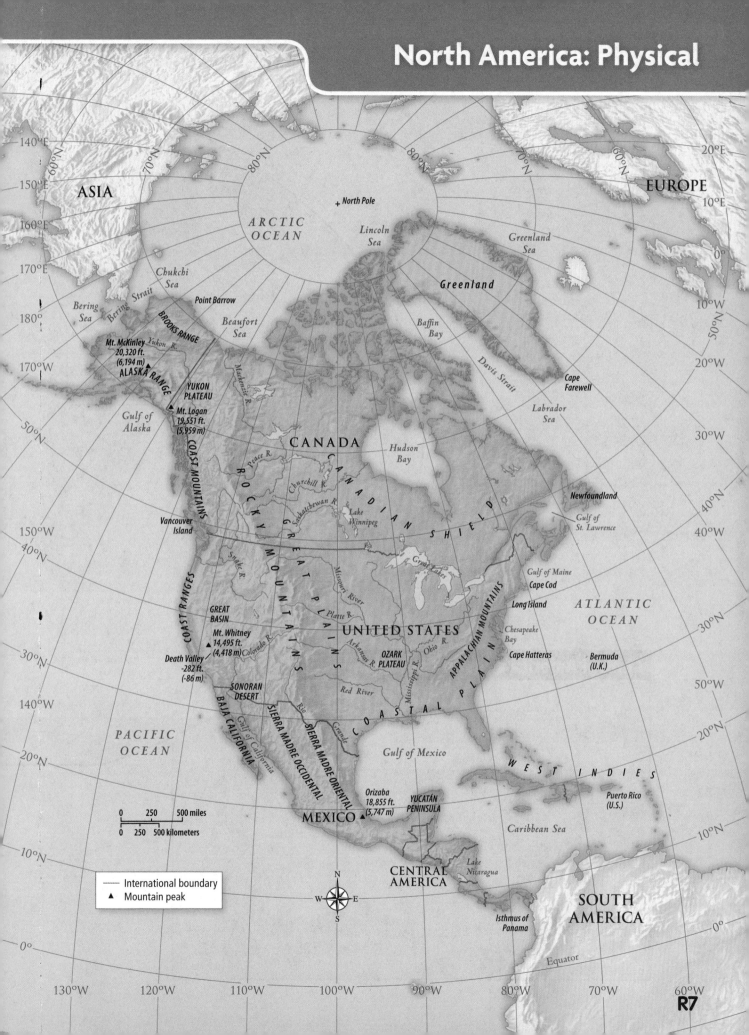

ASIA

EUROPE

ARCTIC
OCEAN

+ North Pole

Lincoln
Sea

Greenland
Sea

Chukchi
Sea

Point Barrow

Greenland

Bering
Sea

Bering Strait

Beaufort
Sea

Baffin
Bay

BROOKS RANGE

Yukon R.

Mt. McKinley
20,320 ft.
(6,194 m)

ALASKA RANGE

YUKON
PLATEAU

Mackenzie R.

Davis Strait

Cape
Farewell

Mt. Logan
19,551 ft.
(5,959 m)

Gulf of
Alaska

CANADA

Hudson
Bay

Labrador
Sea

Peace R.

COAST MOUNTAINS

Churchill R.

ROCKY

Saskatchewan R.

Lake
Winnipeg

Vancouver
Island

CANADIAN

SHIELD

Newfoundland

Gulf of
St. Lawrence

Snake R.

GREAT

MOUNTAINS

PLAINS

Missouri
River

Great Lakes

COAST RANGES

Gulf of Maine

Cape Cod

GREAT
BASIN

Platte R.

UNITED STATES

Long Island

ATLANTIC
OCEAN

Mt. Whitney
14,495 ft.
(4,418 m)

Colorado R.

Arkansas R.

OZARK
PLATEAU

Ohio R.

APPALACHIAN MOUNTAINS

Chesapeake
Bay

Death Valley
-282 ft.
(-86 m)

Cape Hatteras

Bermuda
(U.K.)

SONORAN
DESERT

Rio Grande

COASTAL

Red River

Mississippi R.

PLAIN

PACIFIC
OCEAN

SIERRA MADRE OCCIDENTAL

SIERRA MADRE ORIENTAL

BAJA CALIFORNIA

Gulf of California

Gulf of Mexico

W E S T   I N D I E S

0   250   500 miles

0   250   500 kilometers

Orizaba
18,855 ft.
(5,747 m)

YUCATÁN
PENINSULA

Puerto Rico
(U.S.)

MEXICO

Caribbean Sea

International boundary

▲ Mountain peak

CENTRAL
AMERICA

Lake
Nicaragua

SOUTH
AMERICA

N

W   E

S

Isthmus of
Panama

Equator

140°E 150°E 160°E 170°E 180° 170°W 150°W 140°W 130°W 120°W 110°W 100°W 90°W 80°W 70°W 60°W

60°N 70°N 80°N 80°N 70°N 60°N 50°N 40°N 30°N 20°N 10°N 0°

20°E 10°E 0° 10°W 20°W 30°W 40°W 50°W

World: Political

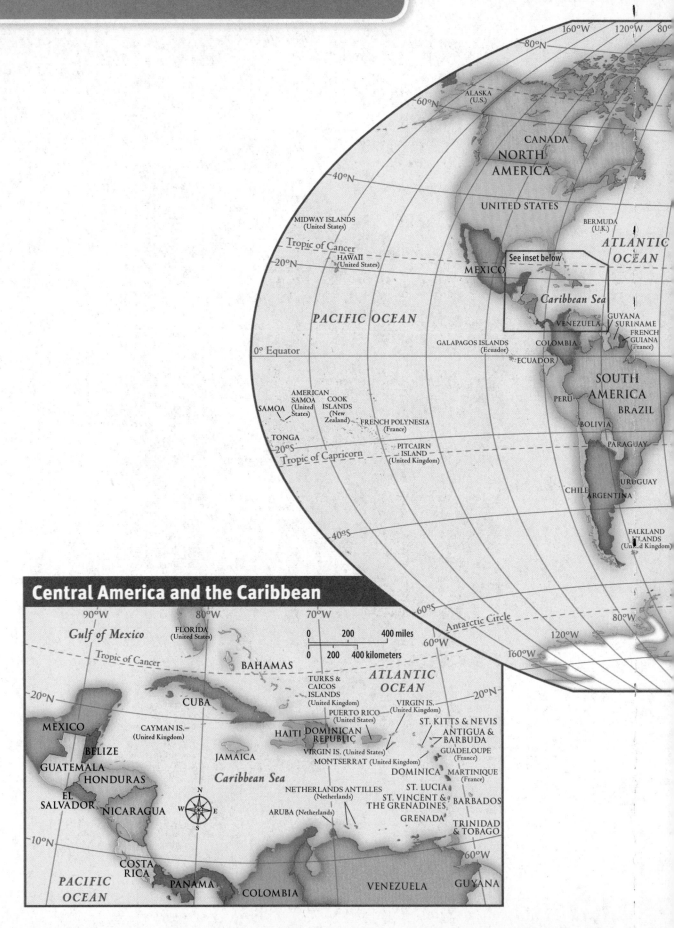

ALASKA (U.S.)

CANADA

NORTH AMERICA

UNITED STATES

BERMUDA (U.K.)

ATLANTIC OCEAN

MIDWAY ISLANDS (United States)

See inset below

Tropic of Cancer

HAWAII (United States)

MEXICO

Caribbean Sea

GUYANA
SURINAME
FRENCH GUIANA (France)

VENEZUELA

PACIFIC OCEAN

GALAPAGOS ISLANDS (Ecuador)

COLOMBIA

ECUADOR

0° Equator

SOUTH AMERICA

PERU

BRAZIL

AMERICAN SAMOA (United States)

COOK ISLANDS (New Zealand)

FRENCH POLYNESIA (France)

BOLIVIA

SAMOA

PARAGUAY

TONGA

PITCAIRN ISLAND (United Kingdom)

Tropic of Capricorn

URUGUAY

CHILE
ARGENTINA

FALKLAND ISLANDS (United Kingdom)

Antarctic Circle

Central America and the Caribbean

90°W

Gulf of Mexico

FLORIDA (United States)

80°W

70°W

0   200   400 miles
0   200   400 kilometers

Tropic of Cancer

BAHAMAS

ATLANTIC OCEAN

TURKS & CAICOS ISLANDS (United Kingdom)

20°N

CUBA

VIRGIN IS. (United Kingdom)

20°N

MEXICO

CAYMAN IS. (United Kingdom)

PUERTO RICO (United States)

ST. KITTS & NEVIS

BELIZE

HAITI DOMINICAN REPUBLIC

ANTIGUA & BARBUDA

JAMAICA

GUADELOUPE (France)

GUATEMALA

VIRGIN IS. (United States)

HONDURAS

MONTSERRAT (United Kingdom)

DOMINICA

MARTINIQUE (France)

Caribbean Sea

EL SALVADOR

NICARAGUA

NETHERLANDS ANTILLES (Netherlands)

ST. LUCIA

ST. VINCENT & THE GRENADINES

BARBADOS

N
W   E
S

ARUBA (Netherlands)

GRENADA

TRINIDAD & TOBAGO

10°N

60°W

COSTA RICA

PANAMA

COLOMBIA

VENEZUELA

GUYANA

PACIFIC OCEAN

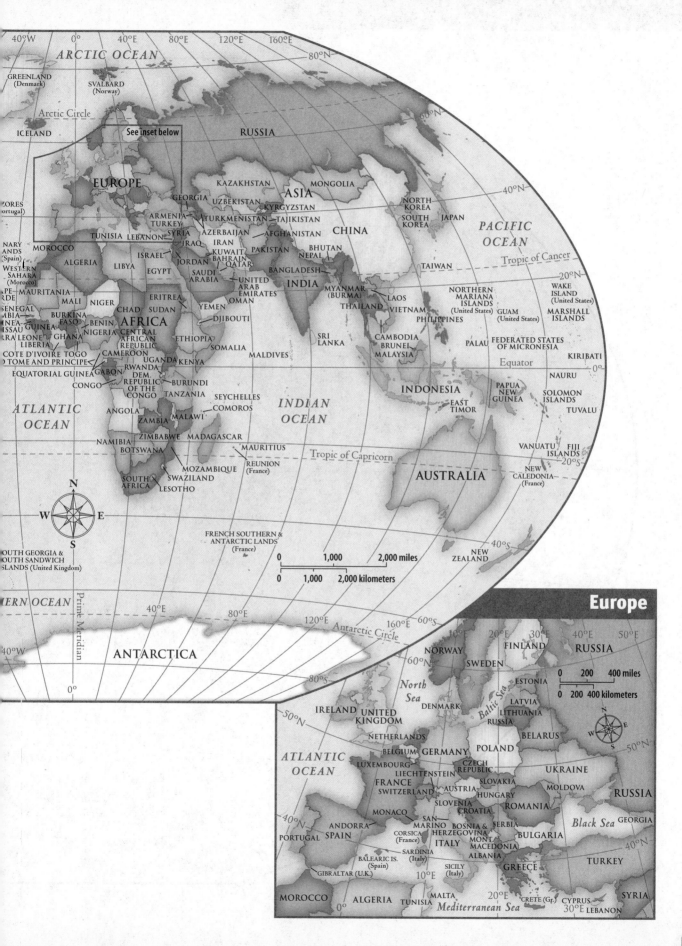

ARCTIC OCEAN

40°W   0°   40°E   80°E   120°E   160°E

80°N

GREENLAND
(Denmark)

SVALBARD
(Norway)

Arctic Circle

RUSSIA

60°N

ICELAND

See inset below

EUROPE

KAZAKHSTAN   MONGOLIA

ASIA

40°N

NORTH
KOREA

ZORES
ortugal)

GEORGIA   UZBEKISTAN   KYRGYZSTAN

ARMENIA
TURKEY   TURKMENISTAN   TAJIKISTAN

SOUTH
KOREA   JAPAN

PACIFIC
OCEAN

NARY
ANDS
(Spain)

MOROCCO

TUNISIA LEBANON

SYRIA
IRAQ

AZERBAIJAN   AFGHANISTAN

CHINA

IRAN

Tropic of Cancer

WESTERN
SAHARA
(Morocco)

ALGERIA   LIBYA

ISRAEL
JORDAN
EGYPT

KUWAIT
BAHRAIN
QATAR

PAKISTAN

BHUTAN
NEPAL

TAIWAN

20°N

PE
MAURITANIA

SAUDI
ARABIA

UNITED
ARAB
EMIRATES

BANGLADESH

INDIA

MYANMAR
(BURMA)

NORTHERN
MARIANA
ISLANDS
(United States)

WAKE
ISLAND
(United States)

SENEGAL
MBIA
NEA
ISSAU
RRA LEONE

MALI   NIGER

CHAD   SUDAN

ERITREA

OMAN

YEMEN

DJIBOUTI

LAOS
THAILAND   VIETNAM

GUAM
(United States)

MARSHALL
ISLANDS

BURKINA
FASO

BENIN
NIGERIA

AFRICA
CENTRAL
AFRICAN
REPUBLIC

ETHIOPIA

SRI
LANKA

CAMBODIA
BRUNEI
MALAYSIA

PHILIPPINES

FEDERATED STATES
OF MICRONESIA

GHANA

CAMEROON

SOMALIA

MALDIVES

PALAU

KIRIBATI

COTE D'IVOIRE TOGO
O TOME AND PRINCIPE

UGANDA KENYA

Equator   0°

EQUATORIAL GUINEA
CONGO

GABON
RWANDA
DEM.
REPUBLIC
OF THE
CONGO

BURUNDI

TANZANIA

SEYCHELLES

INDIAN
OCEAN

INDONESIA

EAST
TIMOR

PAPUA
NEW
GUINEA

NAURU

SOLOMON
ISLANDS

ATLANTIC
OCEAN

ANGOLA

ZAMBIA   MALAWI

COMOROS

TUVALU

ZIMBABWE   MADAGASCAR

NAMIBIA
BOTSWANA

Tropic of Capricorn

MAURITIUS

20°S

VANUATU   FIJI
ISLANDS

N

SOUTH
AFRICA

MOZAMBIQUE
SWAZILAND
LESOTHO

REUNION
(France)

AUSTRALIA

NEW
CALEDONIA
(France)

W   E

S

FRENCH SOUTHERN &
ANTARCTIC LANDS
(France)

0   1,000   2,000 miles

40°S

NEW
ZEALAND

OUTH GEORGIA &
OUTH SANDWICH
SLANDS (United Kingdom)

0   1,000   2,000 kilometers

ERN OCEAN

Prime Meridian

40°E   80°E   120°E   160°E   60°S

Antarctic Circle

40°W

ANTARCTICA

80°S

0°

Europe

NORWAY   FINLAND   RUSSIA

60°N

SWEDEN

0   200   400 miles

North
Sea

DENMARK

ESTONIA

Baltic Sea

LATVIA
LITHUANIA

0   200   400 kilometers

N

IRELAND   UNITED
KINGDOM

RUSSIA

W   E

50°N

NETHERLANDS

BELARUS

S

ATLANTIC
OCEAN

BELGIUM GERMANY

POLAND

50°N

LUXEMBOURG

CZECH
REPUBLIC

UKRAINE

LIECHTENSTEIN

FRANCE
SWITZERLAND

AUSTRIA

SLOVAKIA

MOLDOVA

HUNGARY

RUSSIA

MONACO

SLOVENIA
CROATIA

ROMANIA

40°N

ANDORRA
PORTUGAL   SPAIN

SAN
MARINO

BOSNIA &
HERZEGOVINA

SERBIA

Black Sea

GEORGIA

CORSICA
(France)

ITALY

MONT.
MACEDONIA

BULGARIA

40°N

BALEARIC IS.
(Spain)

SARDINIA
(Italy)

ALBANIA

TURKEY

GIBRALTAR (U.K.)

SICILY
(Italy)

GREECE

10°E

MOROCCO   ALGERIA   TUNISIA

MALTA

CRETE (Gr.)   CYPRUS

SYRIA

20°E

30°E   LEBANON

Mediterranean Sea

R9

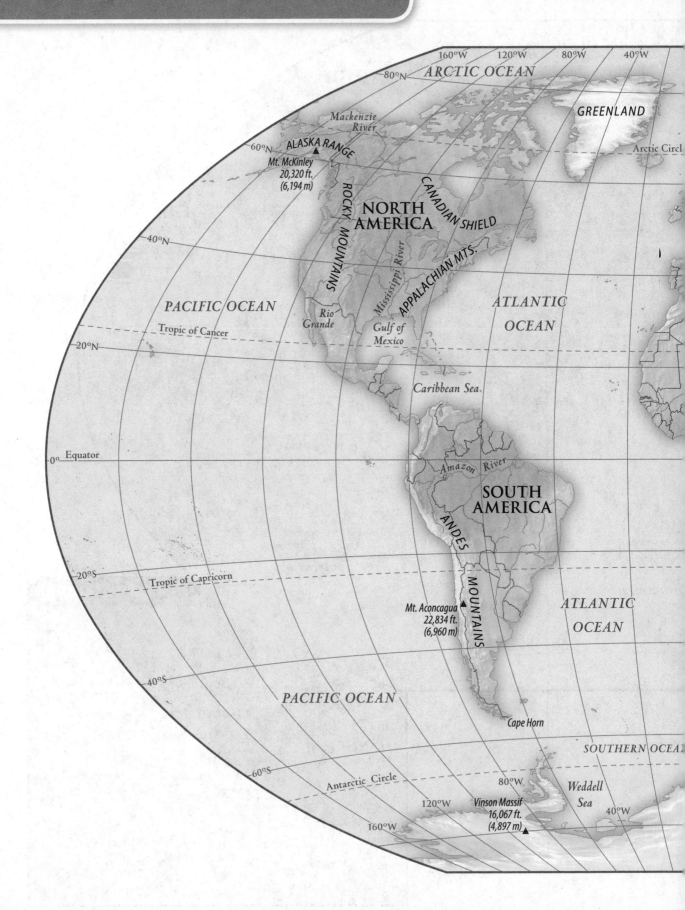

ARCTIC OCEAN

160°W 120°W 80°W 40°W

80°N

GREENLAND

Mackenzie
River

60°N ALASKA RANGE
Mt. McKinley
20,320 ft.
(6,194 m)

Arctic Circle

NORTH
AMERICA

CANADIAN SHIELD

ROCKY MOUNTAINS

40°N

APPALACHIAN MTS.

Mississippi River

PACIFIC OCEAN

ATLANTIC
OCEAN

Tropic of Cancer

Rio
Grande

20°N

Gulf of
Mexico

Caribbean Sea

Equator

Amazon River

0°

SOUTH
AMERICA

ANDES

20°S

Tropic of Capricorn

Mt. Aconcagua
22,834 ft.
(6,960 m)

MOUNTAINS

ATLANTIC
OCEAN

40°S

PACIFIC OCEAN

Cape Horn

SOUTHERN OCEAN

60°S

Antarctic Circle

80°W

Weddell
Sea

120°W Vinson Massif
16,067 ft.
(4,897 m)

40°W

160°W

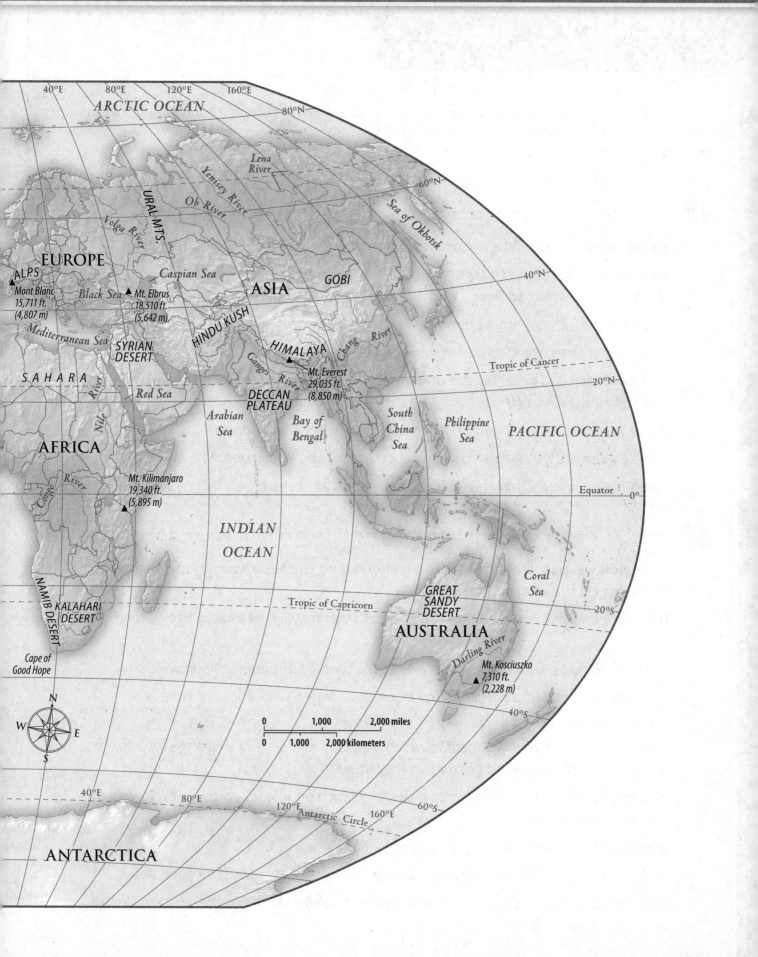

ARCTIC OCEAN

40°E 80°E 120°E 160°E

80°N

Lena River

60°N

Yenisey River

Ob River

URAL MTS.

Sea of Okhotsk

Volga River

EUROPE

40°N

ALPS
▲
Mont Blanc
15,711 ft.
(4,807 m)

Caspian Sea

ASIA

GOBI

Black Sea ▲ Mt. Elbrus
18,510 ft.
(5,642 m)

HINDU KUSH

Mediterranean Sea

SYRIAN DESERT

HIMALAYA

Chang River

Tropic of Cancer

S A H A R A

Ganges River

Red Sea

▲
Mt. Everest
29,035 ft.
(8,850 m)

20°N

Nile River

DECCAN PLATEAU

Arabian Sea

Bay of Bengal

South China Sea

Philippine Sea

PACIFIC OCEAN

AFRICA

Congo River

Mt. Kilimanjaro
19,340 ft.
(5,895 m)
▲

Equator 0°

INDIAN OCEAN

NAMIB DESERT

KALAHARI DESERT

Tropic of Capricorn

GREAT SANDY DESERT

Coral Sea

20°S

AUSTRALIA

Cape of Good Hope

Darling River

Mt. Kosciuszko
7,310 ft.
(2,228 m)
▲

N
W   E
S

40°S

0   1,000   2,000 miles
0   1,000   2,000 kilometers

40°E 80°E 120°E 160°E

60°S
Antarctic Circle

ANTARCTICA

Glossary

This Glossary will help you to pronounce and understand the meanings of the vocabulary terms in this book. The page number at the end of the definition tells where the term first appears.

A

abolitionist (ab ə lish′ə nist) a person who wanted to end slavery in the United States

absolute location (ab′ sə lüt lō kā shən) the exact location of a place expressed by longitude and latitude or street address

alliance (ə lī′əns) an agreement between nations to support and protect each other

amendment (ə mend′mənt) an addition to the U.S. Constitution

Anaconda Plan (an ə kon′da plan) the Union's three-part plan for defeating the Confederacy and ending the Civil War

annex (ə′neks) to make a country or territory part of another country

anti-Semitism (an tē′se mə ti zəm) discrimination against the Jewish people

assassination (ə sas ə nā′shən) the murder of an important person

B

biological weapon (bī ə ′lä ji kəl ′we pən) a harmful agent used as a weapon to cause death or disease on a large scale

biotechnology (bī ō tech nol′ə gē) the study of cells to find ways of improving health in living things

blockade (blok ād′) is an action that prevents the passage of people or supplies

bohemian (bō ′hē mē ən) a person (often an artist or writer) who does not have a traditional lifestyle

bond (′bänd) a form of investment in which buyers loan money in exchange for a fixed amount of money they will get back in the future

boycott (boi′kot) a form of organized protest in which people refuse to do business with a company or nation

budget (buj′ĭt) a plan for spending and saving money

budget deficit (buj′ĭt ′de fə sət) the amount by which spending exceeds revenue

buffalo soldier (bəf ə ′lō sōl djər) an African American soldier serving in the western United States after the Civil War

C

carpetbagger (kär pət bag ər) the Southern name for Northerners who went south during Reconstruction to help local governments or schools

cartogram (kär'tə gram) a map that shows information by changing the sizes of places

casualty ('ka zhəl tē) soldiers or others killed, wounded, sick, or missing

cattle drive (kat'əl driv) the movement of large herds of cattle, by cowboys, from ranches to railroad stations

censure (sen chər) to formally disapprove of some action

checks and balances ('cheks ənd 'ba lənsəs) a system which ensures that no one branch of government has too much power

civil defense (siv'əl di 'fens) the system of protective measures conducted by civilians during wartime

civil war (siv'əl wôr) an armed conflict between groups within one country. In the United States, the war between the Union and the Confederacy from 1861 to 1865

climate (klī'mit) the weather of an area over a number of years

climograph (klī'mō graf) a graph that shows information about the temperature and precipitation of a place over time

coalition (kō ə 'li shən) a group formed for a common purpose

Cold War (kōld wär) a war fought with ideas, words, money, and sometimes force between the United States and the Soviet Union

communism (kom'yə niz əm) a political system in which business, property, and goods are owned by the government

commute (kə 'myüt) to travel back and forth regularly

containment (kən 'tān mənt) the policy or process of preventing the expansion of a hostile power or ideology

convoy ('kän vói) a group of vehicles that travel together to provide better protection

corporation (kôr pə rā'shən) large businesses in which people invest their money and share ownership

counterculture ('ka u˙n tər kəl chər) ideas and values that are different from the larger society

Glossary

D

debate (dē bāt′) a formal argument about different political ideas

demilitarized zone (dē ′mil ə tə rīzd zōn) a region where no military forces or weapons are allowed

détente (dā ′tänt) an easing of tension between nations

discrimination (di skrim ə nā′shən) an unfair difference in the treatment of people

dividend (′di və dend) a share of the profit a company makes paid to shareholders

double bar graph (dub′əl bär graf) a graph that compares information with parallel rectangles

draft (draft) the selecting of persons for military service or some other special duty

E

Electoral College (ē lek ′tȯr əl ′kä lij) the system by which each state has a certain number of electoral votes based on the number of representatives it has in Congress

Emancipation Proclamation (ē man si pā′shən prok lə mā′shən) the official announcement issued by President Abraham Lincoln in 1862 that led to the end of slavery in the United States

espionage (es pē ə näzh) spying to gather government secrets

exoduster (ek′so dus tər) an African American from the South who went to Kansas in the 1870s

expatriate (ek ′spā trē ət) a person who gives up his or her home country and chooses to live in another country

F

fascism (fash′izm) marked by strong national pride and a strong ruler with almost complete power.

federal (fed′ər əl) another word for national

Freedmen's Bureau (frēd məns ′byū r ō) A government agency created in 1865 that provided food, schools, and medical care for newly freed African Americans and poor whites in the South

free state (frē stāt) state where slavery was banned

G

genocide (jen ō sīd) the planned destruction of an ethnic, political, or cultural group

geographer (jē og′rə fer) a person who studies geography

Gettysburg Address (get′iz burg ə dres′) a speech made by President Lincoln at the site of the Battle of Gettysburg in 1863

global grid (glō′bəl grid) a set of squares formed by crisscrossing lines that can help you determine the absolute location of a place on a globe

Global Positioning System (GPS) (glō′bəl pə zish′əning ′sis təm) a group of satellites that use radio signals to determine the exact location of places on Earth

globalization (glō′bəl i zā′shun) a trend where companies do not consider national boundaries when they decide where to buy and sell goods and services

Great Migration (grāt mī ′grā shən) the movement of African Americans from the South to the North

H

historical map (his tôr′i kəl map) a map that shows information about the past or where past events took place

Holocaust (′hō lə kȯst) the genocide of more than 6 million Jews during World War II

homesteader (hōm′sted ər) a person who claimed land on the Great Plains under the Homestead Act of 1862

hostage (′häs tij) is a person who is held as a prisoner until money or demands are met

I

impeach (im ′pēch) to charge an official with wrongdoing

inflation (in flā′ shən) a rise in prices of goods and services

initiative (in ′ish ət iv) the right of citizens to place an issue on a ballot for a direct vote

integrate (′in tə grāt) to bring together people of all races

interdependent (in′tər di pen′dənt) countries that rely on each other to meet the needs and wants of its people

interest (in′tər ist) money that is paid for the use of borrowed or deposited money

Internet (in′tər net) a worldwide system of computer networks

internment camp (in tərn′ment kamp) special camps, usually during war time, where people were forced to live and give up their jobs, their businesses, and their homes

isolationism (ī sə ′lā shə ni zəm) not becoming involved in issues concerning other countries

Glossary

K

kamikaze (kä mi ′kä zē) a Japanese word meaning "divine wind"; refers to suicide attacks in which pilots purposefully crashed their planes, taking their own lives, to sink or cause damage to their opponent's vessels particularly in World War II

L

labor union (lā′bər ūn′yən) a group of workers who unite to improve working conditions

large-scale map (lärj skāl map) a map that shows a smaller area in great detail

latitude (lat′i tüd) an imaginary line, or parallel, measuring distance north or south of the Equator

League of Nations (lēg əv nā shəns) an organization formed after World War I to prevent further wars

liberate (′li bə rāt) to free an area or person

longitude (lon′ji tüd) an imaginary line, or meridian, measuring distance east or west of the Prime Meridian

M

malice (ma′ləs) to want to harm someone

manifest destiny (man′ə fest des′tə nē) belief in the early 1800s that the United States was to stretch west to the Pacific Ocean and south to the Rio Grande

map scale (map skāl) a line like a measuring stick drawn on a map that uses a unit of measurement, such as an inch, to represent a real distance on Earth

mass production (′mas prə′dək shən) the process of making large numbers of one product quickly

meridian (mə rid′ē ən) a meridian is any line of longitude east or west of Earth's Prime Meridian

microchip (′mī krō chip) a tiny computer part that processes information quickly

migrant farm worker (mī′grənt färm wûr′kər) a laborer who moves from one farm to another as the seasons change

Missouri Compromise (mə zûr′ē kom′prə mīz) an agreement in 1820 that allowed Missouri and Maine to enter the Union and divided the Louisiana Territory into areas allowing slavery and areas outlawing slavery

mobilize (′mō bə līz) to assemble for action

Glossary

monopoly (mə'näp ə lē) total control of a type of industry by one person or company

muckraker (mək rā kər) a journalist who wrote about dangerous working conditions or dishonest businesses and politicians

N

nanotechnology ('na nō tek 'nä lə jē) technology that uses atoms to make structures that are about a million times smaller than the head of a pin

nationalism (nash nəl iz əm) loyalty to one's country

nativism (nāt iv izm) the belief that those born in a country are superior to immigrants

O

offshoring ('of 'shȯr ing) the movement of businesses to other countries that have the resources or technology to manufacture products or provide services at a lower cost

opportunity cost (äp ȯr tün'ə tē kost) the value of the second best choice when choosing between two things

P

parallel (par'ə lel) a line of latitude; see latitude

pardon (pär dən) to forgive an offense

patronage ('pā trə nij) a system in which people get political jobs because they had donated money to or were friends with politicians

Peace Corps ('pēs 'kȯr) an agency created by President John F. Kennedy that trains and sends American volunteers overseas to work with people in developing countries

poverty (päv'ər tē) the condition of being poor

price incentive ('prīs in 'sen tiv) something that encourages people to buy or sell a good or service

Prime Meridian (prīm mə rid'ē ən) the line of longitude labeled 0° longitude. Any place east of the Prime Meridian is labeled E. Any place west of it is labeled W; see longitude

productivity ('prō dək 'ti və tē) the amount of goods and services that are produced

profit (prof'it) the money made on goods that exceeds the cost of production.

progressive (prə gres'iv) people who believed in using new and creative ideas for social progress and change

Glossary

prohibition (prō ə 'bi shən) laws that would ban the production and sale of alcohol

property rights (prä'p'r tē rīts) the rights to own or use something

public works (pəb lik 'wərks) projects such as highways, parks, and libraries built with public funds for public use

R

ratify (rat' ə fī) to officially approve

ration (ra'shən) limiting how much of goods people can buy

recall ('rē 'kȯl) a special election during which voters decide whether or not to remove an elected official

recession (rē 'se shən) no economic growth for six straight months, a general slowing of economic activity, and high unemployment

referendum (ref ə 'ren dəm) a direct vote on a proposed law

relative location (rel'ə tiv lō kā shən) the location of a place in relation to another place

reservation (rez ûr vā'shən) territories set aside for Native Americans

S

satellite (sat ə līt) an object that circles a larger object such as a moon

scalawag (skal i wag) a white Southerner who worked with Northerners and African Americans during Reconstruction.

scarcity (skâr'si tē) a shortage of available goods and services

secede (si sēd') to withdraw from the Union

segregation (seg ri gā'shən) the practice of keeping racial groups separate

sharecropping (shâr'krop ing) a system in which farmers rented land in return for crops

slave state (slāv stāt) state where slavery was allowed

slum (slum) a rundown neighborhood

small-scale map (smȯl skāl map) a map that shows a large area but not much detail

Spanish-American War (span'ish ə mer'ikən wôr) the war between the United States and Spain in 1898 in which the United States gained control of Puerto Rico, Guam, and the Philippines

specialization ('spe shə lə 'zā shən) businesses or people that make or sell only one or a few goods or services.

speculation (spək yə'lā shən) risking money in the stock market in order to make a large profit in a short amount of time

stalemate (stāl māt) a situation in which neither side is able to gain much ground or achieve victory

stock (stäk) shares of ownership in a company

stock exchange (stäk iks chānj) a place where shares in companies are bought and sold through an organized system

strike (strīk) a way to protest working conditions by refusing to work

suburb (səb 'ərb) a residential area outside a large city

suffrage (suf'rij) the right to vote

T

tariff (tar'ef) a tax placed on imports or exports to control the sale price

tenant (ten ənt) someone who pays rent

tenement (ten'ə mənt) rundown building

terrorism (ter'ə ris əm) the use of violence by non-governmental groups to achieve political goals

total war (to'təl wôr) attacking an enemy's soldiers, civilians, and property

transcontinental railroad (trans kon ti nen'təl rāl'rōd) a railroad that crosses a continent

treason (trē'zən) the act of betraying one's country

Treaty of Versailles (trē'tē əv vər sī') the agreement that ended World War I

trench warfare (trench wôr faər) fighting from ditches built on either side of a battlefield

trust ('trəst) a way of organizing a number of businesses so that a few people, called trustees, control them

U

United Nations (yu' 'nī təd 'nā shənz) a global organization created after World War II that works to achieve world peace.

V

voluntary exchange ('vä lən ter ē iks chānj) all the businesses and consumers who freely buy and sell goods and services

Glossary

prohibition (prō ə 'bi shən) laws that would ban the production and sale of alcohol

property rights (prä'p'r tē rīts) the rights to own or use something

public works (pəb lik 'wərks) projects such as highways, parks, and libraries built with public funds for public use

R

ratify (rat' ə fi) to officially approve

ration (ra'shən) limiting how much of goods people can buy

recall ('rē 'kó l) a special election during which voters decide whether or not to remove an elected official

recession (rē 'se shən) no economic growth for six straight months, a general slowing of economic activity, and high unemployment

referendum (ref ə 'ren dəm) a direct vote on a proposed law

relative location (rel'ə tiv lō kā shən) the location of a place in relation to another place

reservation (rez ûr vā'shən) territories set aside for Native Americans

S

satellite (sat ə līt) an object that circles a larger object such as a moon

scalawag (skal i wag) a white Southerner who worked with Northerners and African Americans during Reconstruction.

scarcity (skâr'si tē) a shortage of available goods and services

secede (si sēd') to withdraw from the Union

segregation (seg ri gā'shən) the practice of keeping racial groups separate

sharecropping (shâr'krop ing) a system in which farmers rented land in return for crops

slave state (slāv stāt) state where slavery was allowed

slum (slum) a rundown neighborhood

small-scale map (smôl skāl map) a map that shows a large area but not much detail

Spanish-American War (span'ish ə mer'ikən wôr) the war between the United States and Spain in 1898 in which the United States gained control of Puerto Rico, Guam, and the Philippines

specialization ('spe shə lə 'zā shən) businesses or people that make or sell only one or a few goods or services.

speculation (spək yə ʹlā shən) risking money in the stock market in order to make a large profit in a short amount of time

stalemate (stāl māt) a situation in which neither side is able to gain much ground or achieve victory

stock (stäk) shares of ownership in a company

stock exchange (stäk iks chānj) a place where shares in companies are bought and sold through an organized system

strike (strīk) a way to protest working conditions by refusing to work

suburb (səb ʹərb) a residential area outside a large city

suffrage (sufʹrij) the right to vote

T

tariff (tarʹef) a tax placed on imports or exports to control the sale price

tenant (ten ənt) someone who pays rent

tenement (tenʹə mənt) rundown building

terrorism (terʹə ris əm) the use of violence by non-governmental groups to achieve political goals

total war (toʹtəl wôr) attacking an enemy's soldiers, civilians, and property

transcontinental railroad (trans kon ti nenʹtəl rālʹrōd) a railroad that crosses a continent

treason (trēʹzən) the act of betraying one's country

Treaty of Versailles (trēʹtē əv vər sīʹ) the agreement that ended World War I

trench warfare (trench wȯr faər) fighting from ditches built on either side of a battlefield

trust (ʹtrəst) a way of organizing a number of businesses so that a few people, called trustees, control them

U

United Nations (yu ʹnī təd ʹnā shənz) a global organization created after World War II that works to achieve world peace.

V

voluntary exchange (ʹvä lən ter ē iks chānj) all the businesses and consumers who freely buy and sell goods and services

Ford, Henry, 140
Ford Motor Company, p140
Forten, Charlotte, 42
Fourteen Points, 132
Fourteenth Amendment, 41, 44, 47, 56
Fourth Amendment, 12
France
  map of, m129
  and NATO, 192, m192
  and the Panama Canal, 126
  and the West German Republic, 191
  and World War I, 129, m129
  and World War II, p154, p162, 164, 176, m177
  and the Yalta conference, 189
Franz Ferdinand, Archduke of Austria, 129
Free Speech and Headlight, 57
Freedmen's Bureau, p38, 39, 40–41
Freedom of assembly, 12
Freedom of religion, 12
Freedom of speech, 12
Freedom of the press, 12
Freedom Rides, 217
Freedom to petition, 12
Friedan, Betty, 220, p220

G

Gates, Bill, 251
Gaza Strip, 236
General Electric, 84
Genocide, 183
George, David Lloyd, 130
Germany
  immigrants from, 73
  postwar division of, 185, m190, 191
  reunited, 235, p235
  and Treaty of Versailles, 163, 164
  and the West German Republic, 191
  and World War I, 129, m129, 130, 132, m132
  and World War II, 164–165, 166, 175–177, p182, 183–185
  See also Berlin, Germany
Gershwin, George, 138
Gershwin, Ira, 138
Ghost towns, 71
GI Bill, 200
Gilded Age, 83
The Gilded Age: A Tale of Today (Twain and Warner), 83
Global grid, m50, 50
Globalization, 246, p246
Gold, 71, 80, p120, 121
Gompers, Samuel, 88
Goods, 246
Gorbachev, Mikhail, 233, p233, 234, 235

Gore, Al, 237, m237
Gorgas, William, 127
Government
  diversity in, 245
  federal government, 13, 107
  local government, 13, c13, 104–105
  minorities serving in, 245
  as sector of the economy, c18, 19
  state government, 11, 12, 13, c13, 87
  women serving in, 149, 245
Grand Canyon, m77
Great Britain
  independence from, 11
  and NATO, 192, m192
  and the West German
Republic, 191
  and World War I, 129, m129
  and World War II, 164, 165, 166, 175
  and Yalta conference, 189
Great Depression
  and consumerism, 141
  crash of the market, 144, p144
  and the Dust Bowl, 148
  and Hoovervilles, 146, p146
  response to, 146–147, p149
  and the Roosevelt
Recession, 149
  spread of, 145
  warning signs of, 144–145
  and World War II, 166, 169
Great Migration, 135, p135, 136
Great Plains
  African Americans in, 75
  and the Dust Bowl, 148
  homesteading on the 74–75, p74
  and Manifest Destiny, 71
  and Native Americans, 79–81
Great Salt Lake, m77
Great Society program, 226
Great Western Cattle Trail, 76, m77
Greece, m129, 190, p190
Greek Americans, 143
Gross national product (GNP), g145
Guam, 124, m124, m178
Guantánamo Bay, 124

H

Hamer, Fannie Lou, 217, p217
Hampton Institute, 101
Harlan, John Marshall, 56
Harlem, New York City, p136, 136–137
Harlem Renaissance, p136, 136–137

Index

Index

Index

State government —Trusts

Index

Index

Index